Focus Group Interviews:
A Reader

James B. Higginbotham
Higginbotham Associates, Inc.

Keith K. Cox
University of Houston

222 South Riverside Plaza • Chicago, Illinois 60606 • (312) 648-0536

AMERICAN
MARKETING
ASSOCIATION

Designed by Mary Jo Krysinski

Library of Congress Cataloging in Publication Data
Main entry under title:
Focus group interviews.
1. Interviewing in marketing research-Addresses, essays,
lectures. I. Higginbotham, James. II. Cox, Keith K.
HF5415.2.F63   658.8'34   79-15536
ISBN 0-87757-123-6

Focus Group Interviews

CONTENTS

PART III

Marketing Applications   96

PART IV

Advantages And Limitations   114

PART I

What Are Focus Group Interviews?

This first section gives a general overview to the subject of focus group interviews. Major topics include:

1. A comprehensive overview of focus group interviews.

2. Practical understanding of focus groups.

3. The mechanics of conducting group interviews.

4. A "flesh and blood" approach to focus group interviews.

5. General discussion by a group of moderators.

Group Interviewing

WILLIAM D. WELLS *Graduate School of Business, University of Chicago, Chicago, Illinois*

Group interviewing—interviewing people in groups rather than individually—entered the marketing research scene shortly after World War II as part of "motivation research" [3]. Like most motivation research techniques, it was instantly condemned by the conservative research establishment as "unscientific" and therefore untrustworthy. It has prospered nonetheless, and today in many marketing research organizations, group interviews are nearly as common as interviews done by the traditional survey questionnaire.

Group interviewing has proved so durable because it has some important assets that allow it to compete effectively with other ways of getting information. Some of these assets are undiluted virtues; some are not.

One asset is that group interview studies can be, and often are, fast and cheap. A three- or four-interview study can be conducted, analyzed, and reported in less than a week in an emergency, and at a cost much lower than that of most other ways of learning about attitudes and behavior. This means that an efficient group-interviewing facility can be extremely valuable when time and cost constraints are severe. It also means that group interviews will sometimes be employed when a more expensive, more time-consuming method would be more appropriate—the research equivalent of Gresham's law.

A second, related advantage is that the group interview is a superb mechanism for generating hypotheses when little is known. Even when time and funds are ample for the most painstaking research, the researcher must get some background somewhere before he can cope with a problem in any useful way. When other information sources are sparse or lacking, or when the researcher needs immediate, personal contact with the subject matter to spark his own thought, group interviews are highly productive idea breeders.

A third important advantage is that the group method drastically reduces the distance between the respondent who produces research information and the client who uses it.[1] In a typical large-scale survey, the respondent talks to an overworked and undertrained field interviewer who cannot possibly fully appreciate the client's problems or the context of the research. The field interviewer's version of what the respondent said goes to a coder who is similarly in the dark. The coder's work goes to an assistant analyst who does further injustice to the data, next through an analyst to a supervisor, then maybe to someone who knows what the study is about. With so many chances to lose information and add noise, it is not surprising that clients who order surveys sometimes get mostly what they do not want.

In a group interview study, on the other hand, the number of interviews is so small and the time consumed is so short that the client can participate in most or all of the interviews himself, either by providing feedback to the interviewer on the relevance of the material being produced, or by asking questions himself as the interview unfolds. Besides its obvious feedback value, client participation promotes acceptance of the research by the person who counts most. As a true participant, the client can see with his own eyes and hear

---

[1] Hereafter "client" means anyone who uses the information the interviews produce. He may be a client in the usual sense. He may also be another investigator who will use the results of group interviews as a basis for further research. Or he may be the investigator himself.

with his own ears. Once the study is completed, nothing makes a finding more compelling than the memory of having been there, actively involved, when it emerged.

Some researchers feel that clients, like unruly children, must be protected from their own impulses—in this case, their impulse to influence the course and nature of the research. When that assertion is true, a group interview study is probably not a good idea.

A fourth advantage of the group interview technique is its flexibility. Survey interviewers work from a rigid question schedule. A good group interviewer works from a list of topics—listening, thinking, probing, exploring, framing hunches and ideas as he proceeds. He also "listens with the third ear," trying to achieve a grasp and an intuitive understanding of what is being said. He looks at the respondents, watches posture, listens to voice tone, and tries to decide when respondents are "putting him on." He is not an automatic, mechanical, wind-up question asker, as survey interviewers necessarily and properly are.

A fifth advantage of the group interview, an advantage shared with the individual depth interview, is its ability to handle contingencies. Much of consumer behavior is "if . . . and . . . otherwise." "If it is one of the three brands I sometimes use *and* it is on sale, I buy it; *otherwise*, I buy my regular brand." "*If* the day is hot *and* I have to serve the whole neighborhood, I make bug juice; *otherwise*, I give them soda or Coke." "*If* I know that we're going to take a long trip with a lot of high-speed driving *and* the tires are getting a little worn, I replace them; *otherwise*, I leave them on until I trade in the car." Single survey questions can obtain all these elements separately; but unless the relationships are already fairly well known, it is hard to design questions that pick up those contingencies that link the events.

A sixth advantage is that group interview respondents stimulate one another. One respondent's remarks may lead another to pursue a line of thinking he would not have followed in an individual interview. A bold respondent may encourage a less outgoing one to voice feelings and opinions that he never would have revealed had someone else not had the courage to express them first.

Finally, a group interview study has an important advantage over the standard questionnaire study in that the findings emerge in a form that most clients fully understand. The typical survey report is a thicket of percentages. Unless the client has the researcher's eye for numerals, he is apt to find a percentage-ridden report arid and impersonal. The typical group interview report (like the typical individual depth-interview report) is crammed with real people. Instead of mysterious symbols and dull tables, there are direct quotations in which believable people give their views at length and in their own words. For many clients, this is the texture of the world.

These advantages—speed, relatively modest cost, ready production of hypotheses and ideas, direct connection between respondent and client, flexibility, sensitivity to contingencies, intragroup stimulation and comfortable results—make the group interview a formidable contender when research-method decisions must be made. Each of these advantages carries a penalty, but none should be ignored.

PREPARATION

Understanding the Problem. Although it seems almost too obvious, it is probably worth emphasizing that the value of a group interview study depends to a very great extent on the interviewer's appreciation of the client's problems. Before doing anything else, the interviewer talks to the client. He finds out what the client already knows or thinks he knows and what he thinks he wants to know.

This step is exceedingly important because the group interviewer does not normally have his questioning route prescribed. He must hunt for answers in the interview like a hound following a scent. If the interviewer doesn't recognize the wisp of an answer, that trail may never be taken.

For this reason, the term *interviewer* used in this chapter has a somewhat different connotation from the term *interviewer* in the preceding and later chapters. Here, the interviewer is not only skilled at interviewing but also very well aware of the purpose and objectives of the research. He is the client's proxy. He does what he thinks the client would do if the client had the time, inclination, and skill to do it.

The Questions. Once the client's problems are understood, it is helpful to cast them into a set of questions—not questions to be asked of the respondents, but rather, questions to be asked of the research results. For example:

> What do dog owners think about their dogs? Do they regard them as animals or as members of the family? Do dogs have "personalities"? If so, what are the major types? How do dog owners decide what form of food to buy? What part does the dog play in evaluating a food? What roles do children play? Is price important? Under what circumstances and in what way? How do dog owners select a specific brand? Do they think they should buy a variety, or do they think they should be consistent? Why? What dogfood advertising can respondents remember? What is their reaction to this advertising?

This detailed set of questions has two purposes. It ensures that both client and interviewer have thought about what they really want to know, and it ensures agreement on specific objectives before the study begins. Though this sort of preparation is obviously desirable in any study, it is especially important in group interview research because a group study does not normally have its scope and objectives specified by a preset questionnaire.

The Outline. Once the questions to be answered by the research have been established, the interviewer can prepare a topic outline. Instead of a specific set of questions to be asked in a predetermined order, the group interviewer uses a set of notes on major issues, a set of cues to help ensure that all important points are covered. Novice interviewers often feel uncomfortable with so skimpy a guide because they feel the need to ask questions continuously, and they fear they will not be able to frame just the right question at just the right time. Experienced interviewers know that it is far more important to listen and react perceptively to what respondents are saying than to emit a volley of questions, regardless of how elegantly they are phrased. The novice interviewer should remember that all his respondents have had many years of practice at giving sensible answers to stupid questions, and he should not be afraid of asking some himself. Sometimes a fumbling, stumbling question will elicit a long, detailed, and interesting response because the respondent has adapted the question to his own purposes and can therefore use it as a lead-in to say what he has on his mind.

Recruiting Groups. Group interviewing is now so common that field supervisors anywhere in the country can recruit groups to fit almost any specifications. Their sources include their own staffs or interviewers, their interviewers' acquaintances, local organizations whose members participate in return for contributions to the organization treasury, and as a last (expensive) resort, telephone or door-to-door recruiting.

When recruiting respondents, it is usually helpful to provide for both homogeneity and contrast within specific groups. In marketing research, homogeneity is particularly desirable with respect to social class and stage in the family life cycle. Consumers occupying different stages of the life cycle have such different needs and problems, such different resources, such different sets of experiences and perceptions of reality that they sometimes have difficulty communicating with one another. Especially in conversations about shopping and homemaking, younger, less experienced women are apt to defer to the veterans. When social classes are mixed, the more literate and articulate middle-class respondents may suppress participation by lower-class interviewees who feel unlearned. When the topic is personal, it is usually unwise to mix the sexes.

With this homogeneity, it is often helpful to provide for a spark to be struck by contrasting opinions. One of the best ways to produce contrast is to be certain each group includes both users and nonusers of the client's brand. (This keeps the client interested too.) If the product carries no social stigma, it is also useful to include within the same group both users and nonusers of the product class. But if the product does have social connotations—for example, if nonusers of instant coffee think users are lazy, or if buyers of big life insurance policies think nonbuyers are selfish—mixing users and nonusers may soft-pedal some important ideas.

Group Size. Small groups are inefficient because they provide less than the maximum number of respondent hours per hour of interviewer time. Very small groups lose the mutual stimulation among respondents that makes the group setting unique. When groups are too large, they are difficult to manage, and in very large groups, less forward but potentially valuable respondents hesitate to speak. The ideal group size will depend somewhat on the physical accommodations (for example, the number of chairs that will fit around the table) and on the interviewer's personal style. Most physical accommodations and most interviewers are amenable to groups of six to ten.

It is a good idea to overrecruit. Group interviewing requires appearance by designated individuals in a specific place at a preset time. When an emergency occurs (baby-sitters didn't show up, friends dropped in, the weather got bad, the car wouldn't start), any one of these individuals is likely to decide that personal concerns are more important than market research.

Friends? When respondents are recruited from neighborhoods or organizations, at least some of them will know one another fairly well before the interview begins. Some interviewers object to this because they believe that discussions among friends produce unreal homogeneity of opinion. Some feel that friends may converse with one another, leaving others out, or that respondents are less than candid in the presence of people they see every day. Other interviewers feel that the naturalness and ease of conversation among acquaintances make an interview among friends dramatically more productive. The assets and liabilities of allowing friends to participate in the same group almost balance out.

Sites. Group interviews can be conducted in the client's office building, in some more "neutral" setting (a research supplier's office, a school, a motel), or in respondents' homes.

Conducting the interviews at the client's home base strongly increases the probability that the client will attend, and for this reason alone it is frequently a good idea. In addition, home-base interviewing greatly simplifies the mechanics of setting up tape recorders, motion picture projectors, samples, and props. On the other hand, home-base interviewing—assuming home base is downtown—makes recruiting of certain types of respondents exceedingly difficult. Also, it always reveals the client's identity, with all the biases which this implies.

"Neutral site" interviewing usually incurs out-of-pocket costs for transportation and room rental, reduces the probability the client will participate, and requires transport and setup of equipment in a strange place. In return, it facilitates recruiting some respondents and conceals the client's identity.

Interviewing in respondents' homes makes it relatively easy to recruit interviewees who will not go downtown. It also provides a setting that the respondents find friendly and familiar and gives both client and interviewer the opportunity to see how a wide variety of consumers live. This latter opportunity can be especially enlightening to a client who would not otherwise see the inside of an inexpensive home.

But in-home interviewing has its dangers. It is easy to get lost on the way to the interview site, especially in a strange town, especially at night, and especially in bad weather. At least once during an in-home interview the doorbell (or telephone) will ring. The hostess will leap up, trip over the microphone cord, rush to the door, and conduct a breathless conversation in tones loud enough to disrupt the interview but soft enough to ensure its continuation.

Equipment. Most interviews are tape-recorded for later listening or transcription. Even in this sensitive age, respondents rarely object to this procedure. When the machine is treated routinely, its obvious presence has no notable effect on the conversation. Respondents forget it is there.

The problems posed by tape recorders are mostly mechanical. When a second interview is recorded over the first by mistake, the first one is erased. Extraneous sounds, easily ignored by the ear during the interview, can make large portions of the recording unintelligible.

Mechanical **problems** multiply when interviewing is conducted out of town. Airline baggage handlers seem to have a union rule requiring tape recorders to be broken. Rented recorders stop in the middle of the interview. When interviews are conducted outside the United States, for example, in Canada, the United States Customs may decide—against all reason—that tape-recorded group interviews are "artistic productions." Then trouble knows no end. To all these hazards, the airlines' attempt to protect their planes from hijackers has added still another: the magnetic fields generated by weapon-detection devices will erase magnetic tapes.

Sound motion-picture projectors are cumbersome, obstreperous, and not easily repaired in the field. Different makes and models are threaded differently. When films are to be used, it is most important that projection equipment, especially if rented, be tested beforehand, and that someone be available who knows what to do when the lights go out.

Some organizations specializing in group interviewing have comfortably appointed rooms in which clients can watch and listen to group interviews from behind a one-way screen. The advantage of such a facility is that clients can talk, laugh, smoke, sleep, or make telephone calls without disturbing the moderator or group.

But the one-way vision room has two disadvantages that deserve some thought. First, by removing the client from the group, it prevents the client participation that is so often fruitful. Second, because it is deceptive, it violates the implicit contract between researcher and respondent. Social psychologists have already found that even well-intended deception can lead to outrage [2]. It would be prudent to think carefully before repeating that discipline's mistakes.

Number of Interviews. By questionnaire survey standards, the number of interviews in a typical group study is ridiculously small. When the study is limited to "middle-aged, middle-income homemakers," reports are often written after three or four sessions, and it is a rare study indeed that requires more than eleven or twelve. From the first interview on an unfamiliar topic, the analyst invariably learns a great deal. The second interview produces much more, but not all of it is new. Usually by the third session, and certainly by the fourth, most of what is said has been said several times before, and it is obvious that little is to be gained from continuing.

Exceptions to this general rule occur when there are important regional effects and when the investigation is intended to cover respondents who differ in age, sex, and social class. Then it is essential that each segment be represented, even though some of the material may appear again and again.

THE INTERVIEW

Styles. As group interviewing has developed under different practitioners, interviewing styles have diverged along a continuum that runs from nondirective at one extreme to directive at the other. At the nondirective extreme, the interviewer (frequently called a "moderator," to emphasize his nondirective role) participates only enough to start the conversation and prevent it from wandering too far from topics of interest to the client. The emphasis is on the group, on the dynamics of group interaction, and on the latent significance of what is said. Thus, in describing the "group depth interview," Goldman [1] writes:

> The moderator guides the discussion, keeping it within fruitful bounds, but rarely participates in it himself. When he can lead a group member to ask a question of a group, the moderator will not question them himself.

The rationale for encouraging spontaneous interchange among group members is that this sort of discussion may reveal important material that would not have emerged in response to direct questioning. The approach is based on the notion that people, allowed to be spontaneous in a nonevaluative, nonthreatening environment, will reveal much about themselves that they would otherwise hide. It even is sometimes asserted by those who advocate the nondirective approach that the dynamics of an in-depth group interview will let respondents reveal things of which they themselves were previously unaware. In the Freudian tradition, the search is at least in part for the "real," as opposed to the obvious and overt reasons why.

At the directive extreme, the interviewer maintains control of the discussion, does most of the questioning himself, and terminates the group's verbal interchanges unless they are clearly on the issue. In this style, the effort is to keep the discussion orderly, follow a predetermined sequence of topics, and explore each topic one at a time. No attempt is made to generate group cohesion or to plumb the unconscious.

Nondirective in-depth group interviewing is well described in the Goldman article [1]. The material that follows is biased toward the directive style.

Arrangement of Respondents. It sometimes makes a difference where respondents sit. Since those directly across from the interviewer have the most eye contact, they tend to participate more than others, and respondents immediately to the interviewer's right or left are likely to participate less. It is therefore often helpful to seat the least talkative respondents opposite the interviewer when possible, and to place the most talkative on the sides.

Some interviewers prefer that respondents be labeled so that they can be called by name. Others prefer the relative anonymity of a conversation in which names are not used. This decision is best left to the interviewer to make on the basis of his personal style.

Opening the Interview. The interviewer's initial remarks define the ground rules and set the tone. In an interview to be conducted according to the directive style, the opening comments might be as follows:

> "Today we are going to be talking about a topic that I think you will find interesting and that I'm sure you all know a lot about, and that is shortening [or cigarettes, or tea, or doctors, or whatever]. First I'd like to find out something about when you use shortening, what you use it for, how you use it and so on. Then I'd like to find out something about what you think of different forms of shortening, then different brands. Finally, we're going to be talking about some advertising for shortening that you may have seen, and we'll look at some shortening commercials and talk about them.

> "First I have a couple of requests. One is that you speak up and only one person speak at a time. We're tape-recording this, and if someone speaks very softly, or if two or three conversations are going at once, we can't hear it later. The other thing is, please say exactly what you think. We're just as interested in negative comments as positive ones, and in fact, the negative comments are sometimes the most useful.

> "One thing more. We're not making a radio commercial or a television commercial here, so don't look for the hidden camera. Say exactly what you think, because that's what we want to know.

> "Now, to get started, perhaps it would be best to go around the table one at a time. I'd like to know something about your families—how many children you have, how old they are, what variety they are, and what your husband does for a living."

These opening comments have special purposes. The first is to give the respondents some idea of the scope of the interview and the topics to be covered. This tells them not only what to expect but also approximately what the boundaries are.

The comments about the tape recorder are intended to make note of the machine in a routine way and set the stage for later requests from the interviewer to speak up or to stop sideline conversations. Such requests are often necessary if a good recording is to be made.

The comment about radio and television commercials is useful because most respondents will have seen commercials that portray real or role-played interviews, and if they assume that a commercial is in progress, they will be self-consciously "on stage."

The tactic of starting the interview by proceeding around the table and asking about family serves several ends. It ensures that every respondent will speak at least once—and on a topic that he is certain to know very well. It acquaints the respondents with one another. It puts relevant information about family composition and social class on the tape. And, by giving the interviewer an opportunity to speak briefly with each respondent at the outset, it allows him to show he is interested in more than skeletal replies. Immediately, if a respondent answers sparsely, the interviewer can pose a question or two, probing for information beyond that which is explicit in the question itself. For instance, the interviewer may ask, "How many of the children are living at home?" "Any grandchildren yet?" "I believe you said your husband works for the telephone company. What does he do?" This sort of light probing helps set the stage for what will happen later.

Tracking. If the interview is to follow the directive style, the interviewer then embarks on a topic and endeavors to keep the interview on that topic until it is covered to his satisfaction. For instance, an interview on shortening might open with a general question on the purposes for which shortening is used. That topic would then be pursued until the interviewer believes he has obtained all the information he needs or thinks he can get on that topic from that group.

During the opening stage, the danger is that the interview will digress in seven different directions, because comments on the first topic are virtually certain to contain material on other subjects also of great interest. Even though it is tempting to follow one or more of these other topics while the trial is hot, the practice of tracking requires that these interesting, off-the-immediate-topic clues be filed away mentally and that the immediate topic be maintained as the conversation focus. After the first topic is exhausted, the second is taken up, and so on until all topics have been covered.

Tracking produces a more or less orderly set of interviews in which all subjects are discussed in much the same sequence. It provides some assurance that all topics of interest will in fact be covered, and, as shown later, it provides a framework for a thorough and speedy report.

In the opinion of interviewers who prefer the nondirective style, tracking imposes far too much order and discipline on the respondents. The nondirective interviewer prefers to let topics emerge spontaneously and to foster dynamic, highly involved group interaction in the hope of obtaining material that would not be available in everyday, face-to-face contacts.

Nondirective interviewers often employ techniques derived from sensitivity training and group psychotherapy to further draw out the group. For instance, they sometimes use marathon sessions lasting far into the evening or through much of a day. They may use projective stimuli, like inkblots, pictures, or designs. Or they may assign roles and ask respondents to act out spontaneous dramas that center on the topic under study. All these practices foster respondent involvement, but they tangle the record and make an already difficult analysis problem that much more complicated.

Pacing. In a directive interview, a specific set of topics (and any other obviously relevant issues that emerge unexpectedly) must be covered within a fixed period of time. Most respondents want to know in advance about how long the interview will last and usually make their plans according to what they are told. The interviewer must therefore pace the session so that an interesting subject does not crowd out other equally interesting topics to be covered toward the end. Pacing an interview is much like writing an essay examination. The interviewer must assign an implicit weight to each question and move on, even if not entirely finished, when the question has taken as much time as it is worth. Like the ideal examination, the ideal interview ends at the bell.

One of the advantages of conducting a series of group interviews with continuous feedback from the client is that different interviews can be paced differently. If a topic has already been well covered in previous interviews, the interviewer need only assure himself, by a series of comparatively brief questions and answers, that the opinions of the present group are much like those he has already heard in detail. He can then move on to examine matters that have not been thoroughly discussed before.

Balancing Participation. In the ideal group interview, all respondents contribute everything they know that is relevant to the topic. This means that the interviewer must encourage the less forward respondent who might otherwise sit back and say little or nothing. It also means that a dominant individual or a small, dominant subgroup cannot be permitted to suppress others' contributions. Participation can be balanced by asking direct questions, by asking for further comment from respondents who seem hesitant about expressing their opinions, by calling on respondents who look as though they are about to speak, and, when the issue is especially important, talking to each group member in turn, progressing systematically around the table. Participation will never be absolutely uniform, but it is important that those who have something to say be given every opportunity.

Pest Control. Group interviews are susceptible to two species of pests. One is the genuine expert who knows so much about the subject matter that other group members hesitate to express their own opinions: the ex-dental technician in discussions about dental care, the dietician involved in a food-product discussion, the man with a lifetime hobby of rebuilding cars in an interview on motor oil. Experts can usually be eliminated in advance, provided that the recruiter is forewarned to ask the appropriate screening questions. Even then, an occasional expert will seep through.

The other species of pest is the all-purpose expert who knows everything about everything, from the amount of preservative per ounce of dry cereal to the effects of television on the moral development of children. Pests of this species give their opinions as established fact and attempt to inflict their viewpoints on everyone else in the room.

The genuine expert can sometimes be induced to withhold his opinions at least until other group members have had their chance. If he enters into the spirit of the investigation, he will let others talk just to learn what they think. If not, there is little the interviewer can do except ensure that another expert of the same type does not crop up in the next interview.

The pseudo expert can often be controlled by maneuvers showing that the interviewer is interested in what all group members have to say. The interviewer can cut him (or her) off in mid-phrase, ask pointedly if there are others who want to express an opinion, avoid eye contact with the pest, look bored, study the ceiling while the pest is speaking, pretend to have a severe headache, change the subject abruptly the second the pest has stopped talking, or display other signs of fatigue. Most pests can be controlled by such tactics but, alas, a few cannot. When an uncontrollable pest appears and has his (or her) way, the only consolation is that some group interviews are better than others. In most states, it is illegal for a civilian to use Mace.

Who Is a Good Interviewer? Almost anyone can learn the mechanics of directive interviewing. It helps to start by watching someone who knows how and to listen to one's own tapes, second-guessing what could have been said or done to make the interview more productive.

It is not easy, however, to acquire the background that enables the skilled interviewer to direct the conversation toward relevant talk and away from chatter that is unrelated to the client's problems. Even when the research questions are outlined in advance, it still takes a command of the specific problem and a fairly close acquaintance with marketing problems in general to know when to probe and when to stop.

Nondirective interviewing is a somewhat different matter. Here clinical training, or at least an intimate acquaintance with the clinical approach, is a great help, as is a contemplative, introspective, openly receptive frame of mind. The ideal nondirective interviewer is somewhat like an animate inkblot.

When the topic is delicate, it is always a good idea to have an interviewer of the same sex as the respondents. When the topic is impersonal, the sex of the interviewer does not matter much, except that young, attractive female interviewers sometimes have trouble keeping young male respondents on the track. Adult males often find it difficult to interview adolescent girls, who usually giggle or sulk. Anyone can experience problems when interviewing adolescent boys.

Report Preparation. Reports of group interview studies have followed several quite different patterns depending on the time and cost constraints of the study, the investigator's personal style, and the client's needs and tastes. At one extreme, when time and cost limitations are severe, the interviewer can prepare a brief, impressionistic summary of the principal findings, depending mainly on his own memory. When the interviews are intended to evaluate a new product idea or a new copy concept and when the outcome is so obvious that it needs little support or documentation, this kind of reporting may be enough. Especially when the client has been present and participating, and when the respondents' reactions can lead to only one conclusion, it may be undesirable to report more than the minutes of the meetings.

At the other extreme, the analyst listens and relistens carefully to the tapes, copying down pregnant segments, fitting the respondents' reactions into a more general scheme derived from his understanding of the history and present status of the problem and his own model of human nature. In this kind of report, the respondents' manifest reactions make roughly the same contribution to the final report as the patient's free associations make to a psychoanalyst's case report. When the reporter is sagacious, imaginative, discerning, and skillful, reports in this tradition are rich, stimulating, novel, creative, and fascinating—and infuriating to anyone who is not prepared to take the analyst at his word.

A method between these two extremes—one designed to preserve the most significant interview material more or less intact and still allow for imaginative interpretation—is technically known as the "Scissor and Sort" or "Long Couch, Short Hallway" technique. The first step in this procedure is to have all the interviews transcribed. Although this step may seem costly and time-consuming (typing a moderately long interview takes about a day), investment is more than repaid in the efficiencies a typed transcript brings to report preparation. Typing services in most large cities provide quick protocols at moderate fees. If the interviewer has encouraged respondents to speak up and talk singly and if there are not too many telephone bells, boat whistles, fire sirens, or jet overflights, the protocols will be reasonably accurate.

The next step is to edit, code, and bracket the interview segments that will form the muscle of the report. Respondents do not usually speak perfect prose. They hem and haw, back up, skip words and phrases, and sometimes forget what they were about to say in mid-sentence. In the editing process, much of this verbal meandering (which the typist will faithfully reproduce) can be deleted, leaving a comparatively readable script. The degree of editing is a matter of judgment. On one hand, it is important to make reports as readable as possible, or they will not be read. On the other hand, it is essential to preserve as much as one can of the flavor and texture of the respondents' remarks, including bad English, clumsy attempts at description, and obvious confusion when confusion is what occurred. In many instances, the chief value of the report will be its presentation of what the respondents had to say in the respondents' own words.

The next step is to bracket those transcript segments that are relevant to the problem and to code the bracketed material by subject matter. A bracket may enclose an interchange among the interviewer and one or more respondents covering part of a page, the bottom of one page and the top of the next, or several pages—as long as the bracketed material has some common subject core. The coding, written longhand in the margin, is simply the analyst's notes to himself on what the bracketed segment is about and where in the report it might fit.

The next step is to cut each interview apart, bracket by bracket, and to staple or tape together the segments that extend over several pages. The segments are then sorted by topic (a long couch or a short hallway will do), and the material is ready for the final step.

The last step is writing the supporting and connective tissue. This material usually starts with an introduction describing the study's purpose, the major questions the investigator sought to answer, the size and structure of the sample, and the major features of the group interview technique. Many reports then go on to a two- or three-page summary of the results, and conclude with the main body of the findings.

If the respondents' conversations have been well segmented and sorted, preparing the main body of the report is not difficult. The first major topic is introduced; the first set of interview segments is placed into the report as a series of exhibits, and the segments are summarized and discussed. Single-spacing the quotations and double-spacing the discussion provide a varied format that is easy to follow.

Subsequent sections have the same pattern, that is, introduction, exhibits, discussion, the major difference being that later discussions point out relationships with material that has appeared before.

This method of report preparation preserves the most relevant sections of each interview, and presents the interview material in an organized, coherent framework. It makes the reader's task easy and provides the analyst with an opportunity to highlight relationships, interpret where interpretation is needed, and point out implications. In a practiced analyst's hands, it does not require an unreasonable amount of time.

TRAPS

Seduction. The group interview is nearly the world's worst instrument for producing hard data like share-of-market percentages, brand-switching turnover tables, and media-reach and frequency figures. No one sets out to use group interviews for such purposes, but the sense of immediacy and conviction one gets from listening to real consumers describe and defend their activities and preferences can lead the unwary investigator into thinking that his samples are larger and more representative than they actually are.

For a quick grasp of broad trends, where an error of 5, 10, or even 20 percent may not lead the investigator too far astray, and for a reading of reactions that are apt to be much the same from one segment of the population to another, three to five group interviews may be all the decision maker needs. But when every percentage point counts or when reactions are likely to vary greatly from one population subgroup to another, seduction by vivid anecdote is an ever-present danger. It is little help to say, "All group interview studies should be followed up by carefully designed, precisely executed, large-scale survey research." Maybe they should be, but they won't.

Taste. The technology of taste tests is now well developed. Among the factors that influence the perceived taste of a beverage or food are the taster's orientation to the product, the perceived reactions of others, physical properties of the environment (such as light, heat, and smoke), the product's physical condition (including temperature and freshness), and the order in which samples are served. When group interviews concern foods or beverages, it is tempting to have the respondents taste some samples at the end of the interview to see how they will react. Then, all the variables that are well controlled in the taste-testing laboratory will affect the group-interview taste test in unknowable ways.

Newness. Group interviews are frequently used to screen new-product ideas. If the new product is a minor variation on something with which respondents are already familiar, group interviews will show how the new-product concept, as presented, is perceived. But if the new product is so truly innovative that it falls outside the respondents' range of experience or if acceptance of the new product requires a change in mores (for example, miniskirts), the group interview filter will likely screen the product out. Evaluation by means of group interviews is essentially conservative. It favors ideas that are easy to explain and understand and, therefore, not very new. It works against radical, but maybe highly profitable, change.

Order Effects. When concepts, products, or advertisements are presented to groups for evaluation, each judgment is certain to be influenced by previous judgments. If group members have been highly critical of one thing, they are apt to compensate by being overly uncritical of the next. Order effects occur in individual interviews too, but they are accentuated by the sentiment and cohesiveness that develop in groups, and they can be powerful enough to overbalance everything else.

Delicate Topics. Since group interviews are more "public" than individual interviews, it might seem at first that they are inappropriate for discussing matters generally considered personal. Experience has shown, however, that group interview respondents are surprisingly open in their remarks on their attitudes toward, and use of, contraceptives, deodorants, laxatives, sanitary napkins, liquor, and drugs. If the group leader is unembarrassed and if he (or she) can establish an atmosphere of trust, groups will discuss with surprising frankness many matters that are not usually mentioned in public.

Compared with individual depth interviews, group interviews focus more on shared experiences and less on personal and individual ones. When the topic is delicate, that is doubly true. This characteristic of group interviews has led some investigators to conclude that studies of delicate topics should always include at least some individual interviews. It has led others to argue that since advertising and marketing must operate at the shared-experience level rather than at the individual level anyway, the less deep, less personal material produced by the group interview is about as deep and personal as one should go.

One Final Trap. When concepts, products, or advertisements are presented for evaluation, group members will assume that the material being evaluated is the interviewer's. Therefore, if a friendly atmosphere has been established, respondents will hesitate to be frankly critical unless the interviewer has emphasized that negative reactions are just as valued as positive ones. Obviously, the interviewer must not only say that he is interested in negative comments; he must also show that he means it.

HOW CAN ANYTHING SO BAD BE GOOD?

Group interviewing violates most of the accepted canons of survey research. Samples are invariably small and never selected by probability methods. Questions are not asked the same way each time. Responses are not independent. Some respondents inflict their opinions on others; some contribute little or nothing at all. Results are difficult or impossible to quantify and are not grist for the statistical mill. Conclusions depend on the analyst's interpretive skill. The investigator can easily influence the results.

With these glaring defects, why have group interviews been so widely used? Why have skeptical clients, who tried them only to see what they were like, come back for more? As noted earlier, part of the answer is that group interviews are fast and cheap. When decisions must be made and resources are limited, the alternative to a group interview study may well be no study at all. But a more important, less thoroughly understood part of the answer is that *any* way of gathering information is a series of compromises. The group interview is the product of one selection of compromises; the traditional survey interview is the product of another. What traditional survey research gains in sample size, standardization, and quantification, it loses in lack of contact between respondent and client, rigidity, elapsed time, and high cost. Too often it also produces elegantly quantified "results" that neither investigator nor client really understands.

CONCLUDING COMMENT

Since most of this chapter has emphasized how interesting group interviews are and how useful they can be, it is appropriate to close by recapitulating and reemphasizing what has already been said about the dangers of using group interviews to the exclusion of other techniques.

Group interviews cannot be conducted with large samples of the population, and sampling techniques that ensure representativeness cannot be employed. One must therefore assume that whatever is being investigated is so uniformly distributed that it does not matter much where one dips into the population or that crude attempts at stratification—such as prescreening respondents on education and age—will pick up all of the variation that is really important. Both these assumptions are questionable and, at times, very wrong.

Group interview respondents are not independent. In a four-interview study with 32 respondents, the degrees of freedom are 3, not 31—one less than the number of independent observations. It is therefore deceptive as well as tedious to count the pros and cons on an issue and subject the proportions to statistical test. By the same token, group interview data are not amenable to analysis by the powerful and extremely helpful multivariate statistical techniques discussed in other chapters in this handbook.

The group leader can, does, and should influence the results. A moderator with the wrong bias can therefore make the findings wrong. Similarly, as in the analytic study of any qualitative material, the analysis and interpretation of group interview material are strongly influenced by the analyst's view of the world—so much so that the usefulness of a group interview study may depend as much on the analyst's insight and creativity as on what the respondents say. Bad analyst: bad report.

For these reasons and because of the ever-present danger of falling into one or more of the six traps described earlier, the conservative course is to use group interviews as a preliminary step to generate hypotheses for more rigorous investigation later on.

When that second step cannot be taken, as sometimes it cannot, the user of group interview material should weigh the risks just described.

REFERENCES

1. Goldman, Alfred E., "The Group Depth Interview," *Journal of Marketing*, vol. 26, July 1962, pp. 61–68.
2. Seeman, Julius, "Deception in Psychological Research," *American Psychologist*, vol. 24, November 1969, pp. 1025–1028.
3. Smith, George H., *Motivation Research in Advertising and Marketing*, New York: McGraw-Hill, 1954.

QUALITATIVE RESEARCH TECHNIQUES: FOCUS GROUP INTERVIEWS

INTRODUCTION

The focus group interview, or group depth interview, is a technique which grew out of the group therapy method used by psychiatrists. The concept is based on the assumption that individuals who share a problem will be more willing to talk about it amid the security of others sharing the problem. It offers a means of obtaining in-depth information on a specific topic through a discussion group atmosphere which allows an insight into the behavior and thinking of the individual group members. Rather than using a structured question-and-answer methodology, the procedure is to encourage a group to discuss feelings, attitudes, and perceptions about the topic being discussed.

The focus group interview is one of the qualitative marketing research techniques developed in the 1950's in reaction to the large sample polling techniques which provided lots of numbers but little insight into what was really going on, the "why" behind the numbers. One researcher has described the technique as "A chance to 'experience' a 'flesh and blood' consumer . . . to go into her life and relive with her all of the satisfactions, dissatisfactions, rewards, and frustrations she experiences when she takes the product into her home." [44-p.6]

In spite of being one of the most frequently used techniques in marketing research today, there are no prescribed guidelines for focus group interviews, no book of rules, no formulas, and no stratagems. [44-p.6] The interviews conducted with researchers and the readings examined in the preparation of this monograph revealed a number of disagreements concerning the use and methods involved in conducting research using focus group interviews. The rest of this chapter will describe the technique, its uses, advantages and disadvantages, noting disagreements among researchers where appropriate.

DESCRIPTION

Merton, Fiske, and Kendall distinguish the focus group as following these criteria:

> Persons interviewed are known to have been involved in a particular situation; . . . The hypothetically significant elements, patterns, processes, and total structure of the situation have been provisionally analyzed by the social scientist. . . . On the basis of this analysis he takes the third step of developing an interview guide, setting forth the major areas of in-

Reprinted from Danny N. Bellenger, Kenneth L. Bernhardt, and Jac L. Goldstucker, *Qualitative Research in Marketing* (Chicago: American Marketing Association, 1976), pp. 7-28.

quiry and the hypotheses which provide criteria of relevance for the data to be obtained in the interview. Fourth and finally, the interview is focused on the subjective experiences of persons exposed to the pre-analyzed situation in an effort to ascertain their definitions of the situation. [54-p.3]

The groups are generally conducted with women, especially house-wives, but can be conducted with any homogeneous group of consumers. For example, Dr. Alfred Goldman has conducted focus group sessions for National Analysts with computer engineers, personnel managers, heads of manufacturing companies, paper-making chemists, retailers, models, doctors, lawyers, and persons whose net worth exceeds a half million dollars.[12]

Focus group interviews typically last one and a half to two hours, which gives the moderator sufficient time to develop a good rapport with respondents and thus get very candid answers. Often the moderator is able to get below the conscious level, and the respond-ents reveal their personality, emotions, and true feelings. This tech-nique thus allows the researcher to handle sensitive areas more ef-fectively via the group method than with individual interviews.

The technique is particularly suited for new product prototype testing, studying package changes, advertising strategy changes, and advertising copy formulation. It is a very flexible technique, and the interview session can be used to show various products, demonstra-tions, ads and commercials or even to conduct taste tests or product usage tests as part of the group interview.

The ideal group is 8 to 12 people. Fewer than 8 is likely to bur-den each individual, while more than 12 tends to reduce each mem-ber's participation. With respect to group member selection, Merton, *et. al.* state:

It appears that the more socially and intellectually homogeneous the interview group, the more produc-tive its reports. . . Interviewees of widely differing social status often make comments or refer to ex-periences which are alien or meaningless to the rest. . . . Some continue to be interested in what is being said, but others become restless and ultimately with-draw their attention.[12]

The number of group sessions conducted depends on the topic being considered, the number of segments to be studied, and expense and time considerations. Covering every possible segment is almost always impossible, so the research must concentrate on the few seg-ments most useful to the specific purposes of the study. For example, if the study requires interviews with broad spectrums of age groups from teenagers to retired people, and heavy users and light users are separated, a large number of group interviews will have to be conducted. The objective, of course, is to try to have as few groups as possible, while at the same time realizing the necessity to replicate the focus group interviews for each segment being studied. If there are two with any one age group and they go in totally differ-ent directions, a third session should be conducted.

It is essential to get as much commonality in a group as possible so that the numerous interacting demographic variables do not confuse the issues; to be most productive, all the participants must be on the same wave length. For example, Young and Rubicam, which conducts approximately 600 focus groups per year, almost never puts married, full-time housewives with children at home in the same group as unmarried, working women because their life styles and over-all goals and needs are completely different. They also break teen-age and child groups carefully and rarely interveiw men and women together.[45-p.10]

A number of reseachers think age, then sex are the most important breaks both being better means of separating the group than occupation or income. Great extremes on any of these are bad, however. This is usually not a problem since researchers are typically looking at the middle class only, tending to avoid the extreme of income categories.

Some researchers argue that groups can easily be racially integrated while others feel that separate groups should be conducted with each race. Even those that argue for integration, however, say that one token Black may be worse than no Blacks at all; it is usually better to have two to three Blacks out of ten.

There is much disagreement about the importance of good recruiting to obtain the group members. A minority of researchers feel that because the interview is so subjective and the sample so small and unrepresentative, it does not really matter how you obtain the individuals. A majority of the researchers contacted, however, feel strongly that proper recruiting is essential to the success of the focus group interview. First, it is necessary for the members to have had experience with the product being studied. It is impossible to elicit valuable comments from individuals with no background upon which to draw. Second, people who have participated in group interviews previously (some research firms use a six month limit, some one year, and a very few have no restrictions) should not be allowed to participate. They know what to expect and are too ready to respond, and "show off" for the other participants. As one researcher has put it, "I've heard every excuse and rationalization for repeat respondents, but I will never accept that a repeat respondent can possibly contribute to a session in the same way as a new respondent . . . the only kind of respondent who can make a contribution to my qualitative work is a fresh, spontaneous, involved, honest respondent who has not pre-thought her answers." [45-p.10]

Many researchers believe that an individual should not be allowed to participate in a group containing a friend, neighbor, or relative; they will tend to talk to each other and not to the group as a whole. For that same reason, church groups or organizations should not be asked to send people. The people that arrive in these groups have already established relationships, some being leaders and some being followers.

The physical environment is very important to the success of the focus group interview. The atmosphere should be as relaxed as possible to encourage informal, "off the cuff" discussion. An impressive large table in a big corporate conference room may inhibit many participants and should be avoided. The environment should encourage the individuals to give their opinions and feelings, not their judgments; it is imperative to avoid giving the group members the impression that they are experts and you want their intellectual opinions, and the setup of the room is important in this regard.

Most researchers feel it is important for the client to observe the focus group session. This can be done by having the client actually participate as a group member, or much more commonly, by watching from behind a two-way mirror. It is usually much better to observe from a detached position where there is no danger of disrupting the normal functioning of the group and where the observer can take notes on those findings important to him. A short break may be desirable during the session so the client can specify to the moderator other things which he would like probed in more detail.

DYNAMICS AND THE ROLE OF THE MODERATOR

To give the reader a better feel for the dynamics of the focus group session, an edited transcript (a full transcript from a session usually runs 60 pages or more) from a focus group interview conducted recently with women in Chicago is included in Appendix A. The interview, which originally appeared in *Advertising Age* was one of a series conducted with shoppers throughout the country designed to explore what "typical" consumers think about products and prices in stores today and how they shop.

The one thing on which everyone agrees with respect to focus group interviews is that the moderator's role is of prime importance to the success. This can certainly be demonstrated in the transcript in Appendix A. Rapport, level of verbal ability, relevancy and direction of the discussion are important responsibilities of the moderator. There have been several good articles written telling the moderator how to carry out these reponsibilities effectively. (For example see [47,46])

Proper analysis and interpretation of the data also depend upon the moderator, his experience, insights into group behavior, interviewing techniques, and his knowledge of the subject at hand. Highly skilled moderators are therefore necessary to insure that the information be as free of bias as possible and provide the understanding required concerning the consumers' attitudes, opinions, and buying behavior.

One problem that some moderators have with group interviewing is that they actually conduct separate depth interviews with each of 10 individuals who happen to be sitting at the same table. To avoid this pitfall, a high degree of interpersonal interaction within the group is needed. The degree of interaction can be determined by the focus of the interview. If comments are consistently directed toward the moderator, interaction among the participants is not occurring. If, on the other hand, the discussion centers upon the subject of the research and the moderator has a very minimal role, interaction has been achieved.

Only with interaction can the group interview:

1. provide the desired spontaneity of response by participants.

2. produce the degree of emotional involvement essential to produce "depth" level responses, and

3. produce the kind and degree of rapport which facilitates a "give and take" exchange of attitudinal and behavioral information.

The moderator's skill in achieving interaction among a group of participants who have never met each other before and probably never will meet each other again determines the kinds and the importance of emerging data. Therefore the moderator, often a trained psychologist, must be thoroughly knowledgeable about the category under study and must know when to probe the group members and when to shut up. This special talent can be developed only by specific training and by learning from a great deal of trial and error.

Following are a few key qualifications of moderators adapted from Donald A. Chase, "The Intensive Group Interview" [46]:

1. *Kind but firm* — In order to elicit necessary interaction, the moderator must combine a disciplined detachment with understanding empathy. To achieve this, he must simultaneously display a kindly, permissive attitude toward the participants, encouraging them to feel at ease in the group interview environment, while insisting that the discussion remain germane to the problem at hand. Only with experience can the moderator achieve an appropriate blending of these two apparently antithetical roles.

   It is also the moderator's responsibility to encourage the emergence of leadership from within the group, while at the same time avoiding tendencies of domination of the group by a single member. The kindly but firm moderator must be sensitive to bids for attention and must maintain his leadership without threatening or destroying the interactional process.

2. *Permissiveness* — While an atmosphere of permissiveness is desirable, the moderator must be at all times alert to indications that the group atmosphere of cordiality is disintegrating. Before permissiveness leads to chaos, the moderator must reestablish the group purpose and maintain its orientation to the subject.

   The moderator must be ready and willing to pursue clues to information that may at first appear tangential to the subject for it may open new areas of

17

exploration. He must also be prepared to cope with expressions of unusual opinions and eruptions of personality clashes within the group. The manner in which these are handled may well be the difference between a productive and an unproductive group session.

3. *Involvement* — Since a principal reason for the group interview is to expose feelings and to obtain reactions indicative of deeper feelings, the moderator must encourage and stimulate intensive personal involvement. If the moderator is unable to immerse himself completely in the topic being discussed, the group will sense his detachment, and the depth contribution of the interview will be lost.

4. *Incomplete Understanding* — A most useful skill of the group moderator is his ability to convey lack of complete understanding of the information being presented. Although he may understand what the participant is trying to express, by carefully inserting noncommittal remarks, phrased in questioning tones, the respondent is encouraged to delve more deeply into the sources of his opinion. He is, by this process, able to reveal and elaborate on the kinds of information for which the group interview is designed. The goal is to encourage respondents to be more specific about generalized comments made by group members.

The usefulness of this technique can be endangered if its application is inappropriate. If the "incomplete understanding" is a superficially assumed role, the group will soon detect this artificiality, and will feel that the moderator is playing some sort of cryptic game with the group. The group interview will then deteriorate into a sterile collection of mutual suspicions. Incomplete understanding on the part of the moderator must be a genuine curiosity about the deeper sources of the participant's understanding.

5. *Encouragement* — Although the dynamics of the group situation facilitate the participation of all members in the interaction, there may be individuals who resist contributing. The skillful moderator should be aware of unresponsive members and try to break down their reserve and encourage their involvement.

The unresponsive member offers a real challenge to the group moderator. There are numerous ways in which a resistant or bashful member can be encouraged to participate, such as by assigning him a task to perform, or by providing an opening for his remarks. If this is inappropriately attempted, it may only reinforce a reluctance to participate in a verbal fashion. The ability to interpret nonverbal clues may provide a means of discovering a tactic to broaden the scope of the group's active participation.

6. *Flexibility* — The moderator should be equipped prior to the session with a topic outline of the subject matter to be covered. By committing the topics to memory before the interview, the moderator may use the outline only as a reminder of content areas omitted or covered incompletely.

If a topic outline is followed minutely, the progress of the interview will be uneven and artificial, jumping from topic to topic without careful transitions. This procedure communicates a lack of concern to the participants, for its mechanical nature makes the moderator appear to lack genuine interest in their responses.

At the same time, the interview cannot be allowed to wander aimlessly. Under such conditions, control of the situation soon passes from the moderator to a self-appointed group leader.

The group interview should be conducted the way one walks across a rope bridge. The handrails are gripped firmly and the objective is kept in mind constantly. If the bottom foot rope should break, the walk is continued hand over hand until the destination is reached. This requires an ability to improvise and alter predetermined plans amid the distractions of the group process.

7. *Sensitivity* — The moderator must be able to identify, as the group interview progresses, the informational level on which it is being conducted, and determine if it is appropriate for the subject under discussion. Sensitive areas will frequently produce superficial rather than depth responses. Depth is achieved when there is a substantial amount of emotional responses, as opposed to intellectual information. Indications of depth are provided when participants begin to indicate how they feel about the subject, rather than what they think about it.

There are differing views with regard to the sex of the moderator. Some researchers believe that it is important that the moderator be of the same sex as the group members to insure adequate rapport between the two. Others believe that with a moderator of the opposite sex the participants will not assume the moderator knows what they are talking about (how they wash clothes, for example) and will thus be more specific in their responses.

A problem confronting most moderators is how to control the person who wants to dominate the group and how to stimulate the reticent member. One way to handle the dominant member is to stop the group and poll each person individually on an issue, therefore giving everyone a chance to talk. Also, the moderator may give the person dominating the session a task such as helping the hostess make coffee which takes him out of the room for a few minutes. Reticent persons are often much more of a problem. The moderator must try to determine why they are shy and seek to encourage them to contribute to the session.

The polling technique is often helpful in getting everybody to express his opinion. At the beginning of the focus group interview a question may be asked which requires each member to express something about himself. This tends to reduce the person's reticence and to encourage him to talk. At the end of each session each individual may be asked to sum up what the group resolved. This summary is often very important.

Another helpful device which provides the opportunity to get more input is to call each of the respondents a day or two later to thank him for participating. Often, the respondents have talked to other people after the session, and this may have influenced their opinions. The followup call allows the researcher to find out what they *now* think about the various issues.

It is important to use the same moderator for all the group sessions, even if the sessions are in widely disparate geographical areas. The moderator learns from each session, and becomes more effective in subsequent sessions. He is actually fine tuning his final report with each additional group. Although rarely done, the ideal way to conduct a focus group interview study is to start with several groups and keep going until no new important information is obtained from the session, which may occur after five groups, or after twenty.

ADVANTAGES AND USES

When used properly, the focus group interview technique offers a number of advantages over other techniques. John Hess has described some of the potential advantages of the technique as follows[49]:

Synergism —   combined group effort produces a wider range of information, insight and ideas.

Snowballing —   random comments may set off a chain reaction of responses that further feed new ideas.

Stimulation —   the group experience itself is exciting, stimulating.

Security —   the individual may find comfort in the group and more readily express his ideas.

Spontaneity —   since individuals aren't required to answer

each question, the answers given become more meaningful.

In addition, the company whose products are being discussed may benefit by:

Serendipity — key items or concepts unthought of may be discovered.

Specialization — the use of highly trained interviewers can be condensed through group interviewing.

Scientific scrutiny — sessions may be analyzed in detail after the interviews are completed.

Speed — the use of groups speeds up the interview process and the data accumulation.

Structure— group structuring is not so obvious and leading arrangements can be used that are unavailable in individual interviewing.

Major benefits accrue from focus group interviews. These interviews provide the researcher with an opportunity to learn directly from consumers, in their own terms, their reasons for buying a product, their expectations of its performance, and the rewards which they hope to reap from using it. "No one has done the original thinking for the women. No one has locked her into little boxes by 'pre-thinking' her reactions and responses. She isn't forced into categorizing her spontaneous and uninhibited reactions so she gives them to you as they happen." [44-p.6]

Eugene L. Reilly points out an additional advantage of focus group interviewing. He states that "Our own work in traditional focus group inquiry had caused us to respect the ability of consumers (especially in the early stages of ideation),to assess (through reaction) new product ideas, new concepts, new strategies, etc." [37-108]

Our interviews with researchers yielded a number of different uses for the technique. Those most often used are:

1. To generate hypotheses that can be further tested quantitatively;

2. To generate information helpful in structuring consumer questionnaires;

3. To provide overall background information on a product category;

4. To get impressions on new product concepts for which there is little information available;

5. To stimulate new ideas about older products;

6. To generate ideas for new creative concepts;

7. To interpret previously obtained quantitative results.

To Generate Hypotheses. An individual whom we interviewed indicated that when a client purchases focus group interviews, he is not buying consumer research. "You are really buying the head of the person who will do the research — the key question is can the person organize information and help you define problems?" With focus groups you are looking for definitions of problems rather than for solutions. What is happening is that you have a loosely defined problem area and want the researcher (moderator) to give you a hand with it. The group sessions give him the guidance to help define the particular problems involved. The researcher and the client draw up a discussion guide together; and when the focus groups are done, what you have is a good operational definition of what the problems are and how they can be stated in the form of hypotheses which can be analyzed via quantitative research.

Because of the qualitative nature of the technique, focus groups are most successful when they allow the researcher to design a better subsequent research study using experimental design or other quantitative techniques. In many major consumer research-oriented companies, any time a major quantitative study is to be conducted, focus groups will be used first to help define the issues and generate appropriate hypotheses for testing.

With sample sizes typically smaller than 100, data which are only directional in nature, and numbers which are not projectable, it is important to recognize that the conclusions generated from focus groups are only hypotheses and that quantitative research must be used to confirm the results before they can be used for decision making.

Several examples can be cited to indicate how focus groups have been used to generate hypotheses. A major gasoline producer, concerned about the future growth of sales of gasoline through service stations, wanted to discover what consumers felt about the gasoline station of the future. It wanted to identify possible opportunities for sales of alternative products and services through its retail network. It used 12 focus group sessions in 5 cities throughout the country to select some possibilities which would be worth investigating in some detail, eventually testing the best ideas with test markets and other quantitative techniques.

Another example of the successful use of focus groups for hypothesis generation concerns research on consumer reactions to bank automated tellers. A series of focus group sessions were conducted with potential users, the results indicating that people found the automatic tellers very impersonal and were afraid of losing their money to the machine. The results of the group meetings indicated that the machines should be personalized, the required secret codes should be easy to remember, and an incentive should be given to the consumer to try out the machine. The hypotheses developed were further tested and confirmed, and a program was created which gave the machine a name and personality all its own. Consumers were allowed to create their own secret code, and free McDonald's hamburgers were given as incentives for using the tellers. The machines now experience the highest usage rate of any automatic tellers in the country with 30 percent of the bank's customers using them, twice the national average.

A third example concerns the use of focus groups to study why women were rejecting vegetable protein products. The quantitative studies found that women said they did not like the taste, but other research showed women could not taste the difference between these products and equivalent meat products. The focus group session found that a possible important reason was that the women did not want to deprive their families of meat.

To Structure Questionnaires. Focus groups are used to help researchers learn and understand the consumer language associated with specific product categories or brands. The language consumers use often may not be at all similar to company technical phrases or buzzwords. One researcher interviewed for this study offered semi-moist dog food, porous-tipped pens, and demand deposits as representative of corporation words not very relevant to consumers. A major use of focus groups is often to find out the key phrases or words used by consumers in talking about the particular product or service.

As an example, a soft drink company, before doing a major study on brand positioning, needed to define the needs people are seeking to satisfy with soft drinks. They know it is not just thirst ("when you see a kid down four cans of cola, you know it can't just be thirst") or a craving for sweets. Such things as social facilitation and escape are also important needs, and 20 focus groups sessions were conducted throughout the country to identify a complete, all encompassing set of needs which were then incorporated into a questionnaire which was used in a quantitative study.

Focus groups are also used to identify new areas to investigate in a quantitative study. For example, a soft drink company used focus groups to examine consumer reaction to several different package changes, including a new wide mouth bottle. The participants indicated that they were concerned with the loss of carbonation in the new package, something that the researchers had not been sensitive to previously. Without the focus groups, the quantitative research would not have investigated this important aspect of the package change.

It is sometimes hard for the researcher to know how to structure a particular question, and focus groups can be helpful in this regard. For example, in studying frequency of use of a laundry product, should the question be put in terms of number of times per month, or in terms of proportion of wash loads?

To Provide Overall Background Information. Focus groups are often used by advertising agencies before making a new business presentation to a potential client. The creative and account personnel are thus able to hear first hand what consumers feel about the product category, the potential client's product, their likes, dislikes, and level of satisfaction with existing products. They are able to hear directly from consumers how they buy and how they use the product, together with their reasons for buying and using it.

In a similar manner, companies considering merger, acquisition, or product line extension into an unknown category may conduct focus group interviews with consumers and/or distributors to determine the attractiveness of the expansion and factors they should consider in their evaluation. In short, what is the product to consumers, how do consumers talk about the category, and how do they judge and evaluate the product?

The wealth of information generated is of great value in introducing someone to a new product category, and as a result, advertising agencies often will conduct focus group interviews when new account teams are assigned to an account.

To Get Impressions On New Product Concepts. One of the most common uses of the focus group technique is the examination of new product concepts to check out ideas at an early stage. As one researcher put it, "So many times the people who work on a project and intellectualize about it almost day and night get so caught up in their reasoning that they no longer can 'see' it clearly. As a result, they can miss the most obvious red flags."[44-p.6]

The following examples show how focus groups can be used to help new product personnel understand how their product fits with consumer needs. First, Texize Chemicals, producers of a wide line of household products including Fantastik®, used a series of focus groups for a new product called Glass*Plus®. Quantitative research had shown that housewives were using Fantastik® to clean glass, a use for which the product was not recommended. The company conducted some focus groups to guide their product development effort and found that there appeared to be a need for a product between Fantastik®, a heavy duty cleaner, and glass cleaners like Windex®. Such a product would be one which could clean glass and also be used as a household cleaner. As a result of the initial concept, they were able to develop Glass*Plus®, which after a great deal more consumer research, both qualitative and quantitative, is being successfully introduced, positioned as an all-purpose light duty spray cleaner. Texize, which has been very aggressive in the new products area, uses focus groups to make preliminary examinations of as many as four to five new product concepts each month, conducting over a hundred group sessions each year.

The focus group technique can also be used effectively by industrial products companies to examine the impressions of dealers toward a new product concept. Owens-Corning Fiberglas is one company which has conducted research of this type.[36] The company's Transportation Marketing Division recently conducted a series of 15 focus group interviews with mass merchandise, oil company and private label tire dealers. The research objective was to see what key benefits and merchandising aids would best help dealers sell glass radials. Previous research had shown that consumers would buy fiber glass radials provided they cost less than steel ones. Owens-Corning marketing personnel watched from behind a one-way mirror as a researcher got groups of 3 to 15 dealers talking about the tire business in general and fiber glass radials in particular. The marketers were very surprised by what they saw as they were convinced that product acceptance would be smooth sailing. But dealers talked about the problems they had when glass bias-belted tires were introduced eight years previously. Even though the bias-belted tires had become big sellers, the dealers were worried that they would have similar initial problems with the glass radials. As a result, the marketing team was able to rework sales themes and promotional copy, with a much higher probability of a successful introduction of the new product.

To Stimulate New Ideas About Older Products. Focus groups can also be used to get consumer impressions of existing products. Such things as consumer satisfaction with what is available now, usage habits, which of several forms or package types are best, possible line extensions, and potential product improvements can all be studied with the focus group technique.

To cite an example, a Texize product, Grease relief®, whose original concept came out of focus groups, was studied using groups to examine some of the above questions. The quantitative research the company had conducted had not indicated any packaging problems, but some focus group participants were found to have a strong underlying distaste for the package. The focus group interviews indicated that the housewives did not like to handle it (pick it up off the shelf). Analysis indicated that the phallic shape of the package was responsible. The company then conducted a series of focus group sessions in Atlanta, a strong Grease relief® market, to determine what type of package might be attractive to the consumers. By the end of each session, respondents had made it clear that a dish detergent-type bottle would be best. In spite of this, participants were sent home with a spray package Texize had developed. Another group session with the individuals was planned for one week later. During these followup sessions the participants said the new spray package was a super package and most thoughts of a dish detergent package were generally downrated. Because members of the group are sometimes so far removed from reality in the sessions that the results are not necessarily indicative of how the product will do in the store, the company decided to do further testing. The final result was the successful introduction of a spray package to attract new users and a large economy sized dish detergent-type package without a spray for heavy users. This example shows how qualitative research can be used most effectively, that is, in conjunction with quantitative research, with each type making important contributions. The qualitative focus groups, for example, were able to identify a problem area which quantitative research was unable to uncover. The groups also identified a possible solution, which was then verified and adjusted via a quantitative followup study.

To Generate Ideas For New Creative Concepts. In addition to helping orient new account teams and gathering information useful for new business presentations, a great number of focus group interviews are conducted by advertising agencies to obtain ideas for new creative strategies for their clients. Myril Axelrod of Young and Rubicam states that:

> Group sessions are, for instance, a most valuable way of letting a copywriter know, hopefully before he has become too emotionally committed to an idea, whether his copy is indeed saying what it is intended to say; whether the consumer is "reading" it in the way he wants her to read it; whether it has meaning to her that is relevant to the way she uses the product and to her needs in the category. [44-p.6]

Most large scale quantitative studies are concerned with the majority, the numbers, and not the single interesting idea that might emerge. For example, during one series of group interviews designed to select a slogan for a new service system, the moderator threw open the discussion for the participants' own ideas. One was particularly succinct and clear, even in perfect rhyme. The phrase was tested further and now is on General Electric trucks all over the country. [12] While this type of experience is admittedly rare, the group sessions often will provide the creative personnel with a wealth of ideas to pursue in their creative process.

Another use of focus groups in advertising is to pretest advertising. The Marketing Workshop in Atlanta, and undoubtedly other research firms as well, conduct short focus group sessions as part of their normal process of testing advertising. They hold a 20 to 30 minute focus group interview after they have administered a quantitative questionnaire to evaluate the effectiveness of the commercials. The purpose of the short group sessions is to provide further insights into why the individuals feel the way they do about ads and to get more detailed information on how respondents interpret the ads.

To Interpret Previously Obtained Quantitative Results. Although not one of the more frequent uses for focus groups, it is one which offers much promise for producing valuable information. This can be demonstrated, using as an example a product of a major soft drink company. The product, a ten percent fruit juice carbonated soft drink, had an acceptable taste, a price which was a little high, and was oriented toward that segment of the soft drink market which was concerned with nutrition.

In the test market, the soft drink started strong, held up for a while, and then dropped off rapidly. Some 30 percent of the market had tried one of the three flavors in a very short time period. The quantitative research which had been conducted had not predicted the falloff in sales and slow death of the product. The company wanted to know why this had happened.

The panel data which had been gathered showed that repeat purchases were slow but did not reveal the reasons why. This was primarily because there was a 6 to 8 week lag between the time that the data were gathered and then disseminated. The research department conducted some focus group interviews and found that the product has a taste that sated very easily but that it was a taste which members of the panel described as " a kind thing that you would have at a wedding. " When asked if that was good or bad, people responded, " It's OK for weddings. " In other words, people liked it but thought of it as being only for special occasions. When asked why they were not buying it, they responded, "Because we've already had it." It seemed that one dose every eight weeks or so was enough. If people wanted to get nutrition in what they drank, it turned out they would buy straight juice or vitamins. If they wanted a soft drink, they did not care about the nutrition at all, and they certainly were not willing to pay extra for it.

DISADVANTAGES AND MISUSES

Some of the advantages of the focus group technique also lead to disadvantages and misuses. For example, focus groups apparently are occasionally used merely as evidence to support a manager's preconceived notions, largely because studies using the techniques are usually cheaper to conduct than quantitative studies using an experimental design.

Focus group interviews are easy to set up, difficult to moderate, and difficult to interpret, and are therefore very easily misused. Often one can find evidence in the interviews to support any position, a reason why many managers use them to support their preconceived ideas. It is obviously very important that extreme care be used in the interpretation, necessitating a highly skilled moderator. This is one of the major disadvantages of the technique, especially since there is an extremely limited number of highly qualified moderators.

In addition, to be most effective, good facilities must be used, as described in the previous section. Unfortunately, there are many cities in the country where adequate facilities are not available.

Another problem with focus groups is that they are used for too many things. Some researchers call this the "quick and dirty" syndrome, again because the groups can be conducted quickly and relatively inexpensively. The problem is the research does not indicate how extensive the attitudes expressed really are, and often the necessary followup using quantitative research is never conducted.

Discussing this problem, one of the researchers interviewed for this monograph offered this advice to future users of focus groups: "Don't use the results as information, and don't believe what comes out of the research. Often, you will make bad decisions using the results, and even worse, you will not know you are making bad decisions. The problem is there is no way to put into perspective what one guy said vs. another guy, or the impact of the group itself on the individual statements." This researcher, who is associated with a consumer products company which conducts several hundred focus groups per year, strongly believes that quantitative research is always required as a followup to the focus group.

Closely related to the problem of the inability to draw firm conclusions from the focus groups is the problem of the nonrepresentative sample used. It is so tempting to leave respondents with a questionnaire. Unfortunately, as one research manager indicated, "The product managers will then project these results to a larger population. For example, with 30 people in the focus groups, if 80 percent said X, the product manager would translate this into so many million people."

The data are not at all projectable because (a) the sample is so poor with respect to the way in which the individuals are recruited (seldom are they recruited randomly), and (b) because everyone does not have an equal say. The mouse-type person in the corner may be the heaviest user of your product, yet may not say much during the focus group session.

In the words of one researcher, "All you are really looking for are the few mavericks who will give you good operational definitions for your future study." At the same time, care must be taken not to place the respondents in the role of marketing experts. The purpose of the focus groups is not to get the consumers to make intellectual judgments, but to determine their feelings and emotions about the subject being studied, and to get help in designing a quantitative study to measure the pervasiveness of these feelings. Many firms, however, want to use focus groups instead of quantitative research, and then ask, "How many?" instead of "Why, how, what concepts were presented?" Clients have a tendency to ask, "How many people does that apply to?" This of course, cannot be answered with focus group interviews, one of the major limitations of the technique.

Another danger with group interviews is that so much depends on the experience and the perceptions of the moderator. He has his own biases, and the things that impress a moderator may or may not be typical. Is the moderator reading things into the interview that were not there, or is he overstating or understating the findings? The moderator is usually involved in the study right from the beginning and thus has certain biases. For example, he knows what kinds of things a client is looking for and often has seen much past research which may influence his observations.

The environment in which focus groups are conducted leads to other limitations. For example, it is difficult to test pricing in focus groups. People are overly sensitive to pricing questions and the participants are only able to respond to relative type questions such as, "Is this worth more or less than this?" Because of this, store tests must be used for pricing studies. A related disadvantage is that the participants are not in their kitchens or homes during the focus groups, and they are therefore outside the environment in which they would normally use the product. This may cause some difficulty in responding to some of the discussion topics.

Another disadvantage is the difficulty in recruiting participants for focus group sessions. This, of course, depends on how many groups are actually conducted and the difficulty in recruiting participants; for specialized sessions this may run as high as $1500. Focus groups are thus not a cheap method, although the total investment is smaller than quantitative research projects, which often cost at least $8,000 to $12,000.

A final disadvantage of focus groups is that there are many charlatans in the business of conducting focus groups, and the marketer must exercise great care in selecting a research firm to conduct the interviews. Some factors to consider in this regard are presented in Chapter Four.

SELECTED BIBLIOGRAPHY & REFERENCES

General

1. Achenbaum, Alvin A. "The Gresham Law of Research," in Russell I. Haley, ed., *Attitude Research in Transition.* Chicago: American Marketing Association, 1972, 25.

2. Bauer, R. A. "Exploring the Exploratory Sample." *Harvard Business Review,* (March 1963), 128-131.

3. Berelson, Bernard. *Content Analysis in Communications Research.* Glencoe, II: The Free Press, 1952. 18.

4. Boyd, Harper W. Jr. and Ralph Westfall. *Marketing Research: Text and Cases.* 3rd Edition. Homewood, Illinois: Richard D. Irwin, 1972.

5. Britt, S.H. *Consumer Behavior and the Behavioral Sciences: Theories and Applications.* New York: John Wiley & Sons, 1966.

6. Brown, Lyndon O. "What Motivation Research Is and How It Works: Its Advantages and Shortcomings." *The Pros and Cons of Motivation Research.* Chicago: *Advertising Age,* 1958, 5-20.

7. Brown, Lyndon O. and Leland L. Beik. *Marketing Research and Analysis,* 4th Edition. New York: Ronald Press, 1969.

8. Bruno, Albert V. and Edgar A. Pessemier. "An Empirical Investigation of the Validity of Selected Attitude and Activity Measures," in M. Venkatesan, ed., *Proceedings, Third Annual Conference.* Association for Consumer Research, 1973, 456.

9. Cartwright, Darwin P. "Analysis of Qualitative Material," in Leon Festinger and Daniel Katz, eds., *Research Methods in Behavioral Sciences.* New York: The Dryden Press, 1953, 454-467.

10. Cheskin, Louis. *A Basis for Marketing Decisions Through Controlled Motivation Research.* New York: Liveright Publishing Corporation, 1961.

11. Cheskin, Louis. *Why People Buy: Motivation Research and Its Successful Application.* New York: Liveright Publishing Corporation, 1959.

12. "Coffee Klatch Research: a new look at focus groups," *Ad Day,* (March 15, 1975).

13. Crespi, Irving. *Attitude Research.* Chicago: American Marketing Association, 1965.

14. Demby, Emanuel H. "From the Qualitative to the Quantitative and Back Again." in Ruddell I. Hailey, ed., *Attitude Research in Transition.* Chicago: American Marketing Association, 1972. 94-99.

15. Dichter, Ernest. *Handbook of Consumer Motivations: The Psychology of the World of Objects.* New York: McGraw-Hill Book Company, 1964. 413-417.

16. Diesing, Paul. "Objectivism vs. Subjectivism in the Social Sciences." *Philosophy of Science,* (March-June 1966), 124-131.

17. Dohrenwend, Barbara Snell. "Some Effects of Open and Closed Questions," *Human Organization.* (Summer, 1965), 183.

18. Einhorn, Hillel J. "Alchemy in the Behavioral Sciences," *Public Opinion Quarterly,* Vol. 36 (Fall, 1972), 368.

19. Gopal, M.H. *An Introduction to Research Procedure in Social Sciences.* Bombay: Asia Publishing House, 1970, 205.

20. Green, Paul E., Yoram Wind, and Arun K. Jain. "Analyzing Free Response Data in Marketing Research." *Journal of Marketing Research,* (February 1973), 45-52.

21. Haire, Mason. "Projective Techniques in Market Research," in Phillip R. Cateora and Lee Richardson, eds., *Readings in Marketing: The Qualitative and Quantitative Areas.* New York: Appleton-Century-Crofts, 1967, 159.

22. Haley, Russell I., ed. *Attitude Research in Transition.* Chicago: American Marketing Association, 1972.

23. Hays, William L. *Quantification in Psychology.* Belmont, CA: Brooks/Cole Publishing Company, 1967, 2.

24. Herzog, Herta. "Behavioral Science Concepts for Analyzing the Consumer." in Philip R. Cateora and Lee Richardson, eds., *Readings in Marketing: The Qualitative and Quantitative Areas.* New York: Appleton-Century-Crofts, 1967, 188-193.

25. Jameson, C. and David Jobber. "Sense and Nonsense of Motivation Research." *European Journal of Marketing,* (Winter 1971-1972), 189-199.

26. King, Charles W. and Douglas J. Tigert, eds. *Attitude Research Reaches New Heights.* Chicago: American Marketing Association, 1971, 181-188.

27. Lazarsfield, Paul E. *Qualitative Analysis: Historical and Critical Essays.* Boston: Allyn and Bacon, 1972.

28. Leonhard Dietz. *The Human Equation in Marketing Research.* New York: American Management Association, Inc., 1967. 73.

29. Leonhard, Dietz. *Consumer Research with Projective Techniques.* Shenandoah, Iowa: Ajax Corporation, 1955, 45.

30. McCall, David B. "What Agency Managers Want From Research," *Journal of Advertising Research,* Vol. 14 (August 1975), 7-10.

31. McNeal, James U. "The Disappearing Motive in Motivation Research." *Business Topics,* (Autumn 1964), 26-30.

32. Markin, Rom J. *The Psychology of Consumer Behavior.* New York: Prentice-Hall, Inc., 1969.

33. Mayer, Charles S. and Rex V. Brown. "A Search for the Rationale of Non-Probability Sample Designs." in John S. Wright and Jac L. Goldstucker eds., *New Ideas for Successful Marketing.* Chicago: American Marketing Association, 1966. 295-308.

34. Newman, Joseph W. "Put Research into Marketing Decisions," *Harvard Business Review,* Vol. 40 (March-April, 1962), 105.

35. Nicosia, F.H. and Barr Rosenberg. "Substantive Modeling in Consumer Attitude Research," in Russell I. Haley, ed., *Attitude Research in Transition.* Chicago: American Marketing Association, 1972, 246.

36. "Owens-Corning Listens to Dealers," *Sales Management* (March 3, 1975), 23.

37. Reilly, Eugene L. "Bringing Together the Needers and Providers: A New Rule for Qualitative Research." Russell I. Haley ed., *Attitude Research in Transition.* Chicago: American Marketing Association, 1972. 100-110.

38. Robin, Donald P. "A Philosophical Evaluation of Predicting Human Behavior Through the Inductive Process," *Southern Journal of Business,* Vol. 6 (April, 1971), 25.

39. Rothwell, Naomi D. "Some Limitations and Difficulties of Motivational Research in Solving Advertising-Marketing Problems." *The Pros and Cons of Motivation Research.* Chicago: *Advertising Age,* 1958, 38-44.

40. Sampson, Peter. "Qualitative Research and Motivational Research," in Robert M. Worcester, ed., *Consumer Market Research Handbook.* London: McGraw-Hill Book Company (UK) Ltd., 1972, 7.

41. Tarpey, Lawrence X. "Marketing Research and Behavioral Science," *Business Topics,* Vol. 13 (Winter, 1965), 62.

42. Walters, J. Hart, Jr. "Structured or Unstructured Techniques." *Journal of Marketing,* (April 1961), 58-62.

43. Yoell, William A. "Determination of Consumer Attitudes and Concepts Through Behavioral Analyses," in Lee Adler and Irving Crespi, eds., *Attitude Research at Sea.* Chicago: American Marketing Association, 1966, 23.

Focus Groups

44. Axelrod, Myril D. "Marketers Get an Eyeful When Focus Groups Expose Products, Ideas, Images, Ad Copy, etc. to Consumers." *Marketing News,* (February 28, 1975), 6-7.

45. Axelrod, Myril D. "10 Essentials for Good Qualitative Research." *Marketing News,* (March 14, 1975), 10-11.

46. Chase, Donald A. "The Intensive Group Interview in Marketing." *MRA Viewpoints,* 1973.

47. Goldman, A. E. "The Group Depth Interview." *Journal of Marketing,* (July 1962), 61-68; also reprinted in Joseph Seibert and Gorden Wills eds., *Marketing Research: Selected Readings.* New York: Penguin Books, 1970. 266-271.

48. Green, Paul E., Gary W. White and Kelley A. Clowe. "A Quota Sampling Procedure for Focused Group Interviews." unpublished working paper, University of Pennsylvania, 1975.

49. Hess, John M. "Group Interviewing." in Gerald S. Albaum and M. Venkatesan eds., *Scientific Marketing.* Glencoe, Illinois: The Free Press, 1971. 231-233.

50. "Market Testing by Group Interview." *Printer's Ink,* (December 7, 1962), 66-67.

51. Merton, Robert K., Marjorie Fiske, and Patricia L. Kendall. *The Focused Interview.* Glencoe, Illinois: The Free Press, 1956.

52. Munn, Henry L. and William L. Opdyke. "Group Interviews Reveal Consumer Buying Behavior." *Journal of Retailing,* (Fall 1961), 26-31.

Depth Interviewing

53. Dichter, Ernest. *Handbook of Consumer Motivations: The Psychology of the World of Objects.* New York: McGraw-Hill Book Company, 1964.

54. Merton, Robert K., Marjorie Fiske, and Patricia L. Kendall. *The Focused Interview.* Glencoe, Illinois: The Free Press, 1956.

55. Smith, Joan McFarlane. *Interviewing in Market and Social Research.* London: Routledge and Kegan Paul, Ltd., 1972.

56. Stebbins, Robert A. "The Unstructured Research Interview as Incipient Interpersonal Relationship." *Sociology and Social Research,* (January 1972), 164-177.

57. Woolf, James D. "Depth Interviewing Useful but Overglamorized." *The Pros and Cons of Motivation Research.* Chicago: *Advertising Age,* 1958, 81-83.

Projective Techniques

58. Anderson, Harold H. and Gladys I. Anderson. *An Introduction to Projective Techniques and Other Devices for Understanding the Dynamics of Human Behavior.* New York: Prentice-Hall, 1951.

59. Arndt, Johan. "Haire's Shopping List Revisited." *Journal of Advertising Research,* (October 1973), 57-61.

60. Green, R. T. and B. G. Stacey. "A Flexible Projective Technique Applied to the Measurement of Self-Images of Voters." *Journal of Projective Techniques and Personality Assessment,* (February 1966), 12-15.

61. Greenberg, Allan. "Pictorial Stereotypes in a Projective Test." *Journal of Marketing,* (October 1959), 72-74.

62. Haire, Mason. "Projective Techniques in Marketing Research." *Journal of Marketing,* (April 1950), 649-656.

63. Largen, Robert G. "Critique" to William A. Yoell's article, "The Fallacy of Projective Techniques." *Journal of Advertising,* (Winter 1974), 36-37.

64. Lindzey, Gardner. *Projective Techniques and Cross-Cultural Research.* New York: Appleton-Century-Crofts, 1961. 42-43.

65. Mills, David. "The Research Use of Projective Techniques: A Seventeen Year Survey." *Journal of Projective Techniques and Personality Assessment,* 1969. XXIX, 513-515.

66. Robertson, Dan H. and Robert W. Joselyn. "Projective Techniques in Research." *Journal of Advertising Research,* (October 1974), 27-30.

67. Steele, Howard L. "On the Validity of Projective Questions." *Journal of Marketing Research,* (August 1964), 46-49.

68. Webster, Frederick E. Jr. and Frederick von Pechmann. "A Replication of the 'Shopping List' Study." *Journal of Marketing,* (April 1970), 61-63.

69. Yoell, William A. "The Fallacy of Projective Techniques." *Journal of Advertising,* (Winter 1974), 33-35.

FOCUS GROUP INTERVIEWING

Sidney J. Levy

The focus group interview is currently a very fashionable method of gathering marketing research data. This vogue has grown rapidly in recent years; consequently, there is as yet little formal study of this method (outside the literature of group dynamics and conference leadership), and the marketing research texts do not say much about it. The basic idea of the focus group is a simple one. A group of people is brought to discuss some certain topics, commonly for 1 to 2 hours. The interviewer--leader, moderator--raises various issues, focusing the discussion on matters of interest to the researcher (and his client) in accordance with an outline or general guide.

GATHERING THE GROUP

In convening a focus group, it is necessary to think about how many people should be present, who they should be, how they are chosen and recruited, and where the meeting should be held.

a. The optimal size of a focus group is usually taken to be about 8 people. Actual group sizes range down from 12 people. Generally speaking, four, five, or six are too few people; the conversation may seem somewhat concentrated, too easily turning on the willingness of one or two to do most of the talking. The participants are more likely to feel exposed, on the spot, excessively pressed to participate whether ready or not. The discussion is especially vulnerable to the personalities and biases of the few individuals present, and therefore may be too narrow in consideration of the topic.

At the other end, 10 or 12 people tend to be too many. As the group grows in size, opportunities to address it decline, people have to wait more for their turns, and are frustrated by more views that they have less chance to respond to. They are also more widely dispersed in the room or around the table. The tendancy for the group to fragment becomes great, and, as a result, the problems of controlling the conversation are magnified. There are likely to be distractions, frequent murmuring, dissipation of remarks in side conversations, sly antagonisms. The moderator is pressed toward the role of disciplinarian and classroom behavior, cautioning the group to be quiet, asking for a show of hands, questioning individuals in turn to be sure everyone gets a vote. These problems grow without necessarily enlarging the pool of information or range of themes that emerge.

The exact number of people that will attend is often

Unpublished manuscript.

unpredictable. Twelve are invited in hopes that eight will come, but all twelve may come. Ten are invited and only six show up. In more than one instance, no one arrived.

b. The composition of the group is based on the research problem. Sometimes a varied group is wanted, for the interplay of diverse views on a topic that all can discuss. For example, a group with both men and women, young and mature, can talk about the new bank automatic tellers in a lively, interactive way. However, sharp diversity or division in the group is hazardous. Consider housewives and career women in one group, discussing cooking, a mixture of young upper status North Shore matrons and a few stout ethnic mamas talking about budgeting, or a few technical minded plant engineers meeting with a few lawyers on the subject of trust management. Perhaps the results are potentially intruiging--but they are more likely to be a fiasco as the participants struggle to find some common ground, or fight the battles of age, sex, and class differences.

Usually, the group is selected to be a relatively homogeneous one, brought together because of some unifying element out of which the discussion can grow: dog owners, people without checking accounts, people unfamiliar with a new appliance, mothers of infants, etc. Excessively narrow homogeneity is also a problem, as the more precise the quota or rare the type, the longer it takes to set up the group.

c. Groups are gathered in a variety of ways. Sometimes telephone screening is used. Field workers may just inquire around for people who fit the quota. A list of people may be provided by the client. Some central locations screen passers-by. Some organizations have accumulated files of respondents with known characteristics that can be drawn upon. To avoid failures, some researchers carry out a secret search for verbal people. The problem of no-shows is handled by desperate last minute calling around, by over-recruiting, and sometimes by having reliable contingency friends in the wings.

d. Focus interviews are held in such settings as a moderator's home, a respondent's home, an advertising agency conference room, at the client's office. Hotels, motels, meeting rooms at churches, fraternal organizations, and "Y's" are used. Marketing research organizations or units in advertising agencies sometimes have special facilities, or access to behavioral science laboratories, where tape recording, videotaping, or one-way viewing can go on. There are only a few places that can accommodate the crowd of watchers (sometimes as many as 12) that may want to observe. Ordinarily, it is useful to have a kitchen area adjacent, whether for products that may be tested, or to be able to serve coffee-and to any group. A main general need is finding a locale that is quiet enough to permit a good taping of the sessions. It is easy to forget that street noises, children playing, nearby typewriters, may not hamper the discussion but can ruin the recording.

CONDUCTING THE INTERVIEW

It is apparent that there is no one best way to conduct
a focus interview. The people who conduct them are usually
interviewers who have learned how to do it from their experience, not from the literature on successful discussion
techniques.

a. First comes the introduction of the topic. A most
fruitful approach is to have a somewhat chatty beginning by
the moderator. Too fast a start does not let the group settle
down a bit, relax, get oriented, begin to pay attention. To
accomplish a comfortable start, it seems better if the moderator does not have a canned opening, but explains the subject of the meeting in his words. Clients and researchers
are usually anxious about this and often try to overcontrol
the moderator. They should realize that good discussions
are not dictated or forced.

To avoid preoccupation with guessing the "true" purpose
of the meeting, as much candor as is feasible should be used
in telling the subject matter to be discussed. However, only
general terms are necessary, as telling specifically why the
information is being sought usually distracts the respondents,
leading them to shortcut the conversation by focusing too
much on being helpful and trying to tell the client what to
do about his problem.

b. A good moderator stays on top of the discussion,
striking a balance between friendly permissiveness and the
directness needed to keep the discussion focused and moving
along. The moderator has to be willing to retire and allow
participants to talk to each other, moving in and out as the
relevance of the conversation requires. Relevance is not
always easy to judge on the spot as a speaker works around his
point, so patience is required. But the time constraint is
sharp. Fear of losing rapport commonly makes moderators over-
indulgent, leading to repetition of ideas, whereas most groups
respond well to lively leadership that keeps the talking
vigorous by intervening when needed. Mere technique is in-
sufficient: interest in the topic and alert listening by the
moderator are the important means, not artificial animation.

c. The emotionality of groups is a curious feature.
Some are determined and sturdy, a buoyant conversation will
go on as if it hardly matters what the moderator does. Some
groups are delicate and fragile, r_ding wooing and encouragement. In other instances, the ch_stry is awful, a creeping
lethargy takes hold, the liveliest response is apathy, and
the situation may be hopeless. Sometimes it can be rescued
by "blasting," that is, raising the most dramatic or contro-
versial aspect; by shifting gears and calling for a break; or
by confronting the problem by exploring why the group seems
to be uninterested. Not infrequently groups are over-stim-
ulated, so giddy with the novelty, the attention, the rewards,
the social situation, their self-consciousness, or the ab-
surdity of discussing some unlikely topic for two hours, that

a contagious hilarity takes hold, with exaggerated comments
and hysterical laughter. These reactions need interfering
with, perhaps by shifting attention to something about the
physical arrangements, the taping a comment about getting
"back to work," or again, examining the reaction itself,
asking why the topic seems so funny.

As in individual interviewing, it is useful to conclude
the formal meeting, but keep the recorder running. In this
post-session freedom, respondents often make relevant or insightful remarks.

d. The moderator is like a conductor, orchestrating an
improvisation. The task calls for adeptness and awareness of
what is going on, what people are doing and feeling. It
means giving everyone a chance without taking dull roll calls.
Tact is needed to hold down the rusher who wants to say
everything all at once. The good moderator is prepared for
this, ready to extract from the overflow one of the issues
for discussion, while deferring the others. A major challenge
is control of the dominating person whether eager beaver,
know-it-all, or a garrulous one lacking terminal facilities,
without withering his cooperation. It is too easy to shut
people up, so that they withdraw and refuse to contribute
further. The moderator has to respect the participants'
sensibilities, and know when he can get away with a blunt,
goodnatured "Will you please shut up?" or "Let's hold it
down," or "Not everybody at once." Special skill is needed
to make judicious interruptions, responding to the speaker
while also cutting him off, so that he feels he has made his
point and can yield the floor to others.

e. Questions often arise about matters other than the
behavior of the moderator. For example, what is the effect
of tape recording? Usually people take recording in stride.
It is common, familiar, and lends gratifying importance to the
activity. The tape recorder serves as a kind of assistant to
the moderator, as it can be appealed to in calls for order,
the need to have people keep just one conversation going.
In general, it is best to deal matter-of-factly with taping,
not to make an issue of it, nor to play back people's voices
in hope of reassuring them, as they find themselves unnatural.
Videotaping is less usual and an elaborate idea; it arouses
more self-consciousness and anxiety about one's appearance,
uncertainty that one has come to the meeting properly dressed
or with hair done right, suggesting more exposure, less anonymity. It is also flattering to be "on television," although the moderator may have to be prepared to explain what
will be done with the videotape if people worry about where
they will later be viewed.

f. The role of client participation also raises questions, as it can be a troublesome issue. It is a topic
that needs a good understanding before the meeting. If
client personnel attend, the simplest way is for them to be
unseen and unheard in another room. Often, however, they
want to be present at the meeting. Sometimes they promise not

to say anything, but find it hard to stick to this because
their interest is intense. They are often moved to want to
correct the respondents who express "wrong" or ignorant ideas
about the client's field, product, brand, or organization.
They may take the leadership away from the moderator and then,
suddenly self-conscious, want to hand it back like a hot
potato. One of the funniest consequences is the natural
table-turning that occurs as respondents discover the all-
knowing client in their midst and use his time and money
enthusiastically interviewing him. A customary ground rule
is to have the client take over the meeting after the main
discussion is finished.

JUSTIFYING THE APPROACH

Group interviewing came about as an evolution of the
interest in qualitative behavioral research. As individual
respondents were rescued from being merely ciphers and tabular
inputs, their patterns of views, attitudes, and feelings
became important to the search for psychological insight.
The depth interview depends not on having a systematic interro-
gation, but on giving the respondent a chance to talk freely.
It was a reasonable extension to conceive of interviewing
several respondents at once. The practical necessity for
doing this arose when seeking reactions to television commercials or to new products too cumbersome to carry around
from door to door. In such instances, the value of a small
manageable audience was evident, especially if an illuminating
conversation were held in addition to polling members of the
audience.

In short order other benefits, both real and imagined,
fueled the surge of interest in focus group interviews.
Three central ideas are especially powerful.

a. It is a common belief that group interviewing is
economical. The economy idea has a face plausibility, given
the ratio of respondents to interviewers; it is as if several
interviews are being accomplished in the same time it would
take to do only one. In fact, however, for several reasons
the cost of a group is likely to be as great or greater than
that of interviewing all members individually. Respondents
are more often paid to cooperate, with rates ranging from $5
to $25 or more, depending on how precious or hard to get they
are. Experienced moderators expect from $100 up; and they
may need helpers to serve as receptionists, baby sitters,
kitchen workers, etc., at $2.50 an hour and up. If necessary
to rent a space, $35 to $100 is added. Videotaping will cost
a few hundred dollars, with cameramen running $15 or more per
hour. The more popular focus grouping becomes, the more
these costs rise. Commonly, the analysis and report writing
are prepared by another research worker. Where professional
analytic time for report preparation is added, a report on a
group of eight respondents costs at least $1000--all depending
on who is doing it for whom, and how much it has to be marked
up for that client.

b. The credibility of a group discussion is almost magically reassuring. A group of people chatting seems more natural than an individual being interviewed. It is easy to imagine that the participants are more likely to come out with what is truly on their minds. The interaction is viewed as multiplicative, making each respondent a richer source of information than he would be alone. Also, greater confidence in results obviates doing more research. (Groups are cheap if one does no more research than with one or two groups, substituting that for a larger project.) It has been observed that results of a group discussion will be accepted and acted upon with important decisions by people who would never be content with a research report based on the responses of the same number of people individually interviewed. The issue is not quantity of data, as eight people talking for an hour each provide more data than eight people talking to one another for two hours.

c. Clients like to participate in groups. A most distinctive advantage of focus groups is the chance for clients--marketing managers, advertising agency creative personnel, R&D engineers--to join, and at times, to bypass the research personnel, by directly seeing and hearing respondents conveniently gathered together where they can be observed. In this way, they feel they are getting quick results, the participation, stimulation, and sense of conviction gained from perceiving the live expression of opinions. They enjoy not having to rely on the intervening analysis of a research report.

These three features--economy, faith in the group, and client participation--have led to groups being widely used (and misused) as the method of choice. Focus groups are best used when indicated by the results to be gained from their special nature.

a. A basic value of the focus group is the opportunity for multiple interactions. A good interview makes use of that fact to learn about the social dynamics and immediate interpersonal features of the topic at issue. That might include how people talk about it in conversation, their vocabulary, phrases, inflections, etc., as these are informally stimulated. An interviewer can do this in a personal interview, and does, but in a group another respondent may seem to offer more realistic or more casual cues and modes of expression. Also, a provocative member of the group is not accused of the sin of "leading the respondent," as an interviewer might be. As part of the interaction, respondents may be moved to challenge and defend their views with relative spontaneity. The researchers can observe how controversy comes up and how it is resolved.

b. Each group meeting usually develops a characteristic social tone concerning the subject being discussed, illuminating its significance as a social topic. It is useful to observe whether people can exchange views easily and fluently or whether the subject is socially awkward. Is it exciting, interesting, sobering, readily made absurd, does anger build? Or perhaps uncertainty, wariness, tentativeness seem to dominate.

c.   A focus group discussion is especially useful for gaining a quick overview of main themes, points, issues, variables, etc., that are to be structured into a questionnaire or other subsequent study design.

d.   A focus group is especially valuable for discussion of trends that are social, economic, and style-oriented. As the individuals will usually represent different points of view and points on the trend continuum, their interaction can highlight the interplay of these points. This will be more obvious with a heterogeneous group, and perhaps an interesting, subtler matter with a supposedly homogeneous group.

e.   Given different knowledge about a subject among the members of the group, they will learn from one another, showing something of how information and attitudes are absorbed or resisted.

f.   The social facilitation of a focus group can be useful when the participants' awareness of common ideas, problems, and emotions stimulates a freer expression than might otherwise happen. This suggests that a focus group is potentially a therapeutic experience, making it necessary to interpret the results with some care, as the marketer's interest might not find the same reactions out in the market under more ordinary circumstances.

There are other cautions that should be offered, as argument against the use of focus groups, especially when they are substituted for using any other research approaches. In their current popularity, they are probably over-used, as some market researchers are inclined to use them for almost every project, with inadequate attention or weight given to their limitations or shortcomings.

DRAWBACKS

a.   A true focus group session does not consist of several people being interviewed individually but concurrently. A major obstacle to achieving a fruitful conversation is the "surveyor's urge" to get a vote from everyone, or to inquire about consensus: "Do you all agree, then?" Meetings are often wasted by being run in that manner, not with a conversation going on among the members, but with each one being asked in turn to voice a response to a specific question. When a good discussion gets going, which is the goal, it is a mistake to expect an intensive exploration of each person's pattern of background, experience, outlook, attitudes, choices, etc. Such patterns are visible in pieces, but cannot be pursued as they would be in an individual depth interview.

b.   Each group has a certain composition and a life of its own that has to be allowed to function if it is to achieve its best results. Given this fact, problems also arise that can interfere with getting the information one is seeking despite the skill and competence of the moderator. As noted, there are usually more dominant members, and others who refuse to be drawn out in public. Whether opinionated, knowledgeable, or merely gabby, the more vocal people are useful, often providing just what the discussion needs. Then again, they have been known to kill it. The others in the group may be so intimidated, angered, overwhelmed, or persuaded, that despite the leader's best efforts, they will not speak up.

c. There is only so much time available for the meeting. The whole group is thus at the mercy of the latecomers and the slow talkers. Highly idiosyncratic behaviors or ideas are sometimes expressed that take up a disproportionate amount of time and are not useful to the general discussion.

d. Regardless of focusing and skillful management, systematic coverage of the topics at issue may not be possible. Focus interviews often have much repetition, get hung up on certain issues, and may not permit a balanced analysis. It is thus sometimes hard to say what kind of cross section of information is represented by the content of one or two group sessions.

e. Analysis of the discussion is hindered by problems in identifying who said what, or in relating later comments to earlier comments by the same person. A researcher listening to a taped discussion usually loses a great deal of material due to mutterings, noise, simultaneous talking, changing of tapes, to say nothing of those gruesome occasions when there turns out to be nothing at all on the tape.

f. Focus groups seem able to discuss just about anything, including men's underwear, feminine hygiene, and personal finances. Nevertheless, many people are inhibited by the public nature of the group, and it often seems the harder way to explore private topics. Also, on any topic, pressure to talk, on the one hand, and to give others the floor as well, may interfere with getting into various kinds of details that need a more relaxed and reflective atmosphere. To the extent that the asset of a focus group is its heightened social immediacy, it should not be used when the social aspect is undesirable. Social competition, exhibitionism, problems in self-esteem, veneer, histrionics, negativism, compliance, and so on, can unduly complicate the anlaysis by the distortions they introduce.

g. The foregoing drawbacks and analogous problems may afflict any research method. But the risk in focus interviewing is relatively great, as so many eggs are being put in one basket. Just as any one individual interview can be a poor one, a relative failure, so can a group discussion. Quality variation is less important with a hundred interviews, but it is a truly dismal experience when perhaps only one or two groups have been scheduled, and when many people are involved, including an eager and then disappointed or angry client. Forewarning is useful, to foster realism by anticipating the possibility that the group may not work out very well.

* * * * * *

It is evident that the focus group interview is a complex technique with many pros and cons. Like most tools, it can be used casually or more rigorously. The discussion above was designed to air some of the relevant issues, so that practitioners and managers can assess the potential value to them of this particular research method.

The Group Depth Interview

ALFRED E. GOLDMAN

"Discussion panels," "respondent-oriented interviews," "consumer conferences," and "focused group interviews" have enjoyed increasing popularity in attempting to solve marketing problems. This article describes the mechanics of conducting group interviews and also some of its consequences.

The title of the article, "The Group Depth Interview," reflects a situation in which information is sought from a number of interacting individuals at the same time, using a combination of probing and direct-inquiry techniques.

CONSIDERATION of each of the three elements of the name given to the group-interview technique suggests that, while the label may be as serviceable as any other, under certain conditions it is not wholly accurate. A comprehensive review of group methods is beyond the scope of this article; and the interested reader can refer to the voluminous literature on this technique and its application to marketing, education, and psychotherapy.[1]

Instead, the present article explains what is meant by *group*, *depth*, and *interview* in a group depth interview . . . the mechanics of moderating such interviews . . . and the five requirements of these interviews.

Group

A group is a number of *interacting individuals having a community of interests*. These two criteria of groups must be satisfied in order to derive the benefits of collecting information in a group setting.

Interaction

In the group situation a person is asked an opinion about something—a product, a distribution system, and advertisement, a television program, or perhaps a candidate for office. In contrast to the individual interview in which the flow of information is unidirectional, from the respondent to the interviewer, the group setting causes the opinions of each person to be considered in group discussion. Each individual is exposed to the ideas of the others and submits his ideas for the consideration of the group.

This assumes, of course, that social interaction occurs at some overt level. If the group members do not interact with one another, but each member directs his remarks to the moderator, this is not a group. It might better be described as multiple or serial interviewing, since the advantages of the group setting are precluded. It is the interviewer's responsibility to stimulate the group members to interact with each other rather than with him.

Community of Interest

The establishment of group cohesiveness is dependent in large part on the second criterion of "groupness," namely, *sharing a common interest*.

[1] Suggested sources: H. H. Lerner and H. C. Kelman, "Group Methods in Psychotherapy, Social Work, and Adult Education," *Journal of Social Issues*, Vol. 8, Whole issue No. 2, 1952, pp. 1-88; W. Mangold, *Gegenstand und Methode des Gruppendiskussions verfahrens: Aus der Arbeit des Instituts fur Sozialforschung*, (Frankfurt am Main: Europaische Verlagsanstalt), pp. 176.

Reprinted from *Journal of Marketing*, 26 (July 1962), 61-68, published by the American Marketing Association.

This common interest should, of course, be relevant to the topic under discussion. A number of individuals may be very different in national origin, religious beliefs, political persuasion, and the like; but if they share a common identity relevant to the discussion (shoe buyers, drug manufacturers, purchasers of luxury items), a group can form. This involves some risks that can be minimized by thoughtful selection of group members. For example, in a discussion of a home-decorating product, the inclusion of one or two low-income people in a group of wealthy individuals may serve to inhibit the free expression of the attitudes of all.

How may these two characteristics of a group be exploited in eliciting useful information, and in what way is this information different from that produced by individual interviewing?

1. First, the interaction among group members *stimulates new ideas* regarding the topic under discussion that may never be mentioned in individual interviewing. When a group member does bring up a new idea, however tangential, the group as a whole is given the opportunity to react to it in a variety of ways that indicate its interest to the group.

The idea can be readily and enthusiastically taken up by the group and ultimately accepted or rejected. The idea can be discussed without a decision being reached, with considerable confusion expressed in the process. The idea can be discussed briefly and then dropped not to be mentioned again. Sometimes, and most significant of all, it can be studiously ignored and avoided, despite the moderator's reiteration of the idea. This behavior, when accompanied by indications of anxiety, such as lighting cigarettes, shuffling uneasily in seats, clearing throats, and so on, suggests that a particular idea has provoked sufficient psychic discomfort and threat as to require its rigorous avoidance in open discussion.

2. These possible reactions to a new idea may also demonstrate a second value of group interviewing—*the opportunity to observe directly the group process.* In the individual interview, respondents *tell* how they would or did behave in a particular social situation. In the group interview, respondents react to each other, and their behavior is directly *observed.*

For example, a housewife who hesitantly and timidly describes how she cleans her floors suggests the tenuousness with which she herself regards these procedures. In one group, the timid admission by one housewife that she hated washing floors and did so only when forced to by fear of social rejection brought immediate and firm support from other group members. They then verbally "turned on" the two group members who washed floors more frequently and meticulously. Here the attitudes of women toward washing floors was reflected in the

way they behaved toward each other *in the group.*

A purchasing decision is frequently a social act in that the items are considered in the context of what others think of the product, and what others will think of *them* for having purchased it. The group creates or recapitulates the marketing situation, depending upon the point at which the decision process is intercepted. Here the process of the decision is exposed in the sharing of experiences, rumors, and anecdotes that go on in a group discussion about a product, service, person, or event. Here we are concerned with the *process* of the purchasing decision, not just in the static end-result of that process. Effective marketing requires understanding of this decision process.

3. A third advantage of group interviewing is that it *provides some idea of the dynamics of attitudes and opinions.* The flexibility or rigidity with which an opinion is held is better exposed in a group setting than in an individual interview. Within the two hours of the typical group session, an opinion that is stated with finality and apparent deep conviction can be modified a number of times by the social pressures or new information that may be provided by the group. As the discussion proceeds, some group members modify their initial reaction, some defend their positions even more rigorously, some admit confusion. In this way, the group setting offers some idea of the dynamics of opinion—its initiation and modification, and its intensity and resistance to change. This pattern of modification in opinion is often as rewarding with regard to understanding motives as the one initially stated.

4. Discussion in a peer group often *provokes considerably greater spontaneity and candor than can be expected in an individual interview.* This is its fourth advantage. The interviewer is frequently an "outsider," regardless of how skillful he or she may be. In the group setting it is not unusual for group members, after an initial period of orientation, to ignore completely the presence of the moderator. For example, in a group of small-

• ABOUT THE AUTHOR. Alfred E. Goldman is Director of Research Development with National Analysts, Inc., of Philadelphia. Dr. Goldman received his B.S. and M.A. degrees from the City College of New York, and his Ph.D. in clinical psychology from Clark University.

Since 1950 he has been associated with various state and federal clinics and hospitals where he was particularly interested in group psychotherapy and research. He was Assistant Professor of Psychology at Northeastern University and Research Associate in the School of Public Health of Harvard University. In 1956 he was Director of Psychological Research at Norristown State Hospital. He has published various articles in psychological and psychiatric journals.

business managers, several of them admitted blatant acts of petty dishonesty at the expense of their customers. It seems unlikely that this would have been admitted to an individual interviewer.

Because of the demands on their time, physicians are unusually difficult to interview at length. Yet in group discussions with other physicians, two hours does not seem to tax their interest or cooperation. Physicians who appear impatient, constrained, cautious, or curt when interviewed alone, seem considerably more garrulous, frank, and at times argumentative when in a group with other physicians.

Candor is permitted not only because the members of the group understand and feel comfortable with one another, but also because they draw social strength from each other. The group provides support to its members in the expression of anxiety-provoking or socially unpopular ideas.

An example may illustrate this. At the beginning of a 2½ hour session, a group of jobbers individually expressed loyalty to, and appreciation of, their suppliers. After an hour, most of these same group members joined in the expression of a pervasive and deeply felt antagonism toward their manufacturers—attitudes which they had not previously expressed for a variety of reasons, including fears of economic reprisal by the jobber.

In another instance, members of a minority group at first vehemently denied favoritism in buying from members of their own group. Later, following a profound and emotional discussion of racial and religious intolerance, *all* admitted that they preferred to buy from a salesman of their own ethnic group. By virtue of its community of interests, the group permitted exposure of feelings not ordinarily given casual or public expression.

5. A fifth advantage is that the group setting is *emotionally provocative in a way that an individual interview cannot be*. A group composed of housewives ranging in age from 25 to 45 may serve to illustrate how the group can provoke reactions which elicit interesting and useful insights into the motives of its members. This discussion focused on how these women felt about their weight, and what effect this had on their diets. At one point in the discussion, the youngest and most slender woman in the group said, "Weight isn't a problem for me yet, but I imagine that for older women like yourselves it would be." Immediately, perceiving the unintended offense to the other group members, she explained, "Well, as you get older, you get fatter." This attempt at diplomacy fell somewhat short of soothing the injured self-concepts of some of the other women, but it did serve to provoke quite profound feelings toward "getting old" and how these feelings were expressed in their eating habits. Thus, a member of the group confronted the other group members with

anxieties that the moderator could mention only at considerable risk to continued *rapport*.

Thus, by virtue of the interaction and common relevant interests of its members, the group offers more and qualitatively different information than can be obtained from the sum of its individual human parts.

Depth

The use of the word "depth," in the name given this technique, implies seeking information that is more profound than is usually accessible at the level of interpersonal relationships. While a respondent may be the best authority on *what* he did, he is often an unreliable source of information as to *why* he did it. His response reflects what he wants you to believe, and also what he himself wants to believe. Retroactive distortion helps him to maintain a self-concept of a wise, judicious buyer motivated by reason rather than feeling.

Much of our daily behavior is motivated by subliminal stimuli (sensory impressions of which the individual is only minimally aware). Depth interviewing seeks to bring these motives to light. Technically these motives are *preconscious*, and are distinguished from *unconscious* motives by the more profound depth of repression of the latter.

A study of the factors that determine which of several supermarkets were used by shoppers in a particular neighborhood illustrates the definitive and lasting reaction to subliminal stimuli. Some of the women in each of four group sessions were adamant in their intention not to shop in one of the markets, although they did not appear able to express their reasons in a clear or consistent manner. Some mentioned a vague feeling that the market in question was somehow messy or even dirty. Yet, upon further exploration, these same women agreed that the shelves were neatly stacked, the personnel clean, the floors swept, the counters well dusted. They could not point out anything to support their charges of uncleanliness. Further, they readily agreed that the store they did shop in was more messy than the one in which they refused to shop. A casual reference by one of the women to a peculiar odor evoked immediate recognition from the others. This occurred spontaneously in several of the groups and led to the consensus that it was a "bloody" or "meaty" odor. This process of "consensual validation" suggested that this vague impression of untidiness stemmed not from anything that could be seen, but rather from this faint yet pervasive and offensive odor. Later this information served to bring to the attention of the management an ineffective exhaust-and-drainage system in the supermarket's meat room.

In seeking "depth" material we do not make the assumption that we can in some way get the respondent to express unconscious motives *directly*. A thing is repressed, that is, remanded to the care of the unconscious, if it is too threatening to the self-concept to allow into consciousness. Generally there is little that a moderator can do, or ethically should do, to provoke the overt expression of such threatening material. What is usually done is to infer the nature of these impulses from who says what, in what sequence, to whom he says it, and how he says it.

However, there are certain conditions under which the moderator may wish to explore some facets on an unconscious motive. By focusing on the motives of one group member, the others are frequently provoked to react to the repressed motive, even if that motive is never made quite explicit. For example, in a discussion of an easy-to-prepare "instant" food, one woman made the following slip-of-the-tongue: "Especially when I'm in a hurry, I like foods that are time-*consuming*." The context of the preceding discussion, which centered upon the role that food preparation plays in the housewife's concept of herself, made it quite clear that the eagerness with which this woman embraced "instant" foods was not without psychic conflict. In this case, the moderator inquired into the error without interpreting to her the feeling of guilt that this slip may have revealed. It did serve, however, to stimulate other women to discuss this problem more openly.

Probing for unconscious material should be undertaken with extreme caution. The danger, in most cases, is not that any appreciable damage will be done to a reasonably stable personality; the normal protective mechanisms will adequately protect the ego from ill-advised assaults by the moderator. Rather, the danger of unskilled probing is represented by the risk of completely alienating the offended group member, and thereby limiting the cooperation and spontaneity of the whole group. In these situations, the professional psychologist with clinical experience is more likely to avoid such pitfalls.

Interview

The word "interview" has the least precise meaning of the three elements of the term, group depth interview. An interview implies an interviewer, rather than a moderator. The role of moderator requires using the group as the device for eliciting information. The moderator guides the discussion, keeping it within fruitful bounds, but rarely participates in it himself. When he can lead a group member to ask a question of the group, the moderator will not question them himself.

An interviewer, especially with a structured questionnaire, is frequently restricted to a direct question-and-answer approach, while the moderator has the greatest possible flexibility and freedom in pursuing motivational "pay dirt" and may seek to exploit unique characteristics of a particular group

in the most effective way by whatever devices at his disposal.

The Mechanics of Moderating

The best way to describe group depth interviewing is in terms of the specific mechanics of moderating the group. Many of the techniques considered here have been suggested by those used in group psychotherapy. Although psychotherapy has a radically different primary goal, it shares with group interviewing the goal of eliciting information which the group member himself finds difficult, or impossible, to produce.

All sessions are tape recorded, with the recorder placed in full view. For training purposes and client observation a one-way vision mirror is used. All group members are paid, to compensate them for the expense of traveling to where the session is conducted, and to attract people other than the merely curious.

Rapport

The most important factor in producing usable information from the group depth interview is the relationship between the moderator and the panel members, and that among the panel members themselves.

The first job of the moderator is to structure the roles of all of the participants. The purpose of the session, how long it will last, and the manner in which it will be conducted are all explained in as comfortable and friendly a way as possible. Good *rapport* is crucial in establishing the candidness needed; and this is facilitated when the language of the moderator is not too discrepant from that of the majority of the group. For example, when the group is composed of young, poorly educated subjects of marginal socio-economic level, "they won't dig you if you bug 'em with a lot of high-falutin' jazz."

Verbal Activity

The verbal activity or passivity of the moderator is determined by the nature of the group and its goals. With alert and articulate people the moderator can assume a more passive role—passive, not inert. In an especially talkative group, or at the other extreme, with a very quiet group, a more active role will be required of the moderator, either to inhibit or provoke more discussion.

Relevancy

One of the most important things that the moderator does is to keep the discussion within relevant limits. Here he must be very careful not to rule out that which is apparently unrelated, but may reveal relevant unconscious motives. A general discussion of grandma and grandpa and the "good old days" may have extensive significance in marketing such things as upholstery fabric or canned foods.

Sensitivity to unconscious processes is, of course, important here and a clinical background is helpful, although not essential.

Projective Questions

The researcher who pursues those motives of the buying decision of which the consumer is unaware must give particular thought to developing various "projective" techniques which expose these motives. The answer to a projective question enables the respondent to express needs which he cannot or does not wish to admit. These, of course, must be individually designed to fit the particular marketing problem. For example, in the selection of kinds of housing materials, material design, or fabric pattern, the following question was found to be very effective: "What kind of family would find this pattern appealing, and why?"

Different reactions to various designs may also be provoked by asking the group what well-known person each pattern suggests to them. In this way, a design that suggests Jayne Mansfield may be qualitatively differentiated from those which suggest Liberace, Eleanor Roosevelt, or Marshall Matt Dillon. Similar material may be provoked by *stereotype photographs* and *the illustrative cases method*.

Illustrative Case Method

To explore personal habits, the illustrative case method is valuable. Several people are described who differ from each other according to the intensity or consistency of some behavior. Then the group members are asked to describe the other characteristics of the person. For example, Miss A uses underarm deodorant four times a day; Miss B uses one only in the morning—what kind of people are they? Or Mr. A traded his Chevrolet in for a Pontiac; Mr. B traded his Cadillac in for a small foreign car—what kind of people are they? Intensive probing follows their responses in order to clarify what motivates Miss A or B, or Mr. A or B.

Stereotype Photographs

A related type of stimulus is represented by *stereotype photographs*. These are pictures of men and women who typify a particular age, income, or vocational group. Each of these variables, of course, can be independently varied to suit the objectives of the study. The appropriately selected photographs are exposed singly or all together, and a question might be asked, such as: "Which of these women would be most likely to use instant tea?"

The response is followed up with: "What is there about the woman you picked that makes you think that?" Such answers as: "She looks as though she's always in a hurry and can't be bothered with brewing tea," or, "Not that one! She looks rich enough to afford the best; she would have her maid brew tea," are quite revealing of attitudes toward a particular product.

Serial Association

In evaluating the effectiveness of advertising copy, controlled serial association may be used. Prior to exposure of the first ad, the group members are trained in the difficult job of saying words freely one after the other. In this way, they can learn to respond to the test ads with some spontaneity.

For example, to evaluate the impression of the product conveyed to women by a pictorial advertisement in a magazine, group members were shown the advertisement and requested to associate ideas with it. It became readily apparent that this ad suggested licentious intrigue and adventure. While the symbolic meaning of the ad served to attract and hold the attention of the reader admirably well, the dynamic meaning it attached to this particular product apparently was not the most advantageous.

Deprivation Questions

Deprivation questions inquire into the relative value of various products or services. A question such as, "Which of the following canned foods would you miss most if it were no longer available to you?" is somehow more provocative than, "Which canned food is most important to you?"

Deception

A calculated "deception" is often effective in testing the limits of the respondent's convictions. A rich source of information and attitudes is tapped by the group's responses to the blatantly incorrect statement that all of ten very different fabrics are made of the same synthetic fiber.

There are times when none of these methods appears to stimulate any but the most mundane and obvious generalities. This, of course, may be significant in itself if it is not a facade behind which reside motives that are not being expressed. Some other procedures that may be useful in these difficult cases are *false termination* and *playing the devil's advocate*.

It is a rule of thumb in group psychotherapy that the most important material may be produced in the last few minutes of the session. In this way the person who would like to contribute something that may be embarrassing or threatening to him has only a few minutes during which he must endure the discomfort. Also, he may deliberately inhibit ideas that he feels are irrelevant to the discussion proper.

Following this lead, especially in group interviews in which emotionally loaded material is involved, the session is "terminated" early by thanking the group members for being there and inquiring as to whether there are any other comments. Intensive probing into these "final" comments has been rewarding on a number of occasions.

For example, a group interview devoted to the

motives involved in drinking in taverns as opposed to drinking at home uncovered very little more than mundane and superficial generalities. Following the *false termination*, a group member casually commented laughingly to his neighbor that he is hesitant to drink in a tavern because he holds his liquor poorly and is afraid of making a fool of himself in public. Further probing of this theme with the man who initiated it, as well as others in the group, revealed the specific moral prohibitions against drinking at a bar made by the group member's father. More important, this "casual" comment led to a quite meaningful discussion about the variety and intensity of impulses and emotions that may be expressed in a tavern but are socially unacceptable elsewhere. Anxiety, provoked by the threat of such emotional expression, may be sufficient to limit drinking to the relative "safety" of the home.

Playing the devil's advocate requires that the moderator take a very opinionated role. With the goal of provoking a reaction, the moderator may himself express an extreme viewpoint on the topic under discussion. This is usually sufficient to move the discussion into more productive channels. The same effect can be achieved without involving the moderator, through the use of an accomplice who takes a pre-established and adamantly stated point of view.

Sophisticated Naivete

In most cases, however, the most effective pose is that of sophisticated naïveté. The group members are assigned the role of educating the unknowledgable moderator. He thus forces the group members to explain even the obvious—those unverbalized habits of thought and action that are rarely subject to scrutiny.

Here the moderator may make frequent use of such probes as, "What do you mean?" "I'm afraid I didn't understand that" . . . or, "Remember now, I'm not a buyer; so, would you explain that to me?" Such probing elicited the realization on the part of one dress buyer that in making selections for her extensive clientele she had primarily four of her regular customers in mind.

Parrying Direct Questions

There are occasions in which a *direct question* may put the moderator "on the spot." Often these questions cannot only be diplomatically dodged, but at the same time they may be used to gain additional information. When group members ask, as they frequently do, about identity of the client, this may be used to open a discussion concerning the relative activity in consumer and scientific research of various companies and the interest of these companies in the needs of the consumer. An effective gambit here in response to, "What company is pay-

ing for this anyway?" is something like, "I'm curious about why you ask," or "What's your hunch about who is sponsoring this research?"

Gesture

The use of gestures should not be ignored in conducting the group interview. A raised eyebrow can be an effective probe; leaning forward on the table may encourage more comment by a reluctant or shy person; a shrug of the shoulder can parry many direct questions.

Attention to the gestures of the group members frequently tells more than what is said. Reserve, disgust, disdain, irritation, enthusiasm, and myriad other emotional subtleties are conveyed by gesture. Here is an example. In a discussion of a building material, one woman, while describing her impression of it, continually rubbed her thumb and forefinger together. Here words expressed a mildly favorable opinion, but the gesture revealed a fear of which she was only slightly aware herself. Despite the fact that the material itself was very rigid and hard, probing as to the meaning of her gesture revealed a fear that it would be "crumbly" and soft.

Non-directive Comments

Non-directive comments often help to focus attention on the emotion implicit in a discussion. A non-directive comment such as, "You seem angry about that," or, "That memory seems to give you pleasure," recognizes and accepts emotion, and at the same time encourages the group member to reflect further on his feelings in relation to the topic under discussion. Most people need such encouragement to express strong feelings in a group setting, particularly feelings of tenderness and sentimentality.

Five Requirements of the Group Depth Interview

Five factors are required of the group depth interview in order to serve its research objectives: *objectivity, reliability, validity, intensive analysis,* and *marketing applicability.* While the first four are required of any scientific research, the last is more relevant to marketing studies. Any endeavor that presumes to be marketing research cannot ignore these guideposts of sound inquiry.

1. Objectivity

Avoidance of the bias of the interviewer and client indicates *objectivity.* Respondents are unusually sensitive to the attitudes and opinions of the group moderator; and if these are allowed to manifest themselves without the moderator's awareness, it can grossly affect the nature of the data. To further objectivity, it is usually necessary to disguise the identity of the client, and for the moderator to observe rigorous neutrality (except when being the devil's advocate). Objective summary of attitudes sometimes requires the use of some quantitative technique, such as a scaling device, within the context of the group interview.

2. Reliability

The degree to which the information produced is representative of the population to which it is generalized is called *reliability*. The question of reliability of the sample, or generaliation of the results, directs attention to the purpose of the group depth interview. Its basic function is to indicate "why" rather than "how many." That is, it focuses on understanding the motives of behavior rather than cataloging the number of individuals who behave in a particular way.

The group interview is particularly useful in the developmental phases of a research program. It establishes the range of attitudes without, however, asserting the representativeness of these attitudes. Perhaps the major function of the group depth interview is to generate creative and fruitful hypotheses. It does not generally permit broad generalization and thus, in most cases, it should be followed by a probability survey to substantiate these hypotheses.

In certain cases, small-sample group interviews can produce generalizable results. For example, a group panel had represented in its members jobbers who controlled 50% of all automotive parts distributed in a particular city. The opinions they expressed represented a considerable portion of the automotive parts jobber universe in that city.

In special circumstances which limit a study to a small sample for security reasons, the problem of sample representativeness may be academic. A manufacturer may need to limit a study to a small sample, in order to prevent too many people from knowing about a new product prior to its introduction to the market.

Group interviewing does not preclude quantitatively adequate sampling; but in most cases it makes it very expensive.

Another kind of reliability problem is the representativeness of the time sample. Purchasing decisions for higher-priced items begin as vague, general ideas of the product and become progressively more specific as decision-making proceeds. Intersecting this process at any one point in time may not adequately reflect its dynamic nature. The purchasing decision can be viewed as a learning process that may be altered many times from the initiation of the need to the actual purchase of a product.

One way in which this process may be investigated may be illustrated by a problem involving the assessment of consumer reaction to a radical styling innovation of a major appliance. Six groups of eight members each were shown scale models of the appliances at three different sessions held at weekly intervals. At each session, attitudes were

intensively probed. A gradual shift in acceptance of the radical change was observed over the three week period. However, when those who had been exposed to the product three times were combined in the same group with people who had never seen the product, the effect was immediate and dramatic: the quality and intensity of their attitudes reverted to what they had been at the very first exposure. Since this kind of interaction duplicates what happens in the market place, it produced a valuable insight into this social-learning process and permitted a more effective marketing decision to be made.

This study suggested that while there may be increasing acceptance of the styling innovation with more exposure to it, this preference was not a stable one and could be reversed by contact with someone who was seeing the radically styled appliance for the first time. Here, it was decided that the style was too radical, and a more moderate style was elected.

3. Validity

A source of continual concern to researchers is the *validity* problem, the assumption that a measure really measures what it purports to measure. The group situation attempts to get as close to the actual purchasing decision as possible.

For example, the task given the group member in a problem which concerned purchase of prepackaged bacon was actual selection from among a number of samples the very bacon that she would serve her family, and not merely enumerating the criteria according to which she usually buys bacon.

Similarly, in a discussion of wine preference, the group members ordered and drank the wine of their choice.

When the topic was that of selecting a garment for themselves, women were asked to act out in detail, using a number of blouse samples, the act of buying one for themselves. Here the moderator took the role of salesman.

A problem involving the factors which are important in home decorating was approached by having groups of married couples go through the actual task of decorating a small-scale model home, using reduced-sized flooring materials, wallpaper prints, drapery fabrics, upholstery fabrics, and a wide variety of miniature furniture of various styles. Each couple decorated in the presence of other couples, and each did so with a conscientiousness that left little doubt that this task had considerable ego-involvement. These various devices tend to decrease the discrepancy between attitude expression and actual purchasing behavior.

4. Intensive Analysis

A fourth requirement of the group depth interview is that the often voluminous data be *inten-*

sively analyzed. Discussion material of this kind defies routine analysis. The method of analyses employed here is similar to that by which group psychotherapy sessions are analyzed.

Qualitative analysis of group-interview material focuses on several kinds of data. At the most superficial level are the opinions easily verbalized. They may at times give only some indication of the attitudes that group members are willing to express to others. Subconscious buying motives may be reflected in such data as: what topics are discussed, what kinds of people bring them up and with what degree of intensity, to whom they are said, and, perhaps most important, the temporal sequence in which they are said.

For example, a product that had enjoyed the highest market share in a particular city for fifteen years began to decrease in sales to members of a minority group. The drop in sales did not appear to be attributable to changes in product, package design, or sales policy. In several group sessions, the following sequence of themes was discussed: minority and national groups are becoming more alert and militant all over the world; domination by the more powerful majority must stop; sometimes members of minorities are dealt with unfairly by the police; the company in question makes a good product and is the biggest manufacturer of that product; other companies that also produce a good product are entering the field. These themes, in the context of the total group session, suggested an identification of the minority group member with the smaller producer in opposition to the large "powerful" company. To the extent that their buying behavior was consistent with this psychological identity, the "big" company was being hurt.

5. Marketing Applicability

The group depth interview is designed to *solve marketing problems*. Even if a study satisfies the other four requirements, it is just an "academic exercise" if its findings cannot be put to use in the market place.

A variety of marketing problems in which the group depth interview is applicable have already been indicated. As noted above, the group depth interview is most frequently useful and appropriate in the developmental and exploratory phases of research. Here it is used to make it more likely that the correct questions are asked in large sample surveys to follow.

The group depth interview is also helpful in cases where broad sampling is prohibited by security requirements. For example, when used as a complement to new-product development, group sessions are conducted at several points in the process, to aid management in decisions which are not best left for a point later in the process. In this way, management has available consumer reactions *before* large investments of time and money are committed.

For example, development of a new food product may begin with an exploration of several food concepts in order to expose which of several alternative directions would serve the consumers' needs best. Or, perhaps a manufacturer might wish to know which of several kinds of materials are best suited for a home building item before one of them is committed to intensive laboratory development. When one of these materials is selected by the groups and is developed further, the graphic design of the product also is explored by the group method. In a final research phase the progressively refined and elaborated product may be discussed by various kinds of groups in order to help to guide advertising themes, promotional campaigns, and perhaps distribution systems.

The group depth interview has been used to explore attitudes about corporate images, public relations, personnel-turnover rate, recruiting appeals, health problems, container design, political issues, and many other marketing and social problems. The full potential of the method has yet to be realized.

Marketers get an eyeful when focus groups expose products, ideas, images, ad copy, etc. to consumers

THE FOLLOWING ARTICLE IS PART I OF A TWO-PART SERIES ON FOCUS GROUP INTERVIEWING, largely based on a talk presented to a Marketing Research Association meeting last year by Myril Axelrod, a veteran of more than 17 years in qualitative research exclusively. She says that the full value of qualitative research can only be realized if the researchers have a strong and valid philosophy and if they are thoroughly trained and experienced. In Part I, presented here, she discusses when qualitative research should be used, when it is most valuable, and how it should not be misused. In Part II, which will appear in the next issue of the *Marketing News*, which will be a special issue on marketing research, she will discuss all the elements that go into developing good qualitative research and the pitfalls to avoid in such research. She has directed the Y&R Focused Lab Facility since 1967. Before that she developed and operated all qualitative services of Compton Advertising Inc.

BY MYRIL D. AXELROD
Vice President
Qualitative Research
Y&R Enterprises Inc.
New York, NY.

Myril Axelrod

A SENIOR ACCOUNT EXECUTIVE emerged from the viewing room in a kind of state of shock after a focus group session.

He was an excellent and dedicated account man. I know because I worked with him on one of my earliest projects, when qualitative research was relatively unfamiliar. He had made every effort to do a good job for his client and for his consumer.

Yet, on this occasion, he said, "I've been on this brand for 20 years, and I must say this is the first time I can feel that I really understand the consumer."

The same kind of experience is repeated day after day in our lab. Creatives, brand managers, and clients suddenly realize what they think is right for the consumer and what they expect the product to do for the consumer are not necessarily the way things are.

What is qualitative research? And what is it not? How can it be used fruitfully and successfully vs. how can it be abused? I want to stress particularly, in defining the productive use of this research approach,

> *"Qualitative research is . . . 'A chance to "experience" a "flesh and blood" consumer.' . . . to go into her life and relive with her all of the satisfactions, dissatisfactions, rewards, and frustrations she experiences when she takes the product into her home."—Myril Axelrod*

Reprinted from *Marketing News*, VIII (February 28, 1975), 6-7, published by the American Marketing Association.

how very important it is for both the client and the researcher to understand what to expect or not expect of qualitative research.

It is always excruciatingly painful to see it incorrectly used, improperly executed, misunderstood, mis-sold, or sold "short." And the client, in many cases, has to share the blame because he may not totally understand the true values of this type of exploration.

Any kind of research is always vulnerable. If the research makes the client look good or smart, it's good research; if it makes him look bad, or he doesn't like what it's telling him, the research all too often becomes suspect.

With qualitative research this vulnerability is even greater, and I understand and sympathize with many of the criticisms leveled against it. I can understand how a client can be fearful and cautious and how he can want to bury it under the rug if it doesn't seem to make sense to him. I say I can understand it because I recognize, and sadly bemoan, the handicaps under which he must work.

There are no prescribed guidelines for qualitative research, no books of rules, no formulas, and no stratagems. There is barely a textbook with which one can teach the ABC's of the profession. The results of qualitative research don't have to add up or check out. They can't even be "covered" by a margin of error quotient or fall under the protection of a probability sample.

But, most important of all, there is virtually no way a client can know, once he has "bought" a qualitative job, whether he did, indeed, buy the best he could get or whether he got from it the most he could — or even, and this is particularly frightening, whether he has been correctly guided.

There is no way of knowing what more he would have or could have learned if the job had been done differently; if a different kind of approach had been used in the questioning; if the "tone" of the interviewing had been different; if the moderator had established a different kind of rapport with the respondents; or if the analyst had a broader range of insights, sensitivity, and familiarity in the category upon which to draw. He has reason to be concerned and to enter into this kind of endeavor with reservations.

However, I'd like to help by setting down some guidelines and giving both clients using qualitative research and researchers offering qualitative services some of my impressions of the standards and goals I feel can make qualitative research a more secure and less frightening proposition for the client who buys it and a more satisfying experience for the researcher who sells it.

TO SUM UP WHAT QUALITATIVE RESEARCH IS, the one best brief phrase might be: "A chance to 'experience' a 'flesh and blood' consumer." It is the opportunity for the client to put himself in the position of the consumer and to be able to look at his product and his category from her vantage point.

It allows him to experience the **emotional framework in which the product is being used** — to, in a sense, go into her life and relive with her all of the satisfactions, dissatisfactions, rewards, and frustrations she experiences when she takes the product into her home.

Another particularly honest observer I remember very well was an excellent creative director who also had been at all times very dedicated and sensitive in his job. His first group session was a similar moment of discovery for him. He came out of the viewing room, shook his head in disbelief, and said, "I guess my wife and I are not as much like everyone else as I thought."

Qualitative research is also an invaluable way to discover the **realities of the situation in which a product is used** and to avoid the often costly and disastrous mistake of sitting in an office on Madison Ave. (or, which can be just as disastrous, in Princeton, N.J., or Toledo, Ohio) and deciding that what the lady in Kansas desperately needs is "X." In reality, however, what the lady in Kansas desperately needs and wants is "Y." The way to learn that is to "experience" that product and that product category together with that Kansas lady.

Such an experience provides the opportunity to discover the **goals and expectations the consumer has for a product** but to learn about these from her in her own terms. One of the most valuable aspects of the free-flowing, open nature of qualitative exploration is that no one has done the original thinking for the woman. No one has locked her into little boxes by "pre-thinking" her reactions and responses. She isn't forced into categorizing her spontaneous and uninhibited reactions so she gives them to you as they happen.

This, in turn, allows the researchers (and the client and the creative person) the opportunity to know how and why a product and other products in the category may be meeting or failing to meet the goals the woman has for them. It gives them personal insight into the consumer's own perceptions of her needs and desires and it does all of this in the language and the idiom of the consumer.

I have had a series of clients involved with shampoo or related hair products and something I learned in my very first exploration in this category continues to affect the marketplace performance (sometimes quite disastrously) of a number of shampoo and allied products entries. The crucial insight we gained in our qualitative work was the recognition of what happens to the woman emotionally, the very

broad ramifications of what washing her hair does for her and what she wants to feel like when she has washed her hair. The success or failure of any number of shampoo products has depended on how well that product was able to enhance and "feed to" those emotional feelings or whether, in some way, it interfered with or inhibited those feelings.

Sometimes everything else can add up and seem as if it is exactly right, but if somehow you have left out that one crucial factor — what the woman wants to feel and how it makes her feel — the results will be all too obvious in the marketplace. That's what I call "understanding the emotional framework in which the product is used."

Now, to make this "philosophy" more tangible. In terms of specific assignments, let me review the ways in which qualitative research can be applied to particular needs:

1. **BASIC ORIENTATION INTO A NEW CATEGORY** — Obviously, from all the above, it is apparent that qualitative exploration is an invaluable way of "getting your feet wet" in a category. In our agency it is, in fact, considered an essential part of the orientation for new personnel who come onto an account or who have to deal with a new subject for that account. It is not unusual for a creative or an account man to request several group sessions first so he can "hear consumers talk" about the category.

One of the most interesting projects we ever conducted, for instance, came about because the agency was asked by a client to prepare a public information pamphlet on venereal disease, to be offered as a public service, especially for teenagers. We arranged, with the cooperation of public health agencies, to hold totally open-ended group sessions in which teenagers discussed venereal disease in their own terms and raised any questions and areas of confusion which they had. We even used as moderators professionals trained to "track down" venereal disease and to guide its victims.

The questions and problems raised by the teens became the actual text for the pamphlet, which is today widely requested and circulated. Actually, too, any number of "demo's," "tests," and personal ways of judging or evaluating a product find their way into advertising because a copywriter heard the consumers describe, in their own words, how they evaluate and judge a product when they are actually using it in their homes.

2. **TO ORIENT MARKETING TEAMS** — We have recently worked very closely with a

client exploring possible line extensions. This experience, provides a particularly good example of how qualitative research can be used with great value in orienting marketing teams.

The line extensions being considered are completely outside the company's familiar product lines. They have virtually no background or "history" in any of these new categories with which to be guided, even in their preliminary thinking. Yet a number of the new products appear to be totally logical extensions of the highly successful existing product.

As a preliminary, "educational" step, we have, therefore, been conducting broad, free-flowing discussions of each of the new categories to learn, in a general way, how the consumer feels and acts in the category, what her needs and wants are, and what a successful product in this category should do or not do. Such information will provide clues and hypotheses as to whether a new entry, as proposed, would or would not be compatible and whether it seems to be promising.

In two instances, the research already done turned up possible problem areas which could conceivably be serious enough to discourage an entry in the category at all. This possibility is being further investigated now in other more quantitative research.

3. TO ORIENT NEW BUSINESS TEAMS — Most agencies spend too much time pointing · out their success and accomplishments and too little reflecting any effort to learn about the company's business and the consumers it sells to. Clients probably can verify how much more secure they feel about an agency which has made it its business to go out and discover where their consumer is "at" and what problems they may be having in selling her.

4. TO EXPLORE CONSUMER REACTIONS AT AN EARLY STAGE — Certainly the most prevalent and consistent use of qualitative research, within the agency and the client organization, should be to check out ideas and copy at any early stage. This, however, always should be in the realm of "checking out"; and it always should be considered as a part of the developmental process, rather than as an evaluation tool.

A. Preliminary Feelings About Copy: Group sessions are, for instance, a most valuable way of letting a copywriter know, hopefully before he has become too emotionally committed to an idea, whether his copy is indeed saying what it is intended to say; whether the consumer is "reading" it in the way he wants her to read it; whether it has meaning to her that is relevant to the way she uses the product and to her needs in the category.

Actually, it can be quite painful to sit in the viewing room with a creative person and to discover, along with him, that whatever it was he meant to say, his copy just isn't doing it. Or, even worse, that his great idea, which seemed so clever and charming to his associates, is,

unfortunately, going right over the heads of his audience.

But how much better for him to find this out while there is still time to do something about it, while there is still time to put the responses of a potential "audience" in perspective and even salvage what is valuable. The reason creatives are sometimes so resistant to copy research in general and group sessions in particular is because they feel that, with some group sessions and some clients, one chance remark by one respondent can kill a good ad. But, if the creatives, **and** the client, use the sessions merely to learn about the copy, and to open up their thinking, there is less inclination to resist research.

B. To Pick up Red Flags: So many times the people who work on a project and intellectualize about it almost day and night get so caught up in their reasoning that they no longer can "see" it clearly. As a result, they can miss the most obvious "red flags."

I can think of a dozen examples — the most dramatic being the late lamented "white" whiskey, Frost 880. The press reports on the Frost 880 debacle would have one believe that research failed to anticipate the problems that this product ran into in the marketplace. But this isn't so.

Frost 880 was not our client and we were not involved in any research done specifically for this brand. I can tell you, though, that our own qualitative explorations in the distilled spirits category had set up very strong warnings that would mitigate against a new entry of this kind. Our qualitative research couldn't have shown more clearly that a product, sold as a whiskey, just can't be white. That concept is too far removed from the traditional thinking and expectations of the consumer when he reaches for a whiskey. We also have explored the "pot" phenomenon with teenaged and young adults when the young set was so into drugs the liquor industry began to consider whether it had a future at all with this generation.

On the basis of this work, we were able to hypothesize (and it unfortunately has come to pass) that the youngsters would more than likely return to booze. Now, of course, America is experiencing a serious teen drinking problem. We have been able, in this same way, to also make clients aware of the problems they might run into when they move into an unrelated, and possibly (from the consumers' viewpoint) inappropriate category; when a temporary crisis environment confuses their vision and planning; when a seemingly attractive product could turn out to be just a "flash in the pan."

But, even on the simplest level, for early and, again, I must stress, preliminary hints of problems with a phrase used in a commercial or a print ad; with the musical background of a commercial; with the characterizations, etc., a series of well-conducted, open-ended group sessions can often give reason to at least stop and consider whether to run the risks involved.

C. Alternate Concept Evaluation: Exploring alternate concepts through qualitative research can be extremely useful and many clients investigate new ideas in this way. But here I have some serious problems because of the dangers I can see, and have observed, when the respondents are merely given a choice of possibilities and asked to choose between them. This kind of "voting" for preferences is more often than not just an intellectual exercise. The consumer, in such instances, is merely making an intellectual judgment, and as such, it is no more meaningful than any intellectual judgments a researcher or a client and his associates can make in his offices or laboratories. But, even more important, this method puts the consumer in a marketing expert role in which she doesn't belong, and her contribution, in that role, can be frighteningly misleading.

In my opinion, the way to get meaningful and more honest guidance on which direction to go, is to expose each concept separately in a series of similar groups of respondents and then to observe what each concept does — that is, what kind of effect does it have on the mood of the group? Do they spontaneously apply it to their own needs and their own lives? Do they "relate" to it with genuine interest and excitement?

In this method, the consumer gives input which only she can give — a view of how each of the concepts affects her and how she might apply it in her own life when it appears in the marketplace as an entity and a reality, not as an and-or possibility with five other hypothetical propositions. Furthermore, marketers retain for themselves the function of making marketing judgments because that is their role and only they are equipped for it.

D. Early Checkpoint for New Products: The fact that observers from the new product development groups can listen and observe and can "experience" the product even as the consumer is "experiencing" it, makes this kind of exploration particularly valuable to them. It is essential, however, that this kind of exploration not be used for nose-counting or to get a vote on the viability of the product. It should only be used to help the people involved in the new product understand how it is or is not fitting into the needs of the consumer.

5. TO SPARK PRODUCT/PACKAGING IDEAS — The opportunity to hear the woman report on all of her experiences in a category and to learn about the frustrations she is experiencing in that category also provides most valuable guidance into where to "go" in a category and what kind of new product is indicated.

In packaging, too, no one can be a better guide on how well a package is working and how it can be improved than the woman who uses it. Listen to her talk about some of the disasters she has experienced with the packages she has used and you will know, all too well, what you want to avoid or how you can offer a more acceptable package than your competition.

Sometimes, too, respondents can shake up clients and researchers pretty badly by pointing up, in the most casual way, something so obvious that you can't believe you missed it. Respondents, for instance, who were trying out a new plastic bottle for pancake syrup in group sessions pressed gently on the bottle to pour from it and discovered that it "geysered" so badly that it could be a veritable disaster at the breakfast table.

6. TO "FLESH OUT" OTHER RESEARCH — Qualitative research can be used to provide insights into the reasons why something seems to be happening in a copy test or why a particularly unusual sales pattern seems to be turning up on sales data. Talking to women, in a free-flowing way, about what they are doing in a category and what has been happening in a category can often start some very important thinking for the marketing minds of the client or the agency.

In our company, we often use group sessions for "diagnostic" purposes when a commercial has performed in an unexpected way in an "on-air" test. We expose the commercial in group sessions to learn what seems to have been happening which may have caused the poor score. Sometimes such direction can help the creatives to improve the commercial so that it can be salvaged. Sometimes the information gleaned becomes guidance for pitfalls to avoid in the future.

7. AS A STARTING POINT FOR OTHER RESEARCH — The use of qualitative research as a starting point for large-scale research like market segmentation is broadly accepted and its importance in this role cannot be minimized. One of my favorite clients is given to saying: "Any segmentation study is only as good as the qualitative data that went into it." He insists upon being personally involved in all of the group session work from which the basic questionnaire is developed and the indications of the qualitative phase must make sense to him before he will move on.

He believes that much of the "direction" to be drawn from the study can be perceived at the completion of the qualitative phase (if, of course, the qualitative work is sound and professional) and that the rest of the research verifies and puts numbers on the data. This has, in fact, been our experience, too, in the segmentation work we have done. In each instance the "directions" were evident even after the qualitative phase but amplified and verified in subsequent phases.

In one instance it was even difficult to restrain the client from wanting to "act' after the qualitative phase. It was a funny scene indeed. Four different speakers warned him before he saw the research that he must not be tempted to "run" with it; that it had to be verified and expanded in subsequent phases.

All warnings notwithstanding, when he saw the results of the qualitative phase, he grinned sheepishly and said: "I want to run with it." He went on to explain that he felt he could run with it because it made so much sense on the basis of his 20 years in the business.

The pieces in a qualitative study should make sense and they should fit together and those are the times people sometimes feel they can act on the basis of this kind of research. But this is not the way qualitative research should be applied. It is best used to open up ideas and to start off people's thinking, or, to make some sense out of what seems to be happening — to shed some light on the "why's" and the "wherefore's" of what is happening.

8. TO BETTER UNDERSTAND BRAND IMAGES —The free-flowing and uninhibited nature of a qualitative discussion can lead to extraordinary insight into how you "look" to your public, and, most important of all, how you got that image. We recently explored the image of a prominent and prestigious bank. The bank's directors feared another up-and-coming bank chain would in time displace the bank. They theorized their name was working against them. We did four group sessions in the area and almost immediately it became clear their problem wasn't their name at all but rather a number of quite different aspects of their overall image. All later back-up investigation has totally verified our findings and the bank, for the first time, seems to be able to see itself as it is seen through the eyes of its customers.

This is but one example. Repeatedly we are called upon to explore brand images qualitatively and to open up new channels

It cannot, for instance, give numbers or tell you how many people do this or feel this or think this. After a series of sessions, a feeling may develop that something may be a prevalent and important reaction and that it is something that had better be thought about strongly but be carefully on guard against any attempt to measure the extent of the reaction in any of the same terms used for a quantitative study.

We never use hand counts in our group sessions because they are so ludicrous and totally unreliable. At best, what do you have in a group session? Ten people, 12 at the most, so suppose they divide three and three and two — what does that tell? Furthermore, there's the social psychology of handraising. Sit behind a one-way mirror some time and watch the number grow as people look around to see how other people are voting!

Numbers do not belong in a qualitative study at any time, not with hand-raising and not with written questionnaires. The goal of qualitative research is to learn what the people have to say and to understand what they say and why they are saying it. It is not to find out how many, because at best, the "population" studied is too small to make any findings "significant" by any statistical measure.

However, if you observe a group planned and moderated by a sensitive, skilled moderator, and you "listen" in an open-minded way (often the most difficult part of all) I can assure you that you will know what is coming out that is important without any hand counts.

"Numbers do not belong in a qualitative study at any time . . . remember . . . the 'quality' of the response . . . is important . . . Its purpose . . . is to start you thinking."—Myril Axelrod

of thinking to improve brand or corporate images. Y&R has, in fact, a unit which is devoted exclusively to the improvement of corporate images and how they are projected to the public through name, packaging, design, etc. Virtually all of the preliminary exploration for their work is done in our Discussion Lab.

QUALITATIVE RESEARCH IS NOT for circumventing quantitative research. Speaking now about the dangers of misusing qualitative research, some of which I already have mentioned, I will spell them out as clearly as I can, primarily because there is so much fear that this is happening all too often and all too widely.

Qualitative research is not a "quick and dirty" and cheap way for avoiding quantitative research. It serves completely different purposes and does not, in any way, presume to supply the same kinds of answers as quantitative exploration does.

The key point to remember at all times, is that it is the "quality" of the response that is important in this kind of research — how "involved" the respondent is; how much this seems to relate to her and her behavior in the category; is she really reacting or is she intellectualizing? Again, what matters is what is happening and what effect it is having.

Would you believe that even a point made by one woman can be a crucial insight, provided it opens up thinking and is followed up sufficiently to know how important it really is. Qualitative research allows you the opportunity to find out what she genuinely wants and needs and it helps you to sell it to her in the way that will have the most meaning for her. In total, qualitative research is suggestive, not definitive. It does not give absolute proof or a clear go-ahead. Its purpose, in a phrase, is to start you thinking.

10 essentials for good qualitative research

THIS IS PART II OF A TWO-PART SERIES ON FOCUS GROUP INTERVIEWING. Part I, in the Feb. 28 issue, told when such qualitative research should be used, when it is most valuable, and how it should not be misused. Myril Axelrod, a veteran of more than 17 years in qualitative research exclusively, here discusses the elements that go into developing good qualitative research and the pitfalls to avoid. It should be added that her talk to the Marketing Research Association, upon which this series is based, also discussed another qualitative research technique besides focus groups. But that technique—the individual in-depth interview—is not as widely used because, as she pointed out, such in-depth interviews are extremely time-consuming, expensive, and not always necessary. But when well-done, they can be reused up to 10 years later.

BY MYRIL D. AXELROD
Vice President
Qualitative Research
Y&R Enterprises Inc.
New York, NY.

MANY SKILLS AND FACTORS COMBINE to create good, sensitive, professional qualitative research.

In presenting my observations on the following 10 essentials necessary for such a successful combination, I will be drawing on my own experiences and the elements that I have found through many years of personal practice, as well as observation of other practitioners, lead to meaningful and reliable insights.

1. UNDERSTANDING THE PURPOSE — The first essential is that everyone involved understand the purpose of qualitative research in general and of the specific project about to be undertaken in particular.

Everyone — clients, account people, and creatives — should recognize what this kind of research is and what it is not (it is not a way to avoid quantitative or nose-counting research), what information is being sought, and how insights derived will be used.

Before beginning any project, the qualitative researcher should make completely sure all to be involved have been heard and each has revealed all of his ideas on what he wants to learn from the research. Armed with this guidance, the researcher can: correct any misunderstandings, include everybody's ideas in the interviewing guide and insure they will be covered; and eliminate interruptions during the session from viewing room observers who think the moderator doesn't understand the importance of their "pet" ideas.

Those in the viewing room behind the one-way mirror generally have no idea how distressing intermittent notes coming all through a session can be and how much this can interfere with the work's quality.

The success of any session depends on how "involved" the moderator becomes with the group's participants and conveys to them the feeling that she is interested in them and what they have to say. If, however, the moderator is forced to be constantly aware of, involved with, and concerned about those in the viewing room, her relationship to the respondents suffers.

That is why I urge clients to get all thoughts, ideas, and hypotheses out into the open in the preplanning, to choose a researcher they can trust, to understand how to "listen" to a session and what to expect from it, and then to let that researcher "do her thing."

They shouldn't "bug" her so much that she can't function adequately. If she can't be trusted to get the information the client wants, then he shouldn't hire her.

Of course, before going into the session, the understanding must be mutual. Researchers must understand clients as well as clients understanding researchers. Researchers must be prepared to deal with all the clients' concerns.

2. MAKING THE MOST OF A SMALL SAMPLE — Because qualitative research is small in scope and involves only a limited number of respondents, it is particularly important to concentrate on those population segments that will give the most meaningful information.

Covering every possible segment in a small exploration like this generally is impossible. In fact, it may be misleading and confusing to have three people from one segment, three from another segment, and three from a third in one group.

Though it would be valuable to hear the subject discussed from the vantage points of all three segments, if separate groups can't be conducted for each, concentrate on the key group — the one most useful to the specific purposes of this project or the group with the most experience with the problems being investigated. It is also more productive to get as much commonality as possible in a group, so that numerous "variables" don't confuse the issues.

For instance, we almost never put married, full-time housewives with children at home in the same group as unmarried, working women because their life-styles and overall goals and needs are completely different. We also break teenage and child groups carefully so that the participants in

Reprinted from *Marketing News*, **VIII** (March 14, 1975), 10-11, published by the American Marketing Association.

a group are on a similar wave-length.

We rarely interview men and women together because we agree with what the psychologist Wechsler wryly commented to one of his classes: "Just take it from me and don't ask questions, men are different than women!" Also, men tend to "perform" for the women and vice versa, and that's not what qualitative research is all about!

3. GOOD RECRUITING — Nothing can be more important than good, honest, serious, dedicated recruiting. The best moderator in the world is going to have a doubly hard time doing her job, and often can't do it at all, when she finds herself faced with a roomful of unqualified respondents who have no experience or background in the category from which to draw.

Equally frustrating can be respondents who have been to many sessions and enjoy "playing" with the moderator and "showing off" for the other participants. I've heard every excuse and rationalization for repeat respondents, but I will never accept that a repeat respondent can possibly contribute to a session in the same way as a new respondent.

Almost anyone will respond to someone who wants to hear her problems, listen to her experiences, and find out how she thinks and feels. That kind of promise brings a respondent to a session with the essential eagerness.

The only kind of response valuable in qualitative research is the spontaneous and emotional one. Once the respondent thinks, censors, and intellectualizes, it no longer is a qualitative insight.

Therefore, the only kind of respondent who can make a contribution to my qualitative work is a fresh, spontaneous, involved, honest respondent who has not pre-thought her answers. This puts a particular burden on the field staff and the recruiters. I'm not popular with field personnel. But I do insist on this.

We always have set strict standards for our recruiters. We have been very tough on them if they tried to circumvent them. Some of our rules are:
—No one attends more than one Y & R group session. We keep careful records of names, addresses, phone numbers, and even demographics to check.

—No one participates in our sessions who has attended sessions somewhere else and we try to check on this through a clearinghouse arrangement with other companies and agencies.
—A number of recruiters, not just one or two, send respondents to a session. Each must turn up only one or two people. Thus, a recruiter is not panicked into "cheating" to fill a quota. We have many recruiters. We don't burden any one. This way is better too because respondents come from different areas of the city and have different backgrounds.
—We constantly add new recruiters.
—Recruiters must use a prescreen questionnaire and are prohibited from revealing the session's subject.

Sure, we get cheaters. Some recruiters may even be a party, at times, to the cheating. But we will never countenance it. We constantly police on our own.

4. A "RELAXED" ATMOS-PHERE — The entire setting and the mood of the sessions must be as relaxed and natural as possible. For many years, before it became popular to have a number of session observers, I had no Discussion Lab in the agency but often went to private homes. I did that deliberately because the most real, genuine, and meaningful responses can only be obtained if respondents feel totally natural and comfortable, as if they are sitting in a neighbor's home and talking with friends.

I always try to establish a "coffee klatsch" or "bull session" mood in order that the respondents will open up and talk in their own comfortable way. I always try to avoid any feeling of a question-and-answer period, because I don't want them to feel the need to either give the "right" answer or feel they have to be knowledgeable.

The biggest danger, in qualitative work, is to end up with intellectual opinions. The session's setting can have a great deal to do with how well that relaxation can be achieved and can counteract the feeling of authoritarian inter-rogation.

We have gone out of our way to have our lab on a floor that is not elaborate and fancy and is not actually a part of Y & R at all. Respondents are not recruited for Y & R, but rather for a research organization. Everything has been

done to minimize any association with "big business" or with advertising.

The session room is furnished like a comfortable, not too elaborate, living room. There is also a small kitchen and dining area. Everything is home-like.

This was our compromise between the need to have a lab where we could be sure creative and account people would be able to attend and observe, while avoiding the negative effect of bringing people into a formidable "big business" setting. It's not perfect.

A far better environment still would be a private home. But our sessions are always more comfortable, relaxed, and "down to earth" than they would be around an impressive conference table in a conference room, where our women couldn't feel at ease.

Unfortunately, when not in New York, we rely on out-of-town field services to provide facilities and cannot always get the interviewing environment we like. We avoid facilities which set up groups in a cold, austere, business-like conference room around a long, forbidding table which faces an obvious mirror that is the only decoration in the room and can't possibly be missed by the participants.

Some practitioners, especially since Watergate and other invasions of privacy have been in the news, would like everyone to believe it is wrong to view respondents from a one-way mirror. They say no attempt should be made to hide the facts that there is a mirror and that the session is being observed.

I don't agree. Rather I feel, most strongly, that observing res-pondents for qualitative re-search is not "spying"; it is not exploiting; and it is not "invading" anyone's privacy for illegal or unscrupulous purposes.

The purpose of qualitative research is to try to better understand the consumer in order that her needs and wants can be better served. Those who believe this, as I do, will not believe that it is wrong to try to learn what it is that she needs and wants.

Respondents are always truthfully told that they are being audio-tape recorded, that a general report will be written, and that at no time will their name be connected with anything they say. Therefore, they have no reason to fear what they say.

A comfortable home-like setting, such as this one in the Y&R Discussion Lab, allows respondents to relax and respond from a consumer frame of reference rather than to play the role of advertising experts. The one-way mirror is the glass in the doors at left.

If the respondents are not going to be themselves, the research might as well not be done at all. I take exception with those who say respondents don't even notice a camera after the first few minutes and it has no effect on the session. How do they know? How do they know what else they would have gotten if the respondents did not know they were being observed or photographed?

I hold that the mirror should be as inconspicuous as possible and that there should be no photographing. I also recommend to field service organizations to set up informal facilities so that the consumers can feel at ease and discuss the subject in the same open way they would in their own living rooms.

5. THE ABILITY TO LISTEN-RELATE AND RESPECT THE RESPONDENTS — The moderator's key to successful rapport with a respondent is the ability to listen and make her feel she (the moderator) cares about what she (the respondent) is saying. This is what this field is all about.

In selecting a moderator the primary requirement is how well that person is going to be able to listen — is he or she someone who is really interested in people, who wants to hear what someone else has to say, who can readily establish rapport and gain the confidence of people, who can make them feel relaxed and anxious to talk? This can only happen if the moderator is genuinely that kind of person.

In the sessions, the moderator can't fake it. The respondents pick it up in a minute. It can make the whole difference between a fruitful session and one where the respondents are only going through the motions.

The moderator is there to reflect the responses of the participants and must not, at any time, inject any of her own opinions or prejudices. Yet a moderator who is dynamic, warm, "involved" in her work, and, most of all, believes in her work, can make the whole difference in the session.

It is essential that the moderator "blend" in with the respondents. Though she must always control what is going on so that it does not get too far off the subject or too intellectual, the best kind of moderator is accepted and "relates" as part of the group.

I always remind my moderators that they should just talk to the respondents, not question them. I tell them to get their guide clearly in mind before the session and then carry on as if it were a natural conversation.

I never have women doing sessions with men because I think that men don't talk to a woman in the same way they would talk to a man or in the way they talk when they are among themselves. What we want to know is what they say when they are "talking to the fellas," not what they say because that is going to please or impress the woman moderator.

Furthermore, a woman might not always recognize when a man is saying something especially important — just as a man can't always know that what women are saying is important because he hasn't had those same kinds of feelings himself and they don't ignite a spark of recognition in him. I even try to use my youngest and most swinging interviewers with teenagers so they won't be inhibited by thinking that they are talking to a mother figure or a teacher.

Allied to all of the above is that it is most important to respect the respondents and to have regard for what they say. I never once came out of a session without learning something. It is always a big mistake for a researcher to assume he knows what the respondents are going to say, or, even worse, to write off what they say because he doesn't have regard for them.

In the beginning of every session we tell our respondents that the reason we have asked them to come is because they use products every day of their lives. They have experiences with them that we need to know about. They, in a sense, know more about the products they use than anyone else. And this is the kind of information they can give us.

6. A "FREE-FLOWING" INTERVIEW — A free-flowing interview, where a respondent is able to bring up any aspect of a subject when it is on her mind and the moderator picks up that idea and probes it as it occurs, needs the kind of environment that gives respondents the opportunity to "ventilate" the feelings they have in a totally oppen way. Dealing with a subject as the respondents themselves introduce it also provides the best reading of what is uppermost in their minds and a better insight into the "positioning" they themselves give an idea or a problem.

I am strongly against "authoritarian" interviewing in qualitative research where, as I once heard a moderator brag, "I run my groups like an orchestra. I can get the respondents to say anything I want them to say."

If this was so, it was hardly necessary to "conduct" the groups. It would have been far simpler to just let him report on his points of view and save the time and money. But neither this nor his orchestrated groups would be qualitative research.

7. SKILLED PREPARATION — Nobody working under me has ever gone into a session without a full guide worked out beforehand, covering every possible area to be discussed **and** the best way to introduce these areas so that the questions will be totally open-ended and not influence the answers.

This, again, is one of the most essential elements of good qualitative research — to think through all the possible areas, prepare the questioning in such a way that it will not influence the results, remember as much of this thinking as possible, and then go into the session and keep those ideas in mind to be introduced when they are most appropriate.

Although it is not always possible to do this, and one must at times refer to a guide during the session, I can only urge moderators to concentrate first and foremost on what is happening and on probing through what is happening in the session.

I have seen what happens when a respondent begins with total eagerness to comment and notices the interviewer is so busy looking at her guide that she isn't listening. That respondent and that thought surely were lost forever.

As for the guide itself, questions should be open-ended enough to elicit the respondents' genuine feelings, rather to suggest ideas to them and then just let them play these ideas back. Many times answers can merely be a reflection of the way the questions were asked, or even the point in the conversation at which the question was asked.

I can remember one moderator let the women spend an hour discussing why they didn't want a multi-pack, then questioned them on what packaging they would like for this multi-pack! Is there any doubt why the "findings" on the packages were not very encouraging?

Or, to give another example: A woman, when talking about cleansers, is asked, "Are you concerned about germs in your kitchen?" Sure, she'll say, "Yes." But that kind of questioning hasn't positioned her relative to how it actually affects her habits, actions, or purchases in the category, or, most important of all, what priority this takes in her selection of a cleanser.

Skillful pre-planning with a great deal of thought is clearly essential. Too many think, "What's the big deal? — all you do is go in and ask questions, and everybody seems to feel why shouldn't they go into qualitative research too, they can ask questions as well as anybody else."

But it is not that simple. "Just asking questions" may be the hardest job you ever had, especially if you care about what you are getting and how meaningful it is.

8. CONTROLING GROUP INFLUENCE — The possibility of group influence and the problems of dominant respondents are often raised as limitations of the group session technique. Such situations can and do occur if the moderator is not skilled enough to know how to handle them, which is one of the most important skills the group interviewer has to learn. The interviewer must know how to turn them around before they contaminate the results of the entire group.

In our groups, for instance, as soon as people are starting to echo the same idea, the moderator immediately throws out the question, "Does anyone feel differently?" or "That's one point of view, now how about someone else?"

In this way she makes it socially acceptable to have a different viewpoint. She also plants the idea that this may not necessarily be the right position to take.

No respondent in our groups is permitted to just say, "I agree." She is forced to also answer the probe, "What experiences have you had that make you feel that way?"

Respondents are, in fact, told in the beginning of the session that, even if they are agreeing with someone, we still would like to hear about their experiences because each of them as an individual consumer is important. They are told that, for this reason too, we are particularly anxious to know when they disagree, so they are primed right from the beginning to take their own positions.

That is how we try to control group influence when it is open and obvious. But, there is also the kind of group influence that happens in the respondents' minds that neither we, nor even they, are aware of — something that is said that may start a whole line of reasoning in the respondents' minds.

To guard against this kind of

hidden group influence, we always insist on at least two, and sometimes more, sessions with the same kinds of people. In this way, if similar ideas come out, without the same influences, we can be more secure that they are meaningful.

I would urge all to always repeat a session at least once with the same kind of population and specifications in order to check it out. One session on any subject can be frighteningly misleading and should never be acceptable.

Another skill the competent moderator must learn is the ability to "turn off" both irrelevant conversation and advertising expertise. She must be able to redirect the conversation to its original purpose — to get the respondents to react from their own vantage points as consumers.

She must recognize inappropriate intellectualization and expertise and be able to assure it doesn't get out of hand. She must, at the same time, know how to do this in a way that does not jeopardize her relationship with the group or interfere with its desire to speak openly and honestly.

9. SKILLED ANALYSIS — How the groups are interpreted also can prove to be a far knottier problem than anticipated. Recognizing that the primary purpose of qualitative research is to provide everyone working on the brand with an opportunity to listen to and identify with the consumer, it is important to urge that all such people make it their business to see the sessions from the viewing room.

The danger of that, however, is that, all too often, every viewer has his own "axe" to grind and he is more than likely listening to hear exactly what he wants to hear. That is what makes the task of analyzing the sessions so difficult.

The analyst must be able to hear everything and to also be "listening with a third ear." Let me urge clients who will be observing in back rooms **please** do not jump to conclusions.

Conclusions should wait until there has been an opportunity to talk with the moderator and to consider her analysis and her input. It is very often not what the respondents are saying that is the key to what the client wants, but what is happening, and many times he needs the benefit of someone's repeated experience inside that interviewing room to understand what is happening. The interviewer, with continued exposure to and experience in group work, can help the client understand.

10. EXPERIENCE, KNOW-HOW, TRAINING — The competence of the person who conducts and analyzes any qualitative work can make the total difference in whether the research will have value and make a genuine contribution. And that, unfortunately, is where the whole process all too often breaks down.

I can't begin to tell you what disasters I have seen and listened to in the guise of qualitative research and how I have wept for the client who bought that work!

Not everyone can be a moderator. It requires not only the kind of outward personality that encourages respondents to want to talk to you, but also an extreme degree of sensitivity, a genuine interest in people, an ability to listen "with a third ear," as the psychologists put it, a great deal of training and experience, and most of all, a serious concern with the importance of understanding this craft.

A qualitative researcher is **not** born "full blown" — despite the fact that focused group moderators and qualitative research firms appear on the horizon almost daily and are being hired at startling prices by unsuspecting clients.

In our shop, for instance, our experience has been that it takes a new moderator close to two years of training and almost daily exposure to our hundreds of sessions each year before we consider that person able to work as regular staff moderator capable of handling a project on the level we aim for.

We have a formal training program in which potential moderators work their way through four levels in order to reach senior status. They are carefully evaluated as they reach each level and if they are not meeting the standards, they are dropped from the program — as they would be if they were enrolled in a professional training school.

Actually, one of the most frustrating aspects of my job and that of anyone either buying or offering qualitative services is that there now are no professional requirements for being a qualitative researcher. No special educational or experience goals are demanded.

In fact, even if a student wanted to obtain special training in the skills of this type of research, he or she would have a hard time finding a college or university that offers such training.

We desperately **need** more qualitative researchers but we need good ones, trained ones, truly professional ones. We need to set up demanding college programs, carefully controled internships, goals, and standards which have to be met if qualitative research is to continue as a viable and dependable tool for the marketer.

Moderators focus on groups: session yields 7 hypotheses covering technology trend, professionalism, training, techniques, reports, etc.

BY THOMAS E. CARUSO (with assistance from the participants)
Editor

HYPOTHESIS GENERATION IS ONE OF THE MAJOR USES OF FOCUS GROUP RESEARCH. At the invitation of the *Marketing News*, six experienced focus group moderators met on May 24 for a most unusual session in which they were the respondents and Marji Frank Simon, vice president of the AMA's Marketing Research Division, was the moderator. The session yielded seven hypotheses which, if true, have major implications for such research. Of course, these professional researchers would be the first to point out that one such session should not be used as the only input for decision making.

Some members of the group objected to the *Marketing News* printing no summary, but only an edited transcript of this session as it had done in the Jan. 16, 1976, issue after a similar session with focus group research buyers. The moderators said focus groups aren't research until after they have been analyzed and reported on by professionals skilled in such qualitative research. Edited tapes and transcripts are aids to analysis; they do not represent the major output from such research to serve as input for the making of decisions as to further research. Such decisions, these moderators pointed out, should await the professional researcher's analysis, observations, and report.

Marji Frank Simon

These seven hypotheses hopefully will stimulate further discussion and additional research and development of this research technique which seems to be increasingly relied upon by marketers and researchers:

1. **The technology seems to be taking over the technique.** The push for increasingly more sophisticated ways of recording and reporting respondents' comments may well influence those comments. This is **qualitative**, not quantitative, research. What a respondent says under hot lights and in front of a videotape camera may not be of the same quality as comments made while sitting with "friends" in her own kitchen or living room, which is where the early sessions were held when the technique evolved from the theory and application of social psychological studies carried out for the purpose of therapy.

2. **The proliferation of viewers is leading to a "show" or party atmosphere** bound to negatively affect research buyers' and users' attitudes towards the technique. Sometimes as many as a dozen observers are behind a one-way mirror or in another room watching a videotape monitor. These may include clients, company officers and even their spouses (one executive brought his wife because "it was better than sitting home and watching TV."), advertising creative people, product managers, etc. Many clients also demand to be served food and drinks while viewing the sessions. While the increasing frequency of such abuses worries some, one moderator observed, "I'd rather have them have a party and not listen, than have them listen and take a wrong conclusion home with them."

3. **Researchers have a professional responsibility** to prevent clients from misusing the focus group technique or the information it yields. After the researcher has done his or her duty by providing professional advice, such as a doctor does, the client (patient) is free to ignore it. Unfortunately, so many clients may be ignoring the advice that some researchers may be ignoring their professional responsibility and may have stopped giving the advice. Entreprenurial researchers may also be under financial and other pressures to "give clients what they want."

4. **There seems to be no organized or institutionalized way for new moderators to receive proper professional education, training, and experience.** Indeed, there seems to be no standard for what background is needed to conduct such research or analyze such sessions.

5. **The moderator's sex is a variable to be considered** in dealing with some subjects in focus group discussions. However, the moderator's skill, ability to develop rapport, and other variables generally have a greater impact than sex on groups conducted on all but highly sex-oriented topics. Myril Axelrod, a strong dissenter on this topic, even in her previous *Marketing News* articles, commented that sex is "always a major factor" and that the results "always are better when the moderator is of the same sex as the respondents."

6. **Although different moderators use different methods, certain techniques can be rather generally applied to certain types of situations,** such as serving refreshments to help the respondents relax and establish the rapport and positive group interaction which are the most important considerations in conducting a focus group. Although some of the moderators thought this part of the discussion was rather superficial and sounded like "Group Moderating 101," others pointed out that

Reprinted from *Marketing News*, **X** (September 10, 1976), 12-16, published by the **American Marketing Association**.

these techniques need to be discussed because there is no such college course offered. Among the techniques discussed are ways of dealing with knowledgeable respondents, the warmup period, using big sheets of paper, starting arguments, "wishing," and "false termination."

7. It seems that in reporting the results of the sessions, quantitative words and practices, such as "all," "detailed findings," "conclusions," using percentages, and reporting head counts and votes, should be avoided in favor of "softer words," such as "impressions," "observations," and "hypotheses for further testing." In addition, it seems that what the moderator/analyst says in the report can be as important or more important than what the respondents said in the session and-or in the report.

Since these are not necessarily separate issues, some were interwoven in this conversation on qualitative research. This is especially true of the first three as shown in the following portions of the edited transscript. The *Marketing News* thanks all those involved for volunteering their time and talents, especially Roy J. Quiriconi, president, Q Research Inc., Rosemont, Ill., who volunteered the use of his facilities for the session. (All photos during the session by Thomas E. Caruso, Editor.)

1. Technology

ROY QUIRICONI — It won't be long before terminals will be in client offices. They will plug in and watch us conducting a focus group session.

MYRIL AXELROD — Seriously?

QUIRICONI — In. years to come, I'm sure that's going to be the case.

RICHARD DROSSLER — I'm not sure that is really a good thing. We do a lot of videotaping because we find it easier to analyze the tapes. But we try not to release our videotapes, unless they are edited for an analytical presentation.

MELANIE PAYNE — I worked in a situation where the office covered five floors. When the camera was on, you could sit in an office four floors away and watch. You could have been three blocks away. I'm waiting for the first class-action suit for respondents who say their privacy has been invaded. We are invading their privacy.

AXELROD — That scares me to hell. I think if you're videoing by law you have to tell them. I don't video, I feel very strongly about that. Do you tell them they are being videoed?

QUIRICONI & PAYNE — Yes, we tell them.

MODERATOR MARJI SIMON — Do you tell them when you are audiotaping them?

AXELROD — Oh, I tell them...

DROSSLER — How about the mirror, same thing?

AXELROD — I don't tell them there is a mirror. I explain to them they are being taped because I don't want to take notes while I'm talking with them; I am just writing a general report; and nothing they say will be connected with them or their name. But you can't do that when videoing. You can't say, "Nothing you say will be connected with you," when their picture is there. That makes a difference between the two. As long as they know they're going to be connected with what they say, they will "censor" it before they say it.

JUDY CORSON — Have you ever had anyone say, "Is that a one-way mirror?" What do you say?

AXELROD — Our mirror isn't obvious. Once you tell people there are people observing them, you're not going to get them completely relaxed.

PAYNE — But if it is obvious, how can you avoid it? With a very obvious, large mirror, I always tell them. But I'm rarely in situations where it isn't obvious.

AXELROD — This is research and I'm only interested in getting as honest, relaxed, and comfortable an opinion as possible. I don't want them to posture for me....I just want to hear how these ladies talk to one another when they're discussing a product. I'm not interested in anything personal.

PAYNE — We used to be able to do that. Maybe my clinical training keeps haunting me, because I feel a personal responsibility for the people there. I guess that is why I object to the cameras and mirrors. It's like, "It's none of your (the client's) business until I'm ready...until I've talked to these people. It's the ladies and me."

AXELROD — We wish we could get back to where we did the job without the mirror, but we can't.

MODERATOR SIMON — Why can't we?

QUIRICONI — Well, they all want to come and watch and they want videotape records....

MODERATOR SIMON — Should we discourage them and push it back the other way?

QUIRICONI — The technique is starting to be run by the technology. I was called in to moderate some sessions on the West coast where we couldn't get around the table because the camera couldn't see everybody. So we had to spread out so the camera could get good shots of everybody. And if you're videotaping, it's much easier if the respondents have numbers instead of names so the technical people can edit the tape. I refused to call people by numbers, "No. 6, what do you think of No. 3's comment?"

PAYNE — That's terrible.

AXELROD — Oh my gosh! *1984!*

QUIRICONI — Also in this instance the videotaping had to be done in color which meant we had spotlights in the room on everybody and everyone was perspiring.

BONNIE PERRY — But that's the exception, isn't it?

QUIRICONI — Today it is, but that's where we're going because whoever does the presenting to top management wants it to be a nice slick job. And one of the recruiting specs on this job was that there be "attractive respondents" in the sessions.

MODERATOR SIMON — Is that going to affect the technique?

QUIRICONI — It's affecting it now.

AXELROD — It's a whole lot removed from when you could sit in a house in Ohio and *really* discuss this subject and *really* have these ladies let their hair down.

DROSSLER — The thing to do for that is to split the sessions and say, "All right, we will do this study over here for the results; and then we'll do some 'groups' for demonstration and edit the second videotape strictly for the presentation, which will include only the things that the research groups also said."

QUIRICONI — But many times you can't do both because of time.

DROSSLER — And also remember your client has to pay for it.

CORSON — You can't say, "No." If we were to have a client who said, "We want them all to look nice, etc.," we'd say, "Buzz off, we're not interested." That is the only way things are going to change. We view ourselves as professionals. When we do qualitative research what we're selling is the analysis. Obviously a good job of recruiting, moderating, etc. is all taken for granted.

QUIRICONI — All of us here consider ourselves professionals.

CORSON — Right. Basically, we are the decision makers as professionals, the same as with an attorney or doctor. When you go for advice, they give you advice. Whether you follow it or not, your well-being is going to be based on that. It is up to the professional to decide. If you see you can affect what they're doing and maybe change it, then you probably will continue to work for them. But, if they're going to continue to misuse it as you're saying, then you probably wouldn't.

QUIRICONI — I'm not saying this is a continuing thing; it is isolated. Every once in a while something like this happens. But it could happen more often.

PERRY — We should recognize it is isolated at this point. Your prediction is that it is going to get bigger, but I don't see it going that way. Every now and then there are people who want a demonstration group. We all know it for that. Given the technology, the fact we're doing more groups with videotape, we should focus on: What can we do in our current settings and what are some of the techniques we can use to encourage candor and openness, the kind of thing Myril said she used to have in people's homes?

PAYNE — You can't.

MODERATOR SIMON — Then it's going to be the end of the whole technique?

DROSSLER — No, it isn't that bad. It's surprising to me, whenever we do these things, how little effect they seem to have on the respondents.

CORSON — Right.

PERRY — The things they talk about in some groups, well, I can't imagine people getting more personal and more candid so I have to assume that they are being open. It is true, even with video camera or tape recorder, a mirror, people are still opening up because they want to. They need to.

ALEXROD — The problem in qualitative research is that there is no way of ever knowing if you would have gotten something different if you didn't have the mirror or whether videotaping makes a difference or if you do the group it is going to be different than if I do the group.

MODERATOR SIMON — What kind of setting do you prefer?

QUIRICONI — We tried a couch along with chairs. Since we found the people who sit in the couch, especially the woman in the center, couldn't talk to anybody directly, we went to chairs and try to make it as comfortable and living-roomish as possible. A lot of subtle things can affect group interaction. I'm afraid a lot of inexperienced moderators simply are not aware of them. Table height, for instance. We went to this continental height coffee table to eliminate the psychological and physical barrier a conference table imposes on participants. But there also are facilities in the field that are palaces ... incredibly plush. If you have the camera, hot lights all over the place, and the respondents have numbers on them, you say, "Let's just sit around as if you're in your own living room and forget the camera, forget the perspiration..."

MODERATOR SIMON — I know one company that has buttons in front of each respondent's place that they push for their reactions. If you walk into the viewing room, you can see just how each person is voting.

AXELROD — And they call *that* qualitative?

MODERATOR SIMON — How do you feel about the viewers sending in notes during the session?

PAYNE — Well, it is annoying...

CORSON — We don't have those problems. What we normally do is tell the client, "Anything you want that wasn't covered, *right before we wind up*, send in a note."

QUIRICONI — I've heard of some places that have an aerial under the carpet so the moderator can wear eyeglasses with a receiver.

AXELROD — The whole key is that those people should think you are really involved with them and interested in them and whatever they say. How can you possibly listen to them while getting buzzed in your ear every few minutes on a two-way radio?

2. 'Show' or party atmosphere and

3. professional responsibility

MODERATOR SIMON — How do you feel about refreshments?

CORSON — We have a company policy: no alcoholic beverages.

PAYNE — But you're working in your own facility. We don't have our own facility. We go out every day and our client says, "I want gin, this brand, Scotch, bloody mary mixes, seven kinds of cheese, etc. etc." And they sit back there and have a party because they're out of town on a "vacation." I think it is abominable. It happens more than I wish it did.

AXELROD — Many places we use across the country have a bar in the viewing room. The clients are having a party; and you want to cry because you're so excited about what you're getting; and these people aren't even listening. Back home we won't serve anything.

DROSSLER — About a month ago a client was raving about a facility where the viewing room was remote. He felt it was so great because the viewers didn't have to be quiet.

QUIRICONI — Our viewing room is away from this room. In our other building, our viewing room was adjacent to the discussion room. We could hear them and they could hear us. When we moved here, I put it over there because many times the clients were making more noise than we were in here.

AXELROD — Do the rest of you feel it is so sad when they are not even listening. It's just so frustrating.

DROSSLER — To some extent, the client is paying for this and it is part of what he wants. Some clients come to a group because they want a trip to San Francisco. Let them have it, as long as some people pay attention.

QUIRICONI — We don't serve any liquor. That is disastrous. We have to address ourselves as to how best to function as professionals under all these different circumstances; a real danger is when some clients come in, see one group or two groups, and say they don't need any more research. We caution them; we write notes up front in the reports telling them that it is qualitative, indicative, etc. But there is little attention paid to them.

AXELROD — Part of a researcher's important responsibility is that he insists on being in on it from the beginning. Unless you know all of the thinking that came before the groups and exactly what the people have in their minds, how can you really do an adequate job?

QUIRICONI — Sometimes I have more people in the observation room than I have here. And a product manager will "drop in" for one group or even 30 minutes of one group.

AXELROD — And then he is sure that he has the entire answer. That is really what has been bugging the clients on the higher level too. Every junior guy on the account decides it is a great jaunt he is going to take. I don't know if the problem can be solved. It goes beyond us; it goes to the client organizations. But part of why we have problems is because there are too many people involved. You may be dealing with the researcher, but there are 12 other people he may not have gotten together with before. And they do "drop in."

PERRY — I think of it as a very flexible tool. And clients should be able to use it however it suits their needs. If they want to drop in for a few minutes, watch all of the groups, or wait until they get the report and then go by that, I think that is ok. We can go with it, whatever way they want to do it.

PAYNE — But we are losing control. Are we responsible for what happens? If we are, then we need to have some say in what the project's objectives are, what the purpose is, how it is going to be done, and where we are going to end up. Otherwise, why do you need me?

PERRY — There are different ways moderators can be used. Maybe ideally you would like to be in on the beginning, help design the project, help make sure we are recruiting the right kind of people, write an analytical report, and advise the client — the total thing. But I'm willing to participate in various nuances.

AXELROD — Doesn't it bother you that what you have done may be totally misinterpreted and misused...

PERRY — That can happen anyway. You can't control what they do with it.

CORSON — The client is going to have to live with the data. He is

going to be successful or not based on what he does with it.

DROSSLER — With some clients, we have a policy that they must either attend all the groups including the briefing and debriefing sessions or stay away completely and listen to our interpretation. Other clients are sophisticated enough to know that if they drop in and see a few minutes it is not necessarily going to be representative.

MODERATOR SIMON — Are you talking about them interfering with your operation?

PAYNE — It's all part of the same thing. The whole business is so out of hand. They're done at random because they all seem so casual... the casual atmosphere of dropping in here and there is part of this. You wouldn't do it on any other kind of research.

DROSSLER — It's more expensive, but we try to use a moderator and an analyst, who stays behind the mirror with the clients and tries to head them off from making quick conclusions.

AXELROD — We have to do that too. Then we drag them back into my office to do some kind of pulling it together.

CORSON — What are they using you for?

AXELROD — They are buying me or you because they assume we have a certain amount of expertise because we've done hundreds of these sessions and can bring to bear this experience, but they not only are not waiting 'til they get the report but also 12 people walk out with 12 ideas. You're not fulfilling your role unless you gather them together, at least try to have surface what they think they have gotten, and try to explain to them what you feel has come out of the group.

PAYNE — You don't know right after the sessions. It's complex. It takes time to think it through.

AXELROD — I used to make my people wait until they got a transcript before they analyzed the sessions. But it is much more dangerous to let everybody go running around with their own ideas. Why don't you feel this is important?

PAYNE — Let the buyer beware.

PERRY — Yes, it is part of their responsibility. They're adults. They know what they're doing. If they want to come and get an opinion, that's ok. I don't see how that detracts from my work. I will give my immediate reactions, but the main thing is the report, my considered reactions. That document represents my response to their problem. In the meantime, they have separate thoughts. You can't control people's thoughts.

CORSON — It depends on what they are buying. In our case, they usually don't do anything until they get the report. But some clients buy moderating only and want to draw their own conclusions. You've got to be of service. I wouldn't get frustrated, Myril, because obviously, they're not waiting for the reports from what you're saying.

AXELROD — It is important to me that they get what they should get. It can be dangerous if they run off and come to their own conclusions.

QUIRICONI — If a product manager is under all kinds of deadlines, he is doing something before you even finish the analysis and mail the report.

CORSON — Is that wrong? If you were in his situation would you do something different?

QUIRICONI — Well, I would hope so, that is why we are doing the research.

CORSON — Really, is that why people do research? They do it for all different reasons.

DROSSLER — Sometimes they do it to prove their point.

QUIRICONI — And if he makes a mistake, then he says, "I'm not going to do groups any more, because they're no good."

AXELROD — That's exactly what's happening. That's why the top people in the big companies have said, "Forget the groups, because my brand managers with two days on the job go to see two groups, decide they have all the answers, and say, 'We have made this decision on the basis of group research.'" That's bad news. It's the policy of one of our large clients.

PERRY — What, not to do any more groups?

AXELROD — That's right. The market research department has a dictum against groups. And they are using groups very guardedly because of these problems.

CORSON — Ok, but you're talking about major companies that have a tremendous backlog of data on almost all the categories they work in. They're not necessarily representative of most clients.

PERRY — Overall, the vast majority of clients are quite sophisticated. They understand when to use groups, when not to, and they're using them well. I wouldn't want to go on record with a trend towards irresponsibility in groups because I certainly don't find it.

DROSSLER — We do deal with a lot of unsophisticated clients or clients with unsophisticated presidents or marketing v.p.s who might make decisions based on groups. What we are talking about is a problem with the power of the focus group. The group can effectively demonstrate a point that percentages and analytical discussion sometimes cannot communicate. But if you have one consumer make that statement, it's a powerful communication. We found, for instance, that a client will get mad when the consumer makes some totally dumb statement. Then you have to remind him that is what people think. Sometimes it hurts. But with the analyst behind the mirror with the client you can discuss it when he first hears it, and it can really lead to a better understanding.

QUIRICONI — We had one two-phase study where everybody understood the objectives. Phase I was to develop the questionnaire for implementation, learn consumer language, etc. We did such a great job in Phase I, that they didn't want Phase II. We only did four groups, but they sounded great...

CORSON — Maybe that was appropriate for him.

QUIRICONI — Not really, otherwise why set up Phase II in the first place?

CORSON — You might not have had clear-cut results from Phase I.

QUIRICONI — Four groups don't give you much clear-cut anything. It's very risky to make a major decision on four sessions...

CORSON — Whose risk is that, yours or the client's?

QUIRICONI — It's theirs ... that is their prerogative.

CORSON — Right, that's my point.

QUIRICONI — But as professionals we should be able to keep them from making mistakes in spite of themselves.

CORSON — How?

4. Education, training, and experience

AXELROD — One thing I want to discuss is how to develop moderators so everybody and his brother just doesn't go around doing groups. We have a two-year work-study training program. I take college students as summer work-study trainees. Is anybody else doing anything? If the universities would make an attempt to have people on their staffs who have done groups, who have years of experience...

MODERATOR SIMON — What kind of characteristics does a person need before they should even go into an internship?

DROSSLER — I almost have a formula. We have an airline in California called "PSA." Those are the letters in the formula: A good moderator has to have Personality, Sensitivity, and Ability. Some cannot moderate even though they have the ability because they lack one of the others.

MODERATOR SIMON — How do you judge these things?

PERRY — We make mistakes. It's trial and error. Unfortunately, it is expensive and too bad for the people involved. Until you get somebody involved in it, it is pretty hard to tell.

PAYNE — I find it very difficult to get a situation where you can train anyone.

DROSSLER — You can always do them for free for the client.

AXELROD — I keep my newcomers around for six months just listening, observing, and writing up sessions. And I observe them too before I even take a chance. And then we usually pick up the cost for that group.

MODERATOR SIMON — That's unusual.

QUIRICONI — One way to go about it is to give someone a tape and tell him to listen and write an analysis. See if he has any insight, or if he just says, "Some said this and some said that..."

MODERATOR SIMON — Are analytical skills the same as moderating skills?

QUIRICONI — It's a first step to see if he makes any sense out of what he heard. A screening step.

AXELROD — To see if they are sensitive and have insight, but personality you have to get some other way.

PERRY — I get them in any group situation to talk about anything. Do you feel they will respond? Are they good listeners? Are they sensitive to what is happening in the group? Are they empathetic? Do they communicate some kind of warmth? There is no formula though. It's a real problem.

CORSON — You could find more who could do a good job moderating than could write a good report. Bonnie and I feel just being around and understanding consumer products, if that's the area you're working in, are important. It is the experience and scope.

QUIRICONI — But academically, they should have some psychology or sociology. You wouldn't take somebody who went to bricklayers' school and figure he is going to become a moderator. He might, but he should have some academic background.

AXELROD — What do you mean by academic? Sometimes you can get a person with just good instincts and personality and...

DROSSLER — I was really saying the same thing. Somebody who went to bricklayers' school may have more sensitivity and personality for it than somebody who has the ability.

MODERATOR SIMON — Start with some kind of psychology or marketing, right?

QUIRICONI — Or sociology. If they're interested in people, they would be taking those subjects anyway.

5. Moderator's sex as a variable

MODERATOR SIMON — How do you feel about a man moderating a women's group or a woman moderating a man's group?

PERRY — It works ok.

CORSON — I think so too.

DROSSLER — It depends on the subject and type of people too. I personally get along well with certain kinds of women and not with some other kinds.

CORSON — You might not want to do sessions on feminine hygiene products, for instance.

DROSSLER — True.

AXELROD — When a woman does a group of women and one says something significant, the moderator knows exactly what she is talking about and knows to probe it. Women talk to each other differently when a man is in the group and vice versa. I not only try to match men to a man's group but also to match a younger moderator with younger groups. I have seen teenage groups where they talked as if they were talking to a mother or teacher. But when they're talking to a younger person on their wave length, they talk differently. I feel a woman brings something to bear from her own experience that makes a difference, but this gets me into fights with everybody.

DROSSLER — No man can do groups universally. But on some subjects the perceptions of men and women are not different. And although the moderator wants to be in rapport with the people, he doesn't have to understand the subject in the same way they do. It isn't that you don't understand the subject, but that you don't have to react the same way. The moderator's role is to keep the respondents conversing.

CORSON — I just did some groups on sewing. I have never sewn anything in my life. It worked out really well because at the end these ladies were trying to convert me. I knew enough about what the client wanted so I could probe. But you don't have to do it yourself to moderate.

AXELROD — I think you have to be able to respond emotionally.

PAYNE — It's harder for me to get women down to basics, especially when I want to find a misconception. I want them to explain actually how they do each step, but they think as a woman I know it. It's harder for me to play devil's advocate than it would be for a man.

PERRY — Either sex can do either group. It takes whatever it takes to moderate groups and you can apply it to any topic...

AXELROD — Do you really think a bunch of blue-collar guys is going to sit around and talk to you about drinking beer in the same way they talk to a man?

DROSSLER — That is the subject matter and the nature of the respondent.

QUIRICONI — In most cases, it doesn't make any difference. A good moderator is a good moderator. In a few cases where it may be blue-collar beer drinkers and you really want them to talk as they talk in the saloon, then that is something I couldn't do either.

6. Generally applicable techniques

PERRY — What kind of preparation do you do for groups, especially if it's not in the consumer area, but an industrial area or something you don't know about?

AXELROD — A lot.

DROSSLER — We have done a lot on aircraft, for example. We spent probably a week with the technical people. We had to know a lot about the product because we were talking to knowledgeable respondents. With consumer products, when I'm working with homemakers, I can play the "dumb man" who doesn't know how to make a cake — up to a point.

PAYNE — Definitely up to a point.

DROSSLER — Right, because they realize I wouldn't be in there if I wasn't some kind of an expert.

AXELROD — Generally the people say, "Why should I waste my time educating him."

QUIRICONI — We also have had one of the client's people in the room. I just introduce him as "Jim and I are doing this together. He has more technical knowledge than I do. And from time to time, he will answer a question." The danger is that he may become the moderator.

CORSON — I have one thing you might be interested in. At the beginning of the warmup, we only want the respondents to talk about themselves. Nobody is allowed to talk about other people. That is one way of making people feel really comfortable.

PERRY — Another technique: in the first 10 or 15 minutes I don't do anything that would appear negative to anything anybody says. Everything is ok. I try and create an atmosphere of openness.

DROSSLER — I find too often moderators don't let the group in on what the subject is. We all have the idea that a focus group is supposed to be totally un-structured. I've found it much more productive if you can give the people an idea of what their job is. It keeps people on the track much better.

MODERATOR SIMON — How specific do you get?

DROSSLER — It depends. In consumer areas, unless there is something very specific you want

to find out, you close in on it from a more general way. But with industrial groups, well, these are very knowledgeable people. They can handle the subject. You can be very specific. But even so, the closer you can put a boundary around the subject, the more the moderator can back off...

AXELROD — Are you taking a position against starting with a general discussion where you go all over the lot and then finally zero in, which used to be the philosophy — everything had to start with a wide-open general discussion so that they didn't know what you were after?

DROSSLER — Yes, in general, I am.

AXELROD — I don't feel this is always the correct approach. In many instances, it can even color the discussion on the specific issues you want to discuss. I think the approach should depend on the problem and the main purpose of the project.

CORSON — It's just a tool. Sometimes you want the respondents to bring up the subject. Sometimes you go right into it.

MODERATOR SIMON — At a morning session, do you serve coffee?

PERRY — It helps people be more relaxed.

DROSSLER — We have a lot of groups at about 5:30 p.m. and we serve sandwiches. These groups tend to open up faster than any of the others.

AXELROD — It's part of the informal environment.

DROSSLER — We've also had some good luck with using big sheets of paper. We start putting things up, have people throw their ideas into the pot, and you start lining the wall with these big sheets with ideas on them.

CORSON — This helps not only to facilitate the discussion but also it helps with the analysis because you don't have to listen to the tapes. We started using it because of Synectics and facilitating the discussion and energy level. There is something about seeing their ideas up that gets people going. Lots of times if I introduce a subject and want to get gut feelings, I use a little sheet and just ask them to write down the thing they like the most and the least. We force them to make notes. I don't collect them. But that is a good way to get some gross feelings at the beginning. Then we start filling up the big sheets...

QUIRICONI — Many times they contradict what they're saying. They say something socially acceptable but they don't mean it.

CORSON — We call it "blowing smoke in your face." We confront such people. They may say something like, "I wouldn't buy anything with preservatives in it." After about 10 minutes, you say, "Ok now, then none of us ever buys anything in the grocery store." They laugh.

PERRY — I don't feel compelled to get them to admit it.

DROSSLER — It depends. If the whole group is off on this track and they don't mean it, then you could say something to challenge their position.

MODERATOR SIMON — I know one moderator who uses the technique of being argumentative. How do you feel about that?

DROSSLER — I have seen it work effectively for a certain personality. I personally don't do that and can't because it is not my personality.

AXELROD — You are trying to simulate the mood and frame of mind the person is going to be in when he goes to buy the product. Who ever buys a product when he is mad?

MODERATOR SIMON — How do you get respondents to come up with new ideas or new approaches for anything?

CORSON — Wishing. We've just recently been experimenting with wishing because we found that people find it hard to come up with new ideas but they are real good at wishing for solutions to problems. Out of the wishing comes things we can fix.

QUIRICONI — We've duplicated some of the idea generation techniques that we heard about — how many things can you do with a brick or a coat hanger were two such exercises. Once by accident I took an entire group of women to lunch. They each had two drinks, and when we came back, it was the best group I had moderated.

AXELROD — When you really come back to it, you don't have to use any artificial techniques. It's just sitting around the living room talking to each other.

MODERATOR SIMON — Have you ever tried telling people the session is over and turning off the tape recorder, but you really keep one on?

DROSSLER — We do that all the time.

QUIRICONI — We did something

like that with teenagers. Very tough, right? We did the session and then had one of our women, a very good interviewer, drive them all home. The group just continued in the car. We got more out of what they said in the car than what they said up here.

7. Reporting the results of the sessions

QUIRICONI — I wonder if in our reporting procedures we aren't somehow communicating that the groups are more formal or more quantitative than they are just by the style of reporting and the language being used. I remember 10 years ago, a qualitative report had a content review section and a narrative for maybe five or 10 pages. Now I see a trend to where it is findings, conclusions, and formalized sections. It sounds like more than it really is. I also have seen words like "all the respondents," "most," "many," "half," all kind of quantitative terms in qualitative reports.

CORSON—In our report, what we would call "detailed findings" in a quantitative study, we title "impressions."

PAYNE — Sometimes don't you have to put limits though that "the feeling was almost unanimous"? If everybody really stomped on this idea, then why not say it?

AXELROD — I sometimes say "the prevalent feeling was that..." but always pointing out that there were some who didn't agree. Instead of impressions, I use "observations."

QUIRICONI — What you are doing is generating hypotheses. If you state conclusions, you should say, "these are hypotheses that should be used for further testing." But I have seen group reports that look like a quantitative report — broken down Roman numeral I, A., B., C., etc.

MODERATOR SIMON — Should there be standards for reports on qualitative research?

QUIRICONI — The reports should have more of a "soft" feeling to them.

PERRY — I don't think there should be a standard. Different clients like different styles. We probably all here write reports a little differently. That's ok if a client wants to see it a certain way; some like us to sprinkle lots of quotes throughout and some don't like lots of verbatims.

MODERATOR SIMON — Many qualitative reports not only come that way but also have little tables in the back that say, "four said this..."

AXELROD — That absolutely appalls me. I just cannot believe people do that.

CORSON — How do you get transcripts that make sense?

PAYNE — I personally don't think there is a way ... unless you have sequential questioning. I don't think there is a typist in the world who can pick up everything said by individuals in a group discussion. I really gave it a good go for about a year. I found myself absolutely appalled. Dos would come back don'ts. I never trusted the typist.

AXELROD — I like to have verbatims, especially if I don't do the writeup instantly.

PAYNE — Don't you listen to the tapes?

AXELROD — It would take forever.

CORSON — What I want to know is when you read the transcript how can you tell who is speaking?

AXELROD — If I've done the session, I can. When I read transcripts that other people have done, sometimes I can't tell, but I still get the general tenor of what is going on...When I am doing a session, I say, "Oh, yes, you said before...," so that anybody listening will know she is the one, especially if she is the only dissenter.

QUIRICONI — I moderate groups differently when I am doing them all by myself and when it is going to be on transcript or when clients are viewing. For example, I've been doing them for a long time so I don't have to be hit over the head with the same thing over and over before I know what it means. But a young product manager may not have that same background. He has to hear it a couple of times.

MODERATOR SIMON — Should the moderator write the report?

AXELROD — Absolutely.

QUIRICONI — I believe so, yes, strongly.

DROSSLER — I tend to think the other way since we often use the analyst behind the mirror and the moderator. The moderator must be close to the subject but generally we would have the other person write the report.

AXELROD — I've talked with moderators who have only moderated. They come in, somebody hands them an interviewing guide that someone else has prepared. They don't know anything about the subject. They do the session and go away. Somebody else writes the report. I just couldn't believe it...

PAYNE — Sometimes if we have six groups to do in a series, two moderators might each do three. You don't have to be involved at exactly the same time. But you are involved in the same product and project. Generally one person would write the report and have the responsibility for the analysis but you have someone to share your ideas with. I think that is the key.

PERRY — I think the person who does the group should write the report.

MODERATOR SIMON — Or at least somebody who was there?

QUIRICONI — On paper, each statement has as much weight as every other. If you turn the transcript over to somebody, they lose a lot.

AXELROD — Something happens in that room, a feeling that you just have to experience. Behind the mirror or on videotape, you don't get that emotion.

PART II

Preparing And Planning For Focus Group Interviews

This section covers a number of practical articles dealing with preparing and carrying out the actual focus group interviews. Major topics include:

1. Preparation for the interviews.

2. Clear understanding of client needs.

3. Understanding the group dynamics.

4. The role of moderators.

5. The selection of relevant groups.

PREPARING FOR GROUP INTERVIEWS

Melanie S. Payne, Elrick and Lavidge, Inc.

Abstract

Proper preparation for group interviews is essential to achieve meaningful study results. Responsibility for conducting the groups should be given to a well-trained qualitative researcher whose job it is to understand the research objectives and how the results will be used. Other aspects of preparation include writing the discussion guide and supervising recruitment of respondents. Prior to the groups, decisions must also be made concerning where the sessions will be held and the type of audio or video recording that will be done.

Preparing for Group Interviews

We have just heard from Al Goldman about the development of interviews and the way they are used, and shortly Myril Axelrod will discuss the procedures that should be followed when conducting groups. Once you have decided that groups are the proper research tool to use and before you actually run the sessions, considerable attention should be devoted to preparing for them. Because group interviewing appears to be such an easy thing to do and the process itself seems so casual, the important step of preparation is often neglected and left to chance.

One of the most crucial elements of preparing a group study is to place the responsibility for it in the hands of a well-trained moderator/analyst. This may seem obvious, but because the technique has gained such popularity and because it seems so simple, more people are getting into the act, and they are often the wrong people. I have seen too many instances where, to save money, a company will turn the job of conducting groups over to a secretary. They give the assignment to her because she is a pleasant individual who gets along well with people and she is a good conversationalist. That is not enough, however, because what is required is someone thoroughly grounded in the theory and technique of what group interviewing is all about.

Once the assignment has been placed in the hands of the right person, the first order of business in preparing for a group interview is to gain a thorough understanding of the problem. Occasionally this means helping the client understand the problem, too. Many clients, of course, know precisely what their needs are and how they will use the results, but all too often the person requesting the focus group research does not really know what he wants to find out or what he will do with the information once the study is completed. In this latter instance, he may know simply that he has a problem, and because the group approach is simplistic, he decides that is what he will do, without really thinking through the issues involved.

In either case, it becomes the researcher's job to clearly spell out the reasons the research is being done, the specific areas to be covered in the groups, and how the results are going to be used once the research is completed. Let me give you an example. Assume you have been asked to do some work for a company that has, (1), done virtually no consumer research and, (2), does not have an understanding of what its customer's attitudes about the company's products are. In this instance, your first job will be to educate the client about what the group interview technique can and cannot do. Secondly, when you actually conduct the group discussions you will probably have to devote some of your efforts to gathering basic attitudinal information about the product category in general and your client's product in particular.

The approach just outlined will be very different from one you would use with a client who has a long history of researching his products and now wants some group sessions to help him develop the concept for a line extension of an existing brand. In these sessions you would shorten the background gathering and move quickly to the heart of the matter -- the new product. My point here is that all groups do not follow the same format and the correct approach to use is a function of the nature of the problem to be tackled.

As you gain an understanding of the problem, you should begin making a list of specific questions to be explored in the research. Some of these questions will be raised by the client, others will occur to you, and the combined list will become the skeleton for your discussion outline. The easiest and most useful way to handle the questions is to organize them by areas or topics so they become clustered in logical groupings. For example, if you are doing some research on a new hot breakfast cereal, you might want to begin with a general discussion of what is served at breakfast and then refine that by having respondents describe weekday versus weekend breakfasts. From there you might move on to focus on cereals, both hot and cold, then narrow down to hot cereals only. At this point you would probably introduce the concept for the new product, and you might even have some actual product prepared for respondents to taste. Just like a good story, a group discussion should have a beginning, a middle, and an end. Typically, as in this example, the movement is from the general to the specific.

The discussion guide itself should be fairly simple -- two or three typed pages, double spaced. It is an outline of the key areas and questions to be covered and not an exhaustive dissertation of every conceivable issue that might be probed for. If you understand what you want to do in a group and have the questions pretty well fixed in your mind, you should hardly have to refer to your outline once you are in the group setting itself. I suppose we all have our own little tricks for achieving this goal. My own personal quirk is that I must sit down at the typewriter and personally bat out the discussion guide I am going to use. Even if someone has prepared a perfectly adequate guide for me, I cannot seem to internalize it unless I type it myself.

Another essential element in the preparation of a guide, whether you have my kind of hang-up or not, is an adequate amount of time to think about the topic of your

Reprinted from *Advances In Consumer Research,* **IV** (1976), 434-36.

discussion. I feel that a minimum of a couple days is necessary to allow the topic area to sufficiently sink in. I don't mean to say that one should spend two or three days working on an outline, but you do need time to mull over in your mind what you are going to cover in a session. I find that I do this when I am preparing dinner, or riding the train to work, putting on my make-up, or whatever. No moderator, no matter how experienced he or she is, can be handed a group discussion guide half an hour before a group and be expected to conduct a first-rate interview.

At the same time you are involved in the process of understanding the problem and preparing the discussion guide, recruiting for the group should be getting under way. This will generally be taken care of by someone other than yourself. Just as the moderating should not be handled by an amateur, recruiting too should be supervised by a specialist. It may seem simple enough to gather together several "warm bodies" for a group discussion, but once again I have seen the amateurs who thought this was such a snap fall flat on their faces. So the moral of the story is pay a little more and find someone who knows what they are about to recruit your groups.

Your responsibility in working with the recruiters is to tell them exactly who you want and who you don't want in your groups. Let's look at the exclusions first. You do not want people who work for marketing research companies or advertising agencies or those employed by your client or any of his competitors. This is fairly obvious. You will also want to screen out certain groups who, for some reason, might bias your results. One of the worst examples I ever heard along those lines happened to a researcher who was doing some conceptual work on baby food and wanted to interview mothers of infants concerning feeding practices. The project director did not learn until the group had assembled that all the respondents belonged to the Leche League. These are women who breast-feed their babies and, not only do they breast-feed, they belong to a league of breast feeders. Needless to say, their responses were hardly typical of all young mothers.

The recruiter should have known better than to have pulled a stunt like that, but that little episode which happened more than 10 years ago taught me to never leave anything to chance. You should always stipulate that you want respondents recruited from a wide area, and that you do not want them to come from the same neighborhood or church or club or ethnic group. My own feeling is that it's okay if two people, but no more than two, know each other in a group, that is they may come in pairs if necessary. This is simply being realistic because often a woman will not agree to participate in a session unless she can come with a friend.

The question of professional respondents always arises -- these are the people who make a habit or perhaps even a living of participating in groups. The opposite of the professional respondent is the so-called virgin respondent -- the person who has never taken part in a group session. What you should ask for and can realistically expect lies somewhere between these two extremes. If a recruiter is providing you with the same faces again and again, you had better take your business elsewhere. Keep in mind that if you have seen those people repeatedly you can be pretty sure that they have recently been respondents in someone else's groups, too.

On the other hand, be fair with your recruiter and do not demand that they provide you with virgin respondents. There is simply too much group interviewing being done these days for that to be a reasonable request. I once calculated that with the number of groups being done each week in Chicago, if everyone demanded virgin respondents we would have exhausted the entire population of the city in a period of eight years. I generally ask that respondents in my sessions have not participated in a group within the preceding six months or perhaps within the preceding year. You will find, however, that even with this sort of screening, people enjoy participating in groups so much that they will lie about not having been interviewed so that they can come back soon again.

After you have stipulated whom you don't want attending, you must be very specific about whom you do want. For example, if you are conducting a study on a new brand of frozen french fries, you do not simply ask for people who eat french fries. Rather, you ask for women who have bought, and prepared for their families, at least two pounds of frozen french fries within the past month. Set your qualifications specifically and precisely and you won't be disappointed by coming face to face with a group of women who have little interest in your product category and who, therefore, cannot be the least bit of help to you.

How many respondents to include in a group is another key issue and one that I find myself getting into arguments about all the time. I am going to be very dogmatic on this point and say that no group discussion should ever have any more than eight respondents. If you, as a moderator, are performing your job correctly, six or seven people is perfectly adequate. I am appalled at the trend which seems to be in vogue now to demand ten or twelve respondents per group. What we want to accomplish with these people we have recruited is to carry out a discussion in which everyone participates as a group. With more than eight people, this process simply cannot occur naturally. The group breaks down and you, as moderator, are faced with the chaos of two or more splinter conversations going on simultaneously. To maintain control you then have the choice of policing the group conversation, thereby destroying the dynamic process you wanted to set up in the first place, or you retreat to the position of having to conduct a series of individual interviews in a group setting. Either solution is unsatisfactory.

At the time respondents are recruited for a group they should be told how long it will last. I generally ask people to be prepared to stay two hours even if I don't expect the session to last that long. What you want to avoid is underestimating the time involved. Men and women who come expecting to spend an hour get very fidgety when that hour is up. At that point they will say anything just to get the group over with and get out, leaving you with a lot of results that you can't have very much faith in. Two hours is about the outside limit for a productive group session. Occasionally some respondents get so wound up with a topic they will, of their own choosing, stay on and on. But normally a group will have said all that it's going to say by the end of the second hour.

It is possible to conduct a group interview literally anywhere there is enough room to seat the respondents and yourself. I have done them in church basements and in posh boardrooms and just about anywhere else you can imagine in between. I personally do not feel that the setting is nearly as important as the tone you set and the rapport you establish with the respondents. If they feel you are on the same wave length with them, you'll get a good interview no matter where you are.

The most desirable facility these days, especially from a client's point of view, is an interviewing room equipped with a one-way mirror and a comfortable room from which to view the group in progress. That viewing room should be as soundproof as possible so that the conversations of the observers cannot be heard by the respondents. Some research companies seem to be especially proud of the fact that they have well-stocked open bars in their viewing rooms. I find this not only unnecessary but offensive because it tends to turn the group session into some sort of charade rather than the serious business that it should be.

The furnishings in the interviewing room, per se, should be comfortable, but they need not be elaborate. There are some who prefer a living room atmosphere with coffee tables and easy chairs. My own preference is for a large conference room table that will seat eight or nine people without crowding. I prefer the table because I think it gives respondents something to hang on to -- both literally and figuratively. Many men and women are very nervous when they come to a group discussion because they don't know what to expect. If they can sit down at a table, set down their coffee cups and fill out a short questionnaire covering product usage and demographics, it seems to put them at ease. Theoretically, people can accomplish the same end sitting in easy chairs clustered around coffee tables. But I find that in such a setting there is a lot of fumbling with clipboards, pencils, coffee cups and ashtrays. Also, women feel compelled to pull their skirts down to cover their knees, especially in a room with a very obvious one-way mirror. I prefer to avoid this altogether by conducting sessions around a conference table.

The presence of such a table also sets a somewhat businesslike tone to the session, and I don't think that's at all undesirable. While you want the respondents to be comfortable, this is a research session and not a neighborhood coffee klatch, and they surely know that ahead of time. They are not there just to shoot the breeze; they are being paid for their participation, and their conversations are being tape recorded. So it seems to me that to force all of this into a simulated home setting doesn't really accomplish very much.

I mentioned tape recording, and the extent to which you will record the proceedings is another decision you will have to make. The less gadgetry you have to worry about, the easier your life will be. If the facility you are using is equipped with an overhead microphone and a sound system, this can be an advantage. But if you don't have this, it's no cause for alarm. Any reel-to-reel tape recorder that can pick up the conversation will do. Also, I routinely take along a small cassette tape recorder to use as a back up. These recorders generally run on batteries, which can be a lifesaver if the electricity fails -- something that has happened to me more than once.

In at least 99 percent of the group interviews you do, audio taping is all you should need. But I have found as this group interviewing business becomes more elaborate, clients are requesting video taping more frequently. My guess is that in many of these cases the video tapes end up being stored on a shelf and are never looked at again. Few people have the interest or stamina to sit and stare at eight to ten hours of film after the fact, so if the tape is going to be used at all it should be edited. This is an extremely time-consuming process, and no one can have an appreciation of how much time it takes until he has been through it once. And believe me, once is enough. Both the filming and the editing are expensive, and my feeling is that much of the time and money spent on video tape might have been better invested elsewhere. But it is the client's money, and he can spend it in any way he chooses.

Just remember that if you are planning to videotape you must meet some special conditions, including lots of ceiling light and no windows or back lighting behind the respondents (or you will end up with shadows instead of faces). Also, to obtain a tape that has any visual interest at all, you should hire a professional cameraman whose job it is to follow the discussion with the camera and zoom in and out to pick up the person speaking. The alternative to this is a fixed camera with a wide-angle lens that is visually no better than an audio tape.

In the past 15 minutes I have taken you through approximately two weeks worth of preparation for a group interview. Some of the issues I covered may have seemed obvious, others trivial, but from where I sit, all are essential. Going back to the point I made at the outset, to the uninitiated, the amateur, or the outsider, group interviewing appears to be a simple, casual process that one just waltzes through. But as the case with everything from raising children to making a souffle, if it ends up being done well, it didn't just happen; it was planned for.

RESEARCH AS GIRAFFE*: AN IDENTITY CRISIS

Jane Templeton, Ted Bates, Inc.

For the past ten months -- give or take a month -- I have had on my desk a personnel form requesting me to produce a job description. I've gotten as far as name and title, but the twelve lines (I've counted them) provided for the actual descriptive meat remain blank. Given the usual personal vanity about compressing one's vital and complex function to a simple objective account, and allowing for an innate tendency to procrastinate, ten months is still a long time. Once, out of impatience with the delay, I decided that a flat statement of the operations that fill the time might satisfy, and started with "I conduct and interpret group interviews". That leaves out meetings and white papers, but does cover the bulk of time and motion. However, it dawned on me before the crossing of the first "t" that it was a cop-out and I reached for the O-Pake. To say that I conduct and interpret group interviews is like a tailor saying that he threads needles.

It would be equating, e.g., a panel recruited for casting purposes with a fishing trip for motivational dispositions in a new product area. In casting interviews, we want to know how the panelists feel about particular product-connected areas, and to elicit this information, if possible, without ever touching on those exact questions (so as to preserve some degree of freshness and spontaneity when the studio interviewer asks them). We must also be able to gauge whether, for any particular panelist, the vivacious and responsive lady or gentleman we see in the group interview will continue to scintillate under production stresses, or will go blank or become afflicted with "peanut-butter-mouth" in the studio situation.

When we are trawling for ideas and needs associated with a new product, we are similarly wary of introducing key topics -- but not because we don't want them discussed. We try to encourage the respondents to raise the relevant issues, so we can discover what they are and where they most naturally "fit" into what these respondents currently think about. We try out various broad general areas of discourse with some likely relationship to our product -- working from general to increasing particularity from the responsibilities of the homemaker, say, to nutritional accountability, to breakfast, to breakfast juices .... until somebody's switch is tripped. But once this happens, we pursue the exploration of opinions, attitudes, and feelings as deeply as the group will go (and group tolerances dif-

fer) to find the points at which fundamental internal states intersect with behavior.

And what about creative reconnaisance, which is another challenge altogether? Where to put new business sallies which -- with half an eye to the theatrical use of the videotape -- call for on-the-spot interpretations? Manifestly, naming the tool isn't going to get me off the hook. I could as usefully say that "I do marketing research".

What is it in general, then, that distinguishes the functions of Presearch from the inbaskets of the account research people down the hall, with whom we frequently share projects?

o There are the apparent, easily observable distinctions that Presearch is not (as the account-research people are) affixed to any particular account group, but float from account to account as need dictates. And our "data-gathering" differs in that most of it is done in the agency's "fishbowl", or in similar one-way mirror facilities outside the city. But these distinctions are really extraneous.

o Paradoxically, the essential difference between what "we" do and what "they" do occurs during the one stage in the project when we all appear just the same way: shuffling papers, frowning, and getting cranky about interruptions. We are all "interpreting" data, but Presearch deals, in a different kind of interpretive responsibility than that assumed by our partners at the other end of the floor.

For example, if someone is not copied on a survey report, or left his copy on the New Haven train, or takes issue with the conclusions it propounds, he can always go back to the raw data, to seek his (her) own conclusions. Our "data" are only data to us, and our clients, in or out of the agency, pretty well know it. They know it because:

o We've worked hard to help our internal "clients" in the creative and account divisions to recognize the complexity of group interview data, and many of the agency clients now understand this as well.

o Also because some of them have learned by experience

---

*My first job in advertising was an act of faith on the part of the research director. He coined a title for my function and assigned me to the creative group. When I asked what I would do, he said: "You've done group therapy, haven't you? You should be good at focus groups. They'll tell you what they want to know, and you'll interview a group of consumers and come back with the answers." Aside from instructions on recruiting protocol, this was the sum of my instruction. Soon

after, at an intra-agency presentation, I asked one of the art directors to do a visual flip-chart for me: two giraffes, behind a zoo-enclosure; one of the giraffes has bent his neck over to read the sign, and is saying: "We're Giraffes." Many years later, having watched and listened to many other researcher's conception of "focus groups", I find I've come full circle and am back to the Giraffes.

Reprinted from *Advances In Consumer Research*, **IV** (1976), 442-46.

that our interview materials do not lend themselves to literal interpretation. A typed transcript of a session, for instance, often has the same relationship to the interview guide we originally set down, that a 36-in snake has to a yardstick -- it's hard to line up and check off. The topics suggested in the guide are raised, but not sequentially, and topics tend to be interwoven and reappear, sometimes with very different implications, throughout the interview. Further, the written material may contradict the transcript, or both may be belied by the behavioral observations or by the projective data.

The focus of this paper is interpretation of group material, rather than details of procedure. But at this point, a general summary of our particular m.o. -- what we _do_ do and what we _don't_ -- may prevent confusion. Presearch group interviews:

o Employ a relatively formal setting: a conference table in a large office within the agency (or similar facilities in other cities).

o Employ a one-way mirror and/or videotape, and overhead microphones which are connected to an audio recording system and to a loudspeaker in the observation room behind the mirror.

o Are conducted with panels of, typically, 10 - 12 consumers, using the following format:

   - After panelists enter and seat themselves, and are given refreshments, there is a short Warm-Up , during which everyone including the moderators introduces him(her)self to the rest of the group and "ground rules" for the interview are stated.

   - This is followed by a Predisposition discussion, which concerns itself with the contexts in which the product (we are to explore) is bought, used, and thought about. This will include general reactions to advertising in the product area generally.

   - We then introduce materials: concepts, rough or finished creative executions, products, etc., and ask panelists first to write, privately, their immediate reactions to each of the materials, and then to discuss it. This pattern of "write, then talk" is continued until all materials have been exposed.

   - After all materials have been discussed individually, there is usually a collective and comparative discussion of everything exposed to the respondents.

   - The discussion ends with the Wrap-up: a summary statement of what panelists think the group as a whole has expressed during the interview.

   - Before leaving, panelists complete a brief demographic questionnaire and a self-administered projective instrument (drawings and stories).

In view of the several papers delineating rules and standards for moderating group interviews, to elaborate further on our particular interview protocol would be redundant and, worse, presumptuous. What I am describing is in no way intended as a prescription for "how _to_

do group interviews". It is only a statement of how _we_ do group interviews.

But a clear understanding of the nature of our interpretive grist does require more detailed description of how we conduct our sessions. One of the essentials of our manner of approach is the avoidance of direct questions in all parts of the interview. This type of interchange happens as near to never as conversation permits, which accounts in part for the non-sequential, interweaving flow of discussion. Obviously a direct question procedure would be simpler both to moderate and to interpret. But we feel that answers to direct questions are dangerous. They cannot give us some of the kinds of information (motivational, qualitative) that we are seeking, but more importantly, they tend to provide answers which can seriously mislead us. We have defined four reasons for avoiding the hard-edged frontal question:

o Partly, we eschew direct questioning because this kind of interaction is boring. It produces emotional disengagement from the topic, for everybody concerned, to the point of automatic, unsearching answers. Feelings would still be going on, because feelings do operate constantly in people. Some of the feelings might even be strong (like the itch to get away or to gag the moderator), but the feelings each of the panelists might be experiencing could have low, intermittant, or no relationship to the stated topic in a direct question-and-answer interview. A clever and funny moderator can, of course, make even this format entertaining, but who's been interviewed?

o Also, parallel questioning of individuals in the group is a very efficient anti-personnel weapon, in the sense of group dynamics. Respondents get disengaged -- not only from the topic, but also -- from the other people in the group, so that interpersonal provocation, influence, and drift are no longer discernible.

o Too, asking a question directly does not allow the issues to emerge spontaneously. This deprives the moderator and the behind-the-mirror viewers of the opportunity to see its relative saliency, or to weigh and consider the company which that issue keeps: the ideas immediately associated with it, the feelings that accompany it, the language used to express it, etc.

o Finally, there is a less obvious reason for avoiding direct questioning; less obvious, but central to the different kind of interpretive responsibility assumed by the group-interview researcher: we avoid direct questions because of the difficulties in willingness to respond. Not that the subjects are unwilling to answer direct questions. Rather, they are quite willing (providing the questioning hasn't put them to sleep). In fact, they are willing regardless of whether or not they know the answers. I'm not suggesting malicious uncooperativeness on the panelists' parts, nor am I falling into the trap of "insulting the intelligence" of our respondents.

Remember that the kinds of questions typically addressed by this type of research are uncommonly complex. We go into our groups committed to come as close as possible to answering a brain-buster like:

   "If this storyboard is produced as a television commercial, what reactions would the people in this panel be likely to have to it, and what would they do about it?"

Questions like these are not only complex, but also require attitude projection and behavioral conjecture that I'm not sure anyone can manage accurately by introspection. Simple past, present, and future tenses are hard enough to introspect about, heaven knows, but our questions -- if directly asked of group panels -- would have to be set in some obscure tense like the pluperfect conditional.

"If such and such were to happen, in the following situational context, then would you...?"

Questions of this sort are asked, by the people who request the project. And they are duly set down in the "Background and Purpose" section of the final report. They are also, more often than not, answered -- by the person responsible for the project -- with limitations and caveats reflecting the size and probable biases of the sample. But they are neither asked of nor answered by the panelists themselves, directly. Because if we asked, they would answer. And they not only don't know the correct answers, they don't know that they don't know.

That statement, and the claim which is implicit in it, bear some thinking about. Assuming that panel members want to be cooperative (and we usually assume that), and that they have had twenty or more years to get a good fix on themselves, it is a lot to say that we can learn things about them in a two-hour group interview that even the brightest respondent, with the best intentions imaginable, can't tell us. But we can -- and do.

For starters, the things we principally want to know about them are things that they rarely think about concentratedly: buying and brand behavior, usage, product attitudes, etc. -- things which are negligibly important to them as ordinary citizens in the real world ... and are the very essence of our real world. They have little motivation to search themselves for better understanding of this sphere of their lives. Our motivational stakes in understanding these things, on the other hand, are very high indeed. So we'll try harder.

Also, we bring to the interview situation two kinds of expertise which the panelists don't have. We use our expertise in human behavior and marketing strategies to figure out how internal events like feeling, attention, and memory combine in the ultimate sacrament of reaching a hand into a pocket to buy our product. So when we talk about "interpreting" consumer reactions to get the answers to specific questions or to make specific recommendations, we mean something different from the "interpretation" of a questionnaire survey.

In interpreting survery data, the respondents' actual statements are treated as factual, and interpretations are based on measurements and comparisons of these "facts". In the case of group interview interpretation, "what they say" may be amended or modified, or in some extreme cases, even totally contradicted by the interpretation.

I don't mean that the panel's reactions are ignored. On the contrary, all of the respondents' communications are taken into account, both in aggregate and minute-to-minute. As we perceive it, at least three communicative channels are open either all of the time or intermittantly through the interview, providing us with three kinds -- or levels -- of information:

o The level of public affirmation: This is what panelists actually say. It is their interpretation of what they think and feel, impacting with the social role they are trying to maintain, in conjunction with the expressed views of other panel members. We haven't asked them to go "on record" with flat "yes"es and "no"es, so they are not greatly concerned with consistency (or can't keep track of it). Neither are we. We watch motivational drift closely because an about-face is as useful to us as a to-the-death stance. The language they use in discussing what we are there to talk about is also a part of public affirmation, and since they have usually introduced the topic, their language is relatively uncontaminated by our expectations of how they will talk about it.

o The level of private acknowledgement: This is what they write, on our open-end questionnaire, as soon as they have been shown a commercial, or storyboard, or concept, and before any discussion takes place. If your eyebrows go up about the assumption of some independence between these two levels, I have no hard-headed answer. We do ask everybody to turn the written forms face down before open talk commences, and we begin discussion in a different way than the questionnaire, so that there is no exact parallel. But we can't erase the written answers from their minds. Exactly how or why it works, I'm not sure, but that it works, I'm pretty confident about. Written reactions very often sound as if somebody else came in to write them, when compared to the group interchange, and they rarely track very closely the direction of open disscussion. We think that the written material reflects what they think "in solitary", as opposed to feelings they subsequently "own" under social pressure. Or perhaps the spoken comments mirror more what they want to be heard saying. Fitting written statements into our interpretive scheme, we use content plus indications of intensity of emotion or opinion (underlining, exclamation marks, heavy pressure) and involvement (how much is written, signs of personal projection of product use, etc.)

o The level of personal revelation: This is first of all, what we learn from their non-verbal communications: vocal range and variation, postural changes, facial expressions, constrictive or expansive demeanor*. Three respondents can say the same thing and express quite different inner states. Consider the phrase: "Frankly, it leaves me cold." Assume that one respondent making this comment spits it between clenched teeth, leaning forward, hands gripping the edge of the table; that a second panel member says it in a low voice without inflective melody, suppressing a yawn, leaning back with her hands slack in her lap; and that a third panelist says it almost laughingly, sitting forward hugging her arms, maybe with her hand across her mouth, swinging her chair, and with her eyes sparkling. It's up to the moderator to be aware of such behavioral distinctions, not only in the person speaking at any one time, but in the group as a

_____

*If you were worried about the independence of written/verbal responses, you may be beginning to question what we use as a behavioral baseline against which interview behavior stands out and can be interpreted. We establish this informally, for the group as a whole and for individuals, during the warm-up.

whole. About a group, we may note its speed of warm-up, whether -- and when -- they are autonomous or look to each other or the moderator for guidance, the intensity of controversy, the tendency to return to -- or to avoid -- particular topics.

The figure drawings and stories we regularly ask panels to produce are also sources of the "personal revelation" level of data, and are used to elaborate, underline, or reconcile sketchy, ambiguous, or contradictory impressions.

It will have occured to you, of course, that when we shift our attention from one level of response to another, during the interview, we are confounding the distinction between moderating and interpreting. And of course, you are right. The line is a little fuzzy. Some clearly interpretive operations may go on -- even out loud -- while the interview is in progress. This is a decision based on moderator-judgement. Interpreting is almost sure to raise the feeling intensity of the group, and may generate a certain amount of anxiety. The balance is difficult to describe. Placidity, comfort, and consensus are by no means the only -- or even necessarily the most ideal -- forms or outcomes of a group-exploration But on the other hand, the moderator assumes an obligation to keep feeling-intensity and interpersonal contention within tolerable bounds, and to hold rein on behavioral chaos. If the group is judged to be firmly-knit enough to contain stress, and the individual(s) in questions is (are) self-searching enough not to become over-anxious, then it is interpersonally defensible -- and can also be extemely productive -- to offer interpretive probes like:

"You say that it leaves you cold, but I'm getting a very different message from your voice and manner -- that you really dislike it very much" (or "that something about it amuses or delights you"). Can you clarify those different communications for me?"

When the respondent can assimilate this degree of conflict and has the self-awareness to resolve it, or alternately, when the climate of the group is supportive enough so that other respondents will rush in to help one of its members to better self-understanding, these interpretive interchanges are not only helpful to the moderator (and viewers of the session), but also provide the respondents with the uniquely heady achievement of insight. This explains the apparent paradox that some interviewers which are apparently charged with ambivalent or unpleasant feelings and interpersonal strife are frequently preceived by respondents as joyous, uplifting experiences.

In the closing minutes, during the interview wrap-up it is customary for us to invite interpretation from the panel. At this point, the moderator says something like: "You've all been sitting at the table just as I have. If you had the assignment of summarizing what this whole group felt about _____, what do you think you'd say?" Because our sessions tend to be up-tempo, interpersonally active, even sometimes tense and factional, respondents usually want a degree of closure, and will generally jump in -- often spotting things that neither moderator nor viewers have picked up.

The first formal, unadulterated "interpretive" act takes place during our "post-mortem": a debriefing session which is held immediately after the interview, and is attended by the moderators, any viewers who have hung on staunchly to the very end, and others who are concerned with the project and may or may not have been able to

watch from behind the mirror. During this informal re-hashing, we note the conspicuous themes of the discussion, mention spontaneous impressions of the behavioral flow, perhaps glance at the written responses and the drawings, and negotiate a general sense of the direction of the group, using the contributions of everyone who participates.

Now the major job of interpretation begins. This is part of the job description that gives me the most trouble. It is also the part of the job that gives me the most trouble ... and the most personal "juice". Interpreting one or a series of group interviews places great demands on intuitive and organizational skill, and I never finish a report without the feeling that some small truth has been extracted from tons of pitchblende.

Obviously, the interpretation which is finally made will depend on the purpose for which the groups were scheduled and on the form in which results are to be communicated. But whatever the purpose and intended format of presentation, the act of interpreting our group interview data consists in the bringing together of disparate material (private, written reactions, interactive discussion, observed behavior, drawings and stories), weighing and sifting of all inputs, and organization of these multiple clues into an articulated set of premises and speculations.

To take one example, probably our most frequent assignments are aimed at assessing panelists' reactions to creative material. The way we collect data on the relative power or "goodness" of concepts or executions is very different from standard copy-testing procedures. We don't, for example, measure increments of interest and importance, nor do we construct scales. It follows that the kinds of answers we give to the questions asked of the project will be different kinds of answers, in meaning if not in labelling. For instance:

o Comprehension: We do include in reports some estimate of how well our panels seem to understand the message in a concept or execution, but with one important difference. We assume that in any communication the message that is received is as valid as the one transmitted. If most of the people we talk to "understand" copy to mean the same thing, and if they are positively affected by what they think it means, we say that this is good comprehension. We will say this, even if what panelists understood is not what the copy meant to say (of course noting in the report that there is a gap between what we think we said and what they think they picked up).

o Persuasiveness: We also milk the data for anything they can tell us about the extent to which panel members are convinced by our creative material that they should try the product. Precisely because we don't ask: "Would you buy?", we feel free to place some weight on spontaneous statements of buying intention, especially if they are supported by indications that the respondent has projected the buying or using of the product into his future expectations, e.g. by incorporating it into a larger plan: "I would buy it and use the money it would save me to go to the movies." We also watch -- and use -- things like switching from the conditional to the declarative mode: "I would buy it so that I will be able to save money and go to the movies with it." Facial expression and behavioral responses bear on the state of persuasion as well. Also fanning contention and controversy allows us to observe how much respondents who _are_ persuaded will **argue** with those who are not, or how stoutly they will **resist** the arguments of those definitely opposed.

o "Importance" and "Recall": We combine these ideas in a concept we have privately labelled "Embeddedness". This has to do with the extent to which other, subsequent life events which these particular respondents are likely to encounter will tend to evoke rather than to bury their recollection of the message (the "message" being what the respondent got out of it). If, e.g., the next time the respondent gets into a lather about rising prices, she'll probably remember our product, and if she's a type who padlocks her purse, and lathers often and intensely, then for this respondent, the message is highly "embedded".

"Embeddedness" also includes the quality of "identification" which panelists may feel with the idea, the situation, or the people depicted in the execution. Someone who sincerely gets a shock of recognition: "Hey, that's me" when he looks at a commercial is apt to be reminded of the execution everytime the parallel situation occurs in his own life.

o Believability: Is something that shifts significance according to the product, the degree of belief or unbelief, and the reason for which it is believed or not. We report on it, when it seems to be important, but it has no permanently assigned evaluation. Clearly, a cosmetic product that is "too good to be true" may have created a very positive impression, while "some of your damned advertising doubletalk" in connection with bank services or a food's freedom from additives has not gone down too well.

o Liking: The romance which panelists have with the creative material is by far the untidiest of the creative responses we consider. Presumably, an ad or commercial that isn't sufficiently "liked" won't be allowed to deliver its message. On the other hand, we've all seen "adorable" campaigns that didn't move the product, and "outrageous" ones that did. We have to address "liking" in reports, because it is something that panels talk about, but there is no one standard rule for interpreting what "liking" a commercial or advertisement has to do with purchasing the product. We tend to think that strong feelings in _either_ direction register more clearly and last longer than the most benign low level response. A comment like: "It's short and to the point and no-nonsense" -- whatever pejorative connotations are intended -- is nearly always a kiss of death.

As for how we go about combining our three layers of interview material into estimates of persuasiveness or embeddedness or whatever other judgements we have been asked to make, there are, again, no invariable rules. When written reactions are at odds with socially aired opinions or feelings, we can't assume a priori that one or the other is the more "true". We must take into account the type of product, the experience of using it, the probable impact of social pressure on the product category, and so forth. If the written comments are more positive than the beginning of the discussion, it _may_ mean that respondents are drawn to the product, but must pay lip-service to consumer cynicism. If attitudes expressed in the group tend to become more positive as the discussion continues, we would probably assume that this was true. On the other hand, initial private acceptance followed by public rejection _may_ equally well

show a quick disenchantment with advertising claims perceived as superficial or irrelevant, and in such a case, could indicate more intense net-aversion than when both written and verbal responses are moderately, uniformly negative.

There are no formulae. There are, alas, few precedents. Sometimes, long familiarity with a product or product group will give us a reassuring feeling of solidity, and some readymade hypotheses for explaining contradictions. But even here, we must be alert for signs of change. There is also a kind of cumulative serendipity that permits us to recognize in one product category attitudes that are familiar from another, and to speculate about whether, e.g., a product that used to be almost purely cosmetic is beginning to shift to a medicinal image (since attitudinal patterns are suddenly similar to those habitually seen in drug product interviews).

By-and-large, however, once the interviews are done and the various interview products sifted through, we are alone with the data and whatever tools we have acquired to organize them into a final report. Partly, I am hindered in delivering an adequate job description because I feel I should append a resume. It would be difficult to find a vocation that challenged more completely the sum of knowledge and skills I can muster. My group interviews -- and the reports that summarize them -- are as they are because of my academic and clinical background, and have gotten better as my marketing background increased. Group interviews, generally, have astonishing flexibility, and can absorb whatever one brings to them.

Having begun with the premise that I was setting forth _one_ way -- not _the_ way -- to use group interview research, I find _I_ do have something to say about how one "ought" to approach group interviews. One should approach them with as simple and clear an idea of the objectives as possible, and with an equally clear (though possibly less simple) inventory of one's own skills, blind spots, biases, and expectations as possible. This will instruct the professional as to what he can do very well, where he must exercise caution, and -- when the data are before him -- help him to recognize a moderator-skew when he sees one.

A PERSPECTIVE IN FOCUS GROUPS

Maggie Hannah

Ms. Hannah is the Manager of Qualitative Research for Custom Research, Inc., Minneapolis, Minn. She has been a researcher for advertising agencies, consumer products firms, and has conducted many hundreds of focus groups in all parts of the country.

For approximately seven years I worked for advertising agencies or in the marketing area of consumer products firms. During that period, I often found myself sitting in a dark viewing-room, observing focus groups. While watching these focus groups, often the thought crossed my mind that moderating focus groups certainly looked easy *and* anyone could moderate . . . even me. Well, "poetic justice" has occurred in my career-life, and now I find myself actually conducting focus groups, no longer viewing from the "safety" of the observation room, but instead on the other side of the one-way mirror.

Having now experienced the perspective of focus groups from both sides of the mirror, I would like to share some of my thoughts in regard to what makes a focus group, or qualitative research, an effective research tool.

In my opinion, the following aspects of focus groups must be understood in order to ensure meaningful and productive qualitative research:

1) Client understanding of the function a focus group can serve.
2) Client and researcher/moderator agreement on the objectives/purposes for conducting the particular focus groups.

Client Understanding of the Focus Group Function

It is critical, prior to even initiating a qualitative research project, that everyone involved understand how focus groups can best serve the required research needs. A focus-group offers the client an excellent means of evaluating consumer reactions toward ideas, concepts, and marketing strategies.

Suppose a client is considering a new product concept or a change in current marketing strategy for an established product. Prior to spending heavily against the de-velopment of that new product or spending heavily against the execution of that new strategy, a focus group will allow the client to learn how his potential consumers feel about the idea. The focus group therefore will aid the client in further development of fine-tuning of the proposed concept or strategy . . . prior to making a major expenditure.

It is important that clients understand that the ideal function of a focus group, or qualitative research, is to provide *direction.* Because of the small sample reached through focus groups (i.e. approximately eight to ten respondents per group), the findings from a focus group are not meant to be used as the "final word" upon which to base entire marketing plans or marketing strategies. Rather focus groups ideally should be viewed as a research-vehicle that provides a client with findings which represent the "tip of the iceberg" in terms of the overall marketing research project. Focus groups, or qualitative research, offer reaction to ideas and directional information. Additional large-number, quantitative research is usually recommended as a next-step to supplement and support the qualitative findings.

Focus groups used for this type of directional evaluation appear to be currently in vogue for many clients. This increased interest and usage of focus groups for directional purposes is, in my opinion, a good sign. Using focus groups can best serve his research needs, it is im-definitely serves the client well. Not only will focus groups save him money in the long-run, but also time is being saved in the development of new and different marketing ideas and strategies.

Agreement on the Objectives/Purposes for Conducting the Groups

In terms of undertaking a qualitative research project which involves focus groups, the onus on the researcher/moderator is to make sure the client understands and accepts the benefits *and* the limitations focus group research provides. A researcher/moderator has done the client a disservice if the client is led to believe that focus group sessions will offer *all* the answers. A focus group project may offer directional help, but focus groups will also leave the client with some unanswered questions or

Reprinted from *Viewpoints,* **18 (July 1978), 4-8, published by the Marketing Research Association, Inc.**

concerns — possibly some concerns the client never even considered, which the consumers perceive as critical to acceptance of the concept or strategy.

In order to ensure that the client understands and accepts both the function of the focus groups and how the focus groups can best serve his research needs, it is important that the researcher/moderator force the client to isolate the two or three major objectives he (the client) has in regard to information generated from the focus groups. If the client is unable to limit his major objectives to two or three, it may be too early in the developmental process for focus groups, i.e. the client's needs may be too general and vague to produce meaningful information from focus groups.

Considerations/Steps to Ensure Meaningful Qualitative Research

Having briefly discussed some of the general aspects of qualitative research/focus groups, let me now explain some more specific steps/thoughts I personally consider to ensure my own focus groups will provide my clients with productive and meaningful research.

1) Determine with the client whether focus groups, or qualitative research, is the most effective research to serve his needs.

The decision to conduct focus groups depends greatly on where a concept or strategy is in terms of its developmental stage. For example, if the client has truly reached a point where no further development can be implemented on an idea or strategy without consumer feedback — this is a time when focus groups can be beneficial in helping to determine further direction in the development of the idea or strategy.

Or, if the client is already in the marketplace with a product or a commercial, and the results he expected are not occurring — this may be the time to find out from consumers what their problems/concerns are in regard to the product or commercial. (Ideally, if effective research had been done prior to introduction into the marketplace, the client would not have to consider qualitative research *after* introduction to understand his problems.)

Or, if the client wants to ultimately conduct some quantative testing on a concept or concepts, but needs more definitive information to determine which areas/concerns to cover in the quantitative test — this is a time when focus groups may help provide direction in regard to designing the quantitative questionnaire.

Basically, the responsibility of the researcher/moderator then is (1) to understand thoroughly the client's problems and research needs, (2) to learn what the client wants to learn in order to work with his problem, and (3) to determine whether qualitative research, i.e. focus groups, will actually offer the client the information he wishes vis a' vis his problem(s).

2) Assuming focus groups are appropriate in addressing the client's needs, the researcher/moderator must then work with the client in determining the qualifications for the respondents in the focus groups.

While most clients are aware of their target-markets (i.e. consumers the client wishes to reach), the researcher/moderator can help the client by suggesting market-segments or demographic groups which the client may be forgetting (e.g. working women, large family households, etc.)

Thus, though the choice of people the client wishes to hear from is normally predicated on the client's suggestions, the researcher/moderator has the responsibility, in my opinion, to counsel the client as to whether these market-segments seem most appropriate, based on the client's previously stated interest areas and concerns.

3) The next step is for the researcher/moderator to analyze the client's research needs and present him with a written proposal outlining the research project.

This written proposal serves as a reconfirmation of the client's objectives for conducting the research . . . based on the researcher/moderator's understanding of the client's needs.

Many clients claim they do not need a written proposal. It has been my experience, however, that a written proposal serves three purposes. The first purpose is to place *in writing* the researcher/moderator's understanding of the project. By writing a proposal which contains background information, objectives, information to be obtained, study design, budget, and timing . . . everyone involved with the project has a working-document which fully explains the project.

The second purpose a written proposal serves is to force the researcher/moderator to clarify the project's purposes and objectives both for himself and for the client. If during prior discussion with the client, a misunderstanding has occurred . . . a written proposal will probably call attention to it and enable the misunderstanding to be corrected *before* the focus groups begin.

The third purpose of the written document is to "protect" the researcher/moderator. If after the study is completed, the client questions the design of the study or the information obtained from the study, the researcher/moderator can refer back to the written proposal to determine if indeed the objectives, etal., were completed correctly and according to the proposal. It is important therefore that once the proposal is written, the client read it carefully and inform the researcher/moderator of any concerns or misunderstandings which occur in the written proposal.

4) Armed with a written proposal — which both the researcher/moderator and the client agree upon — the fielding of the study can then begin.

The field service organization used for recruiting the

focus groups plays a major role in the success of the entire study. A field service organization should be chosen which both the researcher/moderator and the client trust. If the client is unfamiliar with the organization, the onus on the researcher/moderator is to select a reputable, dependable, and professional firm — one which the client will find acceptable.

The recruiting of respondents for the proposed focus groups *must* be reliable. The client will learn very little about his concept if he ends up viewing groups where the respondents do not represent the market-segment he desired. In addition, from the researcher/moderator's standpoint, it is maddening to be conducting a group and midway into the group, discover the group members are *not* the people the client wishes to reach.

I cannot stress enough the importance of reliable recruiting. One means of ensuring that a field service organization is professional and dependable is to conduct periodic quality-control checks on the organization. Our firm has one person assigned to this task, i.e. validation of respondents for both qualitative and quantitative work handled by outside suppliers. With this continual monitoring of suppliers' field service operations, I can then comfortably recommend which field operations to use in cities selected by the client.

5) **Prior to conducting the actual focus group sessions, the person who will be doing the moderating and the client should discuss and review thoroughly the proposed discussion outline.**

Within our firm, the person who will do the moderating of the groups is also the researcher who has interface with the client. In my opinion, this is ideal. It means that one person from the research firm has full responsibility for the project, e.g. developing and designing the study, conducting the groups, and preparing/presenting the findings. Greater understanding of the client's needs and concerns can be achieved in this manner.

The discussion outline itself may be totally generated by the moderator, based on the client's information desires. Or, the client may provide the moderator with a discussion outline he (the client) designs. In either case, the client *and* the moderator should both be comfortable with the outline.

Asking the client for his two or three major objectives in regard to the project at this stage (i.e. review of proposed discussion outline) will greatly help the moderator clarify and note the key areas on the outline which need to be probed in depth.

A moderator must be flexible in regard to the final discussion outline. A client may decide five minutes before the first group to concentrate on different discussion areas than previously agreed to. The client, however, should be discouraged from throwing in numerous, additional and new areas of information at the last minute.

Rightfully so, many clients want to get their money's worth out of the group sessions. The client must, however, remember that groups tend to be most helpful and productive when a limited number of areas are discussed in depth. The client who continues to add, and add, and add to his list of discussion areas does both the moderator and himself a disservice. The moderator may feel rushed for time during the group, and therefore may be able to only cover each discussion area superficially. The client may not learn very much about any one area, but may instead obtain only general information about numerous areas. One purpose of any focus group is to obtain in-depth feelings and information — too many topics during a group discussion will defeat this purpose.

Because of a client's tendency to want to learn as much as possible from a group, the moderator must be able at times to say "no" to the client's requests. If the client is unable or unwilling to limit the amount of information he wants to extract from a group, the moderator must diplomatically call a halt to the client's demands — for the good of the ultimate research findings.

6) **In order to ensure that the actual focus groups will be as successful as possible, the moderator must prepare both mentally, and, to a certain degree, emotionally.**

Prior to actually conducting the focus group, I believe the moderator should totally familiarize himself with the discussion outline. The topics of discussion should be so well remembered *and* understood that the outline rarely, if ever, is referred to. I find personally that jotting down key-words on the margins of the outline, prior to the group, can be very helpful in quickly reminding me which areas are of particular concern to the client. Notes such as these tend to be easy to read while standing or moving in front of the group.

In beginning the group, I find that a very brief, introductory period of discussion helps to relax the respondents. This warm-up enables the moderator to establish an atmosphere that is relaxed and non-threatening.

During this warm-up period, I usually explain to the group why the microphone and one-way mirror are being used. (Before the group starts, I *always* check with the client to make sure he agrees that the mirror and microphone should be explained.) I feel that unless the client has strong reasons not to explain the mirror's purpose, the respondents should be informed that they may be observed during the session. By noting the existence/purpose of the mirror, if something does occur behind the mirror during the group, e.g. match is struck, door opened allowing light in, etc., no one in the group will be overly concerned or feel they have been spied upon unknowingly. The tendency among respondents is to look at the mirror while it is being explained and then ignore it. (Also, I have never had a client who was unwilling to permit an explanation of the mirror.)

As I mentioned earlier, not only must the moderator be mentally prepared for each group, he or she must also prepare emotionally. Respondents, for the most part, reflect off the mood of the moderator. If the moderator appears relaxed, enthusiastic, and interested in the topic — the respondents will also relax, be enthusiastic, and display interest in the topic. If the moderator behaves in an uptight, disinterested, and bored manner, the respondents cannot be expected to enthusiastically become involved in the discussion.

I feel that relaxing the respondents in a group environment is a critical responsibility for the moderator. The more relaxed people become . . . the more spontaneously honest and candid the group. Achieving honesty and candor in a group means, in my opinion, more meaningful results for the client. If a group has relaxed and been honest, everyone wins. The respondents leave feeling good about themselves and their opinions. The moderator feels the information obtained was achieved in a pleasant, satisfying manner. And, the client has obtained information which is useful toward addressing his problems/concerns vis a' vis the concept being discussed.

7) To many clients, the analysis or report on the groups is what separates the "men from the boys" in terms of moderators.

Many people are capable of conducting groups and then writing a report on what was said. It is my belief however that a good researcher/moderator conducts the groups *and* then writes a report which includes not only what was said, but more importantly, includes the *implications* to the client of what was said or left unsaid.

If a report is strictly a regurgitation of what the respondents said . . . then transcripts of the tapes from the groups will serve the same purpose. A good report must go beyond what was said and analyze what was *meant* by respondents' comments. During the actual group discussion, a good moderator must therefore not only conduct the flow and direction of the discussion, but must also be processing the meaning and implications of the discussion. It is critical then that the moderator understand his client's needs and problems so thoroughly that during the actual group, the moderator is continually asking himself or herself mentally . . . "what does *that* really mean in terms of my client's concerns."

In order to adequately digest what was said and implied during the groups, a reasonable amount of time is necessary from the conclusion of the groups to the actual preparation of the analysis/report. This period of time will allow everything to "sink in" and be examined carefully by both the moderator and the client, prior to the moderator's writing the report. A reasonable time period to digest the findings in turn will also provide the client with a more thoughtful, and hopefully meaningful, analysis/report.

In an article of this length, it is impossible to fully discuss all the various aspects of qualitative/focus group research that can and should be considered. The preceding thoughts however will provide some insight into the overall functions and benefits of qualitative/focus group research.

In conclusion, it is my belief that any qualitative/focus group research is only as good as the communication and understanding established throughout the project between client and researcher/moderator. On a general level, the client must understand how the research can help him . . . and how it cannot. On a more specific level, the researcher/moderator must fully understand and appreciate the client's problems and needs. If good communication has been achieved, everybody benefits. The client is pleased because at the conclusion of the project, he has obtained meaningful research direction. The researcher/moderator is pleased because he or she has assisted their client by providing valuable and professional service.

THE DYNAMICS OF THE GROUP INTERVIEW

Myril D. Axelrod

Young & Rubicam International, Inc.

Because I am employed by one of the world's largest advertising agencies and work closely with a variety of clients, including many of the major marketers, I have had the opportunity to witness, in recent years, a growing feeling of insecurity with focussed group research and a growing desire to have some kind of yard-stick by which to "measure" the kind of focussed group services that are being bought. At least three of the client "giants" I know of have even gone so far as to issue virtual bans on the use of this kind of research unless it can meet rigid standards of positioning and quality.

Part of the concern about focussed groups, my client sources report, stems from the very serious problem of misuse of the observations drawn from them, and the mistaken impression that such research can be used to circumvent or substitute for larger-scale quantitative exploration or to provide definitive direction in areas where it is not able to do so.

The question of when to use focussed groups and the very important contributions that good focussed group research can and does consistently make will be discussed by other panelists. I won't, therefore, dwell on it, except to express my hope that we, as researchers, will realize how dangerous it can be, both for us and for the client himself, if we foster in any way the desire to "sell" focussed group research for purposes where it is not appropriate, or if we allow the insights drawn from focussed group research to be used as the kind of incontrovertible "proof" it is not intended to be.

My particular assignment for this conference pertains to another aspect of why clients are becoming increasingly fearful about the use of focussed group research--the quality of the focussed groups they have been buying and the absence of any standards or yard-sticks with which they can evaluate what they have bought.

In this area of research, in particular, a client is all too often buying the proverbial "pig in a poke." He has been told that qualitative research is "subjective;" that its value depends on the interpretive skill of the practitioner; that the practitioner has the special sensitivities and the special kind of knowledge that equip him to create the "magic" of the group interview and to draw marvelous wisdom from it.

But how, the client can argue, can he develop the confidence he is supposed to have; how can these special skills be measured or evaluated;

what "checks" or controls are there; what ground rules ought to be met?

Today, unfortunately, there are no ground rules. In fact, within the past few years, I have seen hundreds of new practitioners of the "art" of focussed group interviewing spring full-blown on the scene with no more experience than that they have watched a few groups and are convinced that they can, with no difficulty, do equally well. In the course of a recent talk I had with one of my clients, we went through a list three pages long of research suppliers who had done focussed group work for his company in the past year, and neither of us recognized more than five of the names as trained, experienced, proven practitioners.

A further, very serious complication is the fact that there have never been any prescribed procedures or techniques which qualitative researchers have been required to follow. There are, in fact, almost no textbooks or training materials with which to help a person coming into the field learn the basics of the focussed group interviewing technique. As a result, the sad reality is that every moderator walks into the focussed group room and sets his own rules. It has even come to pass that any practitioner who manages to "discover" a "new and dynamic" gimmick that will make his groups seem different or innovative becomes this year's "hot" researcher.

While I certainly cannot deny that there are always, and should continue to be, new techniques to be learned and new skills to be developed with which to improve the success and effectiveness of focussed group research, I would like to make a plea for some kind of basic framework, some kind of essential starting point that can give this amorphous "discipline" some much needed discipline.

Over and over again, I have attended and even participated in conferences or panels on focussed group research when virtually every practitioner in the room had his own point of view, his own rationale and his own conviction that whatever he was doing was inordinately effective and successful. Yet another practitioner was taking a completely opposite position and advocating a totally contradictory approach. I remember a client sitting next to me at one of these meetings who left the room saying, "If I ever considered using focussed groups, this would certainly convince me to forget it. What they're trying to tell me is that 'anything goes' and that can't be the way it is."

I, for one, don't believe that is the way it is, and certainly not the way it should be.

Reprinted from *Advances In Consumer Research,* **IV (1976), 437-41.**

That is why I would like to spell out for you some of the essential ground rules I try to bring to bear and some of the techniques which I have been applying to focussed group interviewing for a host of years and literally thousands of interviews.

I recognize, as I have suggested, that other practitioners may not concur in all of these points of view; also that there will certainly be approaches or dimensions that they feel are important which I will not cover. However, I would hope that this discussion can possibly become a starting point from which to build some body of basic information on the practice of group interviewing as it is applied in advertising and marketing research.

The first essential for effective group research, in my mind, is:

...KEEP THE CONSUMER IN A CONSUMER ROLE

I feel that it is crucial that the respondents in a group discussion at all times stay in their role as consumers. I believe that their only value in advertising or product research is as consumers, and that the only insights they can give us that will be of value must come from their experiences and reactions as consumers.

One of the greatest failures of qualitative research, in my opinion, is that the consumers who are called in for qualitative research projects are so often placed in the role of advertising or marketing experts. They come to an impressive, big company setting, are placed at an official-looking conference table, presented with a group of alternatives, and asked to make choices, judgements, comparative decisions, which they are not qualified to make and which are rightfully the province and responsibility of the marketing executive.

The only role that consumers should be asked to play is their own, and everything possible should be done to foster that attitude and to keep them in that role.

Our own way of doing this starts with the first contact with the potential respondents. The recruiters who solicit respondents set the mood by explaining the importance of the person's experiences as a consumer and the value of sharing those experiences with the people who are bringing them the products they use and trying to give them the things they want.

This same kind of positioning is also employed at the session itself when we make our introductory remarks. The participants are again told about their value as consumers and reassured about the contribution each has to make in drawing upon his own experiences.

We also ensure that the setting will not encourage an inappropriate role. Our sessions are held in a modest, "lived-in" looking living room located away from the rest of the business of the agency. The respondents sit on couches and chairs, never at a conference table. There are no obvious mirrors, no cameras, no video equipment. We studiously avoid these kinds of equipment because we feel they are overt and disturbing reminders to the respondents that they are expected to be "on."

We want to see our consumers and talk to them in a setting and mood that is as normal and familiar for them as we can make it because, again, we want to be able to capture the experience and feelings they have in their every-day environment. We also want to establish the kind of rapport with them that will further foster this kind of relaxed and natural response.

This, then, brings us to my second essential for effective group interviewing:

...PROVIDE A MODERATOR THE CONSUMER WILL WANT TO TALK TO

To do this, we select and screen our moderators with scrupulous care, emphasizing always the warmth, the genuineness and the sensitivity which the moderator will bring to bear.

Although it is highly important that the moderator in a group session be non-directive and that he studiously avoid bringing his own influence on the responses, the personality and the demeanor of the moderator can unquestionably be a key factor in the effectiveness and even the "validity" of what comes out of the session. (I use the term "validity" here to reflect the honesty and openness of the respondents, and not in any statistical or quantitative context.)

Our experience has shown us time and time again how much more involvement and participation occurs when the moderator is warm and reassuring, when he (or she) has a quality of genuine interest and empathy with the respondents, when he is truly a listener, when he can readily communicate the sincerity and concern that make the respondents want to talk.

We also look for moderators who are "alive," who can keep the respondents alert and involved; moderators who can throw themselves into what is happening and can encourage the respondents, by their own sense of involvement and interest, to recognize that something interesting and exciting is happening.

A focussed group discussion should be exciting for the moderator, for the respondents, and for the listeners, and often it is the moderator who is responsible when it is not. But, even more important, if the moderator has not kept up the enthusiasm and interest of the respondents, the likelihood is that he will not be able to draw out the full range of insights the respondents can offer.

"Why bother?," the respondents might well feel in such a situation--and clearly, the research must suffer.

Essential number three:

...SET A TONE THAT MAKES THE CONSUMER WANT TO TALK

The success and effectiveness of the session is frequently directly related to the "tone" established for the discussion. The philosophy of interviewing to which I subscribe calls, as I have indicated, for a relaxed, informal mood and a free-flowing conversational feeling to the discussion. I believe that the goal of the session should be to draw out those responses and reactions and those insights which would appear if the participants were discussing the subject with their own friends or neighbors, rather than any kind of formal, structured, question and answer situation.

We are, therefore, particularly concerned about the way in which questions are asked or probing is undertaken. The very same probe, we find, can be posed with so different an attitude that the response is almost a total reversal of the answer that might have been drawn if the attitude and the approach of the interviewer had been different.

We feel that it is extremely important to be supportive and reassuring in drawing out respondents. We feel that we can probe almost endlessly and still not "lose" our respondents as long as they recognize that we are not attacking or challenging or trying to make them look ridiculous.

Even when we are pursuing a point fairly relentlessly, we try to do it in a natural, empathetic way and our questioning becomes a kind of interplay of thought rather than an attack. We will even, at times, reassure our respondents with a comment like, "I think I understand, but could you explain a little more?" We also utilize the values of the group situation by calling on others in the group to lend their support by asking, "How about someone else? Perhaps you have had that kind of feeling(or experience), too. Can you tell me a little more about this?"

Sometimes we will be overtly apologetic, explaining that we don't mean to hammer at someone, but we truly want to understand.

We firmly believe that we can get more from respondents who want to talk to us and who are encouraged by our genuine interest to search more deeply into their feelings and emotions.

There are other practitioners who claim that they only get to the "real" stuff when they make the respondents angry, and they studiously go about challenging, provoking and even humiliating the group members. I have never yet seen a consumer buy a product in anger, nor have I seen him respond at the cash register because he is lashing back. And, in my book, the name of the game will always be to try to capture in the group session the emotional frame of reference the consumer is going to experience in the actual buying situation.

Our approach to interviewing also avoids an overtly authoritarian stance, and we attempt to achieve as much spontaneity and free-flowing conversation as possible. At the same time, however, we recognize the very important need for the moderator to stay in enough control that the discussion does not wander off in a totally meaningless direction. To achieve this kind of delicate balance requires essential number four:

...THE MODERATOR MUST MAINTAIN HIS ROLE, TOO

The skilled moderator knows exactly when and how to foster a free-flowing discussion while yet interjecting a new question or a new probe at just the propitious moment, both to maintain the role of moderator and to turn the conversation back to its appropriate course. While I strongly prefer a non-directive approach to one that is restrictively authoritarian, I have seen non-directive interviewers who might just as well not have been in the room at all. And dreary, wasteful sessions they were indeed!

A middle course seems to work best for us. The respondents are encouraged to ventilate all their thoughts and ideas in a spontaneous manner and group interplay is encouraged at all times. But, the moderator is always on top of what is going on and the group is always aware that he is there to keep a structure.

Good group moderators, in my opinion, are like good teachers. They must earn the cooperation and the respect of the group members, and, having gained that good feeling, will have no trouble in maintaining both their own role and the proper function of the session.

The good moderator has also done a great deal of homework. He has had comprehensive discussions with all the people concerned with the project so that he understands totally the objectives of the research; what hypotheses have been raised; what the special areas of concern are. He has also given a great deal of thought to how to approach these various matters in the discussion.

Essential number five, therefore, is clearly,

...THE MODERATOR MUST HAVE DONE CAREFUL HOMEWORK

I can't stress strongly enough, that conducting a focussed group interview involves a lot more than just going in and asking a few questions. In fact, anybody who goes into a focussed group with such an attitude is running the very serious risk of being grossly misled.

The kind of question that is asked, how it is worded, when it is asked, how it appears in the context of the prior discussion, and, as mentioned before, the tone in which it is asked can all have a crucial effect on the kind of response it will bring. Serious, dedicated moderators will consider very carefully the interviewing guide they will use in a session and in introducing areas for discussion. They will work out in their minds the wording that will be the most non-commital and allow for the most meaningful kind of response from the group members.

We, for instance, never go into a session--even though we do many hundreds of sessions a year--without first preparing a written guide which we have thought and re-thought in terms of all its possible ramifications. We will carefully avoid asking a question like, "We would like to have your impression of this commercial," which, you can believe, gives you just exactly that: the consumer's own brand of strictly intellectual advertising expertise.

We've seen it happen over and over again: ask a question that makes a respondent an advertising expert and you've lost his value as a consumer.

We will also debate long and hard about what we are going to introduce first in our questioning and what effect that might have on the areas that will follow.

Often, for instance, a client will suggest that we have what he calls a "general discussion" before we introduce his concept or his advertising. In many instances, this would be an incorrect and misleading approach because it would create an unnatural positioning for the concept. When consumers see an ad on television or in a magazine, they have not been thinking about the category for an hour or three-quarters of an hour before. They haven't intellectualized all of their feelings and taken strong public positions which they might have to reverse after seeing the concept.

In many situations, therefore, we present a concept or an ad as the original stimulus for the discussion and are, in that way, able to get the consumer's fresh and spontaneous responses. Then, later, we are able to work from that reaction into a more general discussion of the category and how the product fits into the category.

In other circumstances, however, the goal of the research is somewhat different, and the key requirement is to get a basic orientation into the category without letting the respondents be aware that we have a particular interest or axe to grind. In that instance, we would work downward from the general to the specific. That approach requires a completely different line of questioning.

Another case in point: we often struggle for a long time to avoid questions that will be so direct, so suggestive that it is inevitable that we will be misled. When I hear moderators asking questions like, "Is there anything unbelievable about that commercial?" or, "Is there anything you don't like about the commercial," I am reminded of the caution I heard a long time ago when I was a young mother. If you say to the kids, "Now don't forget, I don't want you to put beans in your ears," you can be sure they are going to put beans in their ears even if they never thought about it before.

One thing I can guarantee--and I have countless incidents to back it up--if there is something genuinely negative on the respondents' minds, you'll hear about it all too soon, whether you ask or not.

And what about that question that every client thinks he wants to hear: "Would you be interested in buying the product?" Again, what a shockingly easy way to be misled! How much more meaningful it can be to let the consumers talk about the product in their own terms, to let them deal, in an open-ended way, with how it fits into their lives and their needs in the category; to let them demonstrate, through their spontaneous enthusiasm or lack of enthusiasm and the degree of emotional involvement which they manifest, whether or not the product or the concept is viable.

This is why you are doing qualitative research, and qualitative research means that you are examining the quality of the response rather than the response itself.

Although I have spent several of the previous pages talking about the need for a carefully developed and well researched interviewing guide, I am now going to also suggest that, once the moderator goes into the room, he must never fall into the trap of getting caught up in his guide and so dependent upon it that it stymies the free flow of the conversation. He should also carefully avoid referring to the guide while he is ostensibly listening to the respondents.

There is nothing more important in a group than to listen intently and fully, for it is, as I mentioned before, the interviewer's interest and involvement that encourage the respondents to go on. As in the spy stories, the moderator must prepare the guide with scrupulous care, study it with equally scrupulous care, and then, so to speak, he must eat it. By the time he goes into the session, the guide should have become so incorporated into his thinking that it literally has become a part of him.

This is the only way the interviewer can carry on the free-flowing, comfortable, natural "conversation" that makes the discussion valuable. He must be prepared to come into the conversation and open up areas for discussion at appropriate moments while yet not interfering with the spontaneity of the responses and the valuable exchange of dialogue between respondents which is the rationale for the group experience.

This, in turn, points up another essential which the moderator must bring to the session. He must be skilled in the handling of the group dynamics which will occur and know how to use them in a positive way. He must also know how to short-circuit possible negatives of the group situation and minimize possible contamination.

Essential number six, therefore, is,

...THE MODERATOR MUST BE SKILLED IN THE TECHNIQUES OF GROUP DYNAMICS

We, in the qualitative research field, are all too familiar with the criticism that is repeatedly leveled at focussed group research, and particularly with the most prevalent of all, the belief that group members merely pick up from one another and reflect the same ideas.

Several of the clients I have spoken with even take the position that, after the first one or two respondents have spoken, none of the other respondents can be considered "fresh." Someone else I know, who is himself a moderator, thinks it is very humorous to remark that six focussed groups are really just six individual interviews.

While I know that a snowballing effect can certainly occur in the group discussion environment, I also know that it is possible to counteract and minimize such influences with the right kind of moderating and a sensitive repositioning statement by the moderator. Let me give you some examples. We find, for instance, that, as soon as we see an idea starting to "catch on," we can get back on course by asking, "What about someone else? Does someone else feel differently?" With this kind of reassurance, a person who has a different point of view feels free to disagree and express his own position.

We also say, at times, in order to turn a discussion away from a course, "That's one point of view," or, "That's an interesting point; now what about some other thoughts?" Or, we call upon a respondent who has shown signs of another kind of thinking and bring him into the conversation. That then provides the moderator with the opportunity to say, "There seem to be several different points of view that have been brought up. Where are the rest of you on these? What has your experience been?"

In many instances, we also try to avoid group influence by going around quickly at the start of the session to get an immediate, first-thought reaction from everyone. We don't probe at this time or let anyone develop a point of view. Then we go back and pursue the various reactions more totally. But we have first had an opportunity to get all the first-blush ideas out on the floor.

These are some of the ways we use to avoid group influence when it is overt and easily spotted. There are, however, the problems that occur when the effect of a remark or an idea has sparked a whole line of reasoning that might not otherwise have occurred. Even the respondents themselves may not know that this kind of influence has been at work. To guard against this kind of contamination, we always insist on supporting groups, at least one and hopefully more, with essentially the same types of respondents, so that we can find whether the same ideas and reactions repeat, even though the conversation may take a somewhat different turn.

Another much talked about and highly exaggerated hazard of the group interviewing situation is the dominant respondent and/or the non-stop talker. Again, this can only occur if the moderator permits it; and a skilled, competent moderator knows how to deal with such offenders. They require firm and direct intervention, albeit intervention which is civil and good-natured and which doesn't embarrass either the offender or the other members of the group.

If a disruptive or dominating respondent is put down too sharply, other members of the group might be fearful of exposing themselves to the same kind of attack, so they take a safe course and say nothing.

The best technique is usually to break right into a sentence with a reassuring, "That's interesting, but let me just find out what these people over here have to say," or, "Yes, I understand. Let me get some other opinions."

The moderator must also studiously avoid involving the big talker any more than necessary in other parts of the conversation and should direct questions or comments away from this person and toward others in the group wherever possible.

The eager talkers are more often than not counterbalanced by reluctant talkers who need special encouragement and a show of interest on the part of the moderator. It is interesting to see how easily they can be brought into the conversation with reassuring support and some show of recognition from the moderator like, "What about you? You've been very quiet, but I'd really like to know how you feel about some of these things we've been talking about. What ideas did you get when you saw the commercial?"

- The moderator who is skilled in working with group dynamics knows how to draw out individual experiences and reactions.

- He is adept at "using" what is happening in the group to stimulate and broaden the discussion.

- He encourages positive interaction between respondents and recognizes the potential for them to spark one another into deeper and more fruitful introspection. At the same time, he is ever watchful of negative interaction and is quick to head off painful incidents that can interfere with the freedom with which all the respondents will react.

- He knows how to recognize the difference between the intellectual and the emotional-- between what the respondents are saying and what they are experiencing.

- He is constantly aware of the mood and the demeanor of the participants and knows that the strongest "clues" in "reading" the group will come from what is happening and from the emotional affect he perceives in the respondents. He is always listening with a particularly keen "third" ear.

- He knows how to cut right through the expertise and get the respondents back on the track.

- And, most important of all, he knows how to interpret the group for his clients

so that they, too, will be able to take
what is _valuable_ and _genuine_ from the group.

Basically, the good moderator is a "pro," and
he got that way by learning his trade well and
long.

Again, I come back to the very same point at
which I began. We need more practitioners who
are indeed "pros" and who have learned their
trade well and long. We need schools and work-
study programs where they can be trained and
developed. And, we need, desperately, some
kind of quality control.

If we continue in the haphazard, everyone-set-
his-own-rules manner we have been following,
the inevitable result will be that more and
more clients will become disillusioned and
even embittered about this valuable, and in
many cases, irreplaceable research tool.

Some clients already feel that way. Others
are moving in that direction. And what a
crying shame that is!

Clients: Check qualitative researcher's personal traits to get more; Qualitative researchers: Enter entire marketing process to give more

BY JUDITH LANGER
Vice President
Qualitative Research
Lieberman Research West Inc.
Los Angeles

CLIENTS who understand the human side of qualitative marketing research can get more from this type of research. And qualitative researchers who view their role as more than that of a focus group session moderator and enter the entire marketing process can give more to this type of research.

As with any research, a key element in the success of focus groups—now the most popular form of qualitative research being conducted—is the skill of the person conducting it. Just as the role of a *quantitative* researcher extends beyond writing and asking questions, the role of a *qualitative* researcher—a marketing researcher whose principal tool is the depth interviewing technique—extends well beyond moderating focus groups.

What happens in the sessions is only one phase in the total process from problem specification to final report. The qualitative researcher has the responsibility for understanding the marketing issues involved, helping to structure the research to be productive, drawing out consumers, and searching for answers.

From the client's viewpoint, it's important to develop a close working relationship with the qualitative researcher, making the researcher part of the marketing process and not simply an interviewer to whom a list of questions is supplied.

Understanding that the *personal* characteristics of qualitative re-searchers are critical—more so than any list of resume characteristics—can help the client to find better researchers. Understanding the intellectual and emotional process of focus groups also can improve rapport between client and researcher to result in more useful work.

Of course, some people do only moderate focus groups, just as many people serve as interviewers for quantitative research. But, while the survey research interviewer *may* properly be used only to ask predetermined questions, a walk-in moderator cannot be fully effective.

The qualitative research process suffers when a walk-in moderator doesn't really know what to probe for during the sessions. Without an analysis—preferably written—by the moderator afterwards, the client may walk away with a confused, contradictory view of what the sessions meant, and therefore not make proper, or any, use of the qualitative research.

SOME OF THE PERSONAL CHARACTERISTICS and background found in an effective qualitative researcher can be recognized before the researcher officially steps into the moderator's role.

Certain types of academic background and professional experience, indeed, are extremely valuable for a qualitative researcher. Degrees in marketing, marketing research, psychology, and other social sciences do contribute a valuable perspective.

This is not to say, however, that only certain types of academic training can result in an effective researcher. Experience in marketing research generally, qualitative research in particular, and in a client's category or related areas are all to the good.

Yet these, too, may not assure a client of a researcher sensitive to his problems and able to get the most out of the qualitative process. Focus group respondents are directly reacting to the researcher, who should have the ability to establish rapport; give respondents the feeling that they are being listened to with interest, sympathy, and without bias; and have the sensitivity to pick up new thoughts and probe unexpected directions.

In short, moderating is essentially a creative art which must be practiced by those with a certain "flair." These talents relate not just to years of training but to something deeper.

The analytic process is also a personal one requiring sensitivity of observation since the "data" are not clearcut or "hard." Subjective judgment must be used in interpreting answers. Creative judgment is needed to see potential in one comment.

And the qualitative researcher, before, during, and after the sessions, should show an extra element of creativity to come up with ideas. The ability to make inferential leaps from "what was said" to "what it means" is a critical skill of a competent researcher.

GOOD QUALITATIVE RE-SEARCHERS:
● **ARE GENUINELY INTERESTED IN HEARING** other people's thoughts and feelings. A good moderator is someone who in "real life" really is interested in finding out about people.

Reprinted from *Marketing News,* XII (September 8, 1978), 10-11, published by the American Marketing Association.

Asking questions—and listening to the answers—doesn't start when someone sits in the moderator's chair.

● ARE EXPRESSIVE OF THEIR OWN FEELINGS. They don't talk only about concrete, objective events but also give their personal reactions.

● ARE ANIMATED AND SPONTANEOUS. Someone with a dull personality will not be able to control focus groups. Spontaneity is vital for a moderator to take advantage of the great many stimuli during a session.

● HAVE A SENSE OF HUMOR. I don't mean telling canned jokes but finding latent humor possibilities in ordinary situations. This quality, more important than it may seem, is strongly related to imagination, creativity, and spontaneity, all needed in qualitative research.

● ARE EMPATHIC. This ability to understand how others feel and to see life from their perspective is essential.

● ADMIT THEIR OWN BIASES. Complete objectivity is impossible, but we can aim for recognition of our own personal feelings towards the subject with which we're dealing. If qualitative researchers talk about their own experiences or feelings related to a project, a client doesn't necessarily have to get nervous about their objectivity. The key point is whether we can be honest and introspective enough to understand these biases and professionally detach ourselves from them in our work.

● ARE INSIGHTFUL ABOUT PEOPLE. A true researcher is always exploring, asking why. You don't turn on the psychological probing and turn it off afterwards. Good qualitative researchers are truly intrigued with understanding people. This analytical bent shows through in their conversation, whether in personal or professional observations.

● EXPRESS THOUGHTS CLEARLY. The moderator must frame questions quickly, and, if these cannot be stated simply, the session will not succeed.

● ARE FLEXIBLE. They must respond quickly and be able to take new directions before or during sessions. They often face last minute changes and should be adaptable to recommend changes if a technique is not proving productive enough or if a concept needs revising.

Undergoing psychotherapy may contribute in several ways to the development of a sensitive qualitative researcher. The psychotherapeutic process can enable a researcher to see the subjective nature of his or her own feelings, adding insight into human dynamics generally, appreciating the emotional aspects of life as opposed to the rational side alone.

Obviously, many good qualitative researchers have never been through psychotherapy, and it's certainly not the one and only way to acquire sensitivity and insight. But it is an excellent way to pick up some good moderating techniques,

such as nonjudgmental listening, nondirective feedback of feelings to elicit deeper responses ("You seem to be saying . . ."), and even answering questions with questions ("Well, what do you think?").

WHAT'S GOING THROUGH THE MODERATOR'S MIND, as
an individual and as a researcher, during a focus group? By understanding the complexity and intensity of the process, clients may realize that what appears to be easy, really isn't; and, as a result, they may get more from their research.

To get the best results, clients must not only select good researchers who take a broad view of their role but also must fully acquaint them with the project's objectives. It's not enough to know what questions to ask; the qualitative researcher should understand what the *marketing* problems and objectives are.

The qualitative researcher approaches the sessions as an opportunity to learn from consumers, to understand them, and to communicate with them. A productive session begins to generate ideas for solving the marketing problem.

Adding to the intensity of the experience is the fact that most sessions are being observed by the client and/or the agency. The behind-the-mirror audience for a focus group often outnumbers the respondents. This gives the moderator the distinct feeling of being "on stage." Everything will be judged.

Further, the moderator usually is aware of divisions that exist among the observers concerning the hoped-for results. The only way to cope effectively with such pressures is to ignore them and concentrate on meeting the study objectives.

The following questions show the several levels on which the moderator's mind is working during a focus group session:

● What else do I need to ask to understand this respondent's statement—what it means, why he/she feels that way, etc.?

● Am I hearing everything I need to know to understand the problem and answer the objectives of the research? Is there a question not in the topic guide that I should ask?

● When a respondent really irritates me or I disagree strongly with what's being said, am I keeping my own feelings from showing?

● I see one respondent make a face when she hears another's remarks. I must get back to her.

● Since my job includes the creative task of developing ideas, if the concept is getting a negative response, is there any idea I can come up with that will turn it around?

● How can I get the quiet members of the group to feel comfortable and accepted enough to participate easily?

● How can I get a dominating or digressing respondent to stop talking without embarrassing him/her and keep a warm rapport going both with that person and the group as a whole?

● When I have a "know-it-all" respondent who is critical of the others, how do I prevent this person from spoiling the free-flowing atmosphere?

● If a group lacks animation, how can I get the members to loosen up and interact?

● How do I make all the respondents feel free to express their ideas and reveal their personal behavior without fear of judgment from me or the rest of the group?

● When real problems arise—a respondent is hostile, sick, drunk, or doesn't belong in the group (her cousin works for the competition)—how do I handle the problem quickly, nicely, and firmly without losing my relationship with the other participants?

● How much time do I have left? Will I be able to cover everything when just one section of the topic guide could take the full two hours?

● How do I stay fully tuned-in and open to new ideas when I have heard much of this before in previous groups?

● What does all this mean anyway? What am I learning about consumers' feelings, beliefs, and behavior? What ideas does this suggest about solving the particular marketing problem?

● How do I get beyond the intellectualizing to respondents' real feelings? I want to reach the level of unanalyzed impressions and emotions—what goes through people's minds before it becomes censored. The issue is, "What do you feel?" not "What is your opinion?"

IN SHORT, the moderator is actively working at all times thinking about
—What is happening *now,*
—Where the discussion goes *next,* and
—What it will all mean *afterwards.*

All this is to carry out a dual role: 1. To establish and maintain a productive group process and 2. To serve as an analytic researcher whose job is to develop hypotheses that will help solve marketing problems.

Going through this experience, even for professionals who have done hundreds of focus groups, is stimulating, exciting, anxiety-provoking, fun, tiring, and hard.

This paradox in the moderator's role explains our emotional response to it: On one hand, the moderator is in the key position of power—in the spotlight (so to speak) and guiding the flow of discussion. And yet, on the other hand, the moderator is the least important (and rightfully so) because the moderator's personal feelings, thoughts, and opinions about the subject discussed are irrelevant and must be left outside the session room and personal reactions to the individual respondents ("I like her"; "I can't stand her"; etc.) must be submerged.

Understanding the pressures of the moderating experience can help the client work more effectively with qualitative researchers. Some suggestions:

● After a focus group, a "debriefing" discussion with the moderator is an absolute necessity to make sense of what has been heard. Realize, however, how difficult it is for a moderator to provide an "instant analysis." If the researcher doesn't "have the answer" the moment the last focus group ends, allow some time for review and reflection.

● Expect a moderator to ventilate some personal feelings after a session. The moderator isn't a machine. What happens in the session may stir personal feelings—annoyance at a respondent who was a pain, frustration at holding back one's own views on a subject in order to seem natural, or being enthusiastic and interested even though this was the sixth group on the same subject.

● Unless the question is critical, avoid sending in notes during sessions. Some clients want to be able to communicate with the moderator in case important questions have not been asked or a new thought arises that

they wish to introduce. However, it's very distracting and sometimes disruptive. When notes are brought in, respondents wonder what's going on and this makes the moderator feel his or her judgment isn't being trusted.

● One of the more frustrating experiences for a moderator is to be asked, "Why didn't you ask . . .?" when in fact the area was probed. Having sat behind the mirror a number of times, I know just how tedious it can be and how difficult it is not to talk for two hours. Inevitably, observers will be distracted at times, but they should realize this and first find out whether or not the moderator did go into an area before being critical.

● Group sessions often are entertaining because they allow an opportunity for spontaneity. Enjoyment, however, is a byproduct and not the purpose of a group. If a session has provided meaningful answers but lacks excitement and sparkle, the moderator has not failed.

The Focused Group Interview and Moderator Bias

by Frank Kennedy, President
Frank Kennedy Inc.

The nature of the problem

One of the unique features of the group interview and an important source of its strength as a research tool, is the enormous flexibility, scope, and freedom of action permitted the moderator. Not bound by the rigid constraints of a formal questionnaire, the adept moderator constructively uses this freedom to take full advantage of the spontaneous, dynamic give-and-take of the group experience, and to make countless on-the-spot judgments as to what course of action will be most responsive to his research objectives.

Yet, this very freedom——so essential to good moderating——implicitly carries with it a risk and a challenge which is the subject of this paper: the introduction of bias, and the loss of objectivity.

We must recognize at the outset that no moderator can be fully objective; it is inevitable that to some extent subtle biases, pre-conceptions and pressures toward "consistent" findings will unconsciously call for expression during the course of a group interview. Biases and pre-conceptions, once recognized as such, can actually be helpful to the moderator. Yet, unrecognized, these pressures can erode the potential value of the group interview technique.

What must be examined, then, are (a) those factors and needs which provoke these pressures, (b) how they are actually reflected in practice, and (c) what can be done constructively to bring them under control.

Sources of moderator bias

Essentially, there are three quite different pressures at work which threaten to distort moderator objectivity:

—The all-too-human predisposition to welcome and reinforce the expression of points of view which are *consonant with our own.*

—The predisposition to welcome and reinforce the expression of points of view which are *consonant with those of our clients.*

—The predisposition to welcome and reinforce the expression of points of view which are *internally consistent.*

Let us examine each of these potential sources of bias in turn.

(a) Personal bias

What good and bad moderators share in common, of course, are those personal and professional experiences, beliefs, prejudices and emotionally-grounded needs which define our individuality and "humanness." We interface with and interpret new experiences within the context of our past. Our perceptions of reality, and how we manipulate that reality, are inevitably conditioned by needs which transcend the intrinsic properties of "raw" experience.

We are all driven by powerful needs to find reality compatible with our pre-established beliefs, and we all tend to greet dissonant perceptions with selective inattention, if not with anxiety or hostility.

What differentiates the good from the poor moderator is not the absence of needs which predispose us all to bias, but (a) a recognition that these forces exist, (b) an awareness of their power and of how they can subtly influence the course of a group discussion, and (c) mastery of skills designed to minimize their expression.

This is not to say, of course, that the ideal moderator is an unfeeling robot free from hunches, hypotheses, expectations or prejudices. Indeed, every phase of his work, from guide development to moderation and analysis, requires the *constructive* use of hunch, speculation, past experience and provisional hypotheses. Yet the moderator role also requires an effort to make conscious all preconceptions, assumptions and prejudices, and to assure that these potential sources of bias are under continual scrutiny.

Perhaps in the end, the best antidote to moderator bias is the old maxim, "Know Thyself." And perhaps because this goal is so critical during the on-going, dynamic give-and-take of the group experience, moderators with psychological training have a major advantage over those who do not.

In this regard, it should be stressed that it is not the flagrant, obvious introduction of personal bias that must concern us most, since these distortions are usually quite apparent to group participants, observers, and clients alike. It is the subtle, unconscious introduction of bias which is most dangerous, since it typically escapes the attention of even experi-

Reprinted from *Marketing Review*, 31 (Feb./March 1976), 19-21, published by the New York Chapter/American Marketing Association.

enced moderators, and of most psychologically untrained clients. And it is for this reason that no moderator can remain complacent about the issue of bias, or sidestep the need for continual self-scrutiny.

(b) Unconscious needs to "please the client"

A second challenge to objective moderating is the unconscious need to "please the client," and to manipulate group discussions in such a way as to support *client* prejudices and preconceptions. (One prerequisite in this regard is some knowledge of what *will* make the client happy——an issue we'll turn to shortly.)

Bias in favor of client prejudices, preconceptions and hopes is not an easy thing to acknowledge, and for that very reason, it can become a significant roadblock to effective moderating. There is probably no other area of market research in which there is a greater working intimacy between client and "supplier" than in group interview research, with clients frequently going "on the road" with moderators, and sharing with them their observations, reflections, interpretations, and emotional reactions to what is taking place.

A close working relationship between client and moderator during the course of a group interview study can, of course, have considerable value. It encourages a deeper understanding by the moderator of the underlying marketing objectives, and permits him to be fully responsive to these needs. Moreover, by working together, client and moderator may jointly decide to "shift signals," and take full advantage of the flexibility of the technique.

Yet one consequence of such an intimate working relationship is that the hopes, fears, aspirations and preconceptions of the client often become all too apparent. What moderator would not honestly prefer to prepare a report in which he could assert with conviction that a new product concept has merit, that a new advertising theme is responsive to consumer need, or that exciting opportunities exist to capture a critically important market segment? And what moderator could candidly deny that he shares with his client a sense of disappointment when

the advertising or marketing implications of his work are frankly "unfavorable" in character?

It is, of course, true that for most moderators, there are meaningful and gratifying rewards in pulling a client back from the brink of a disaster, or in making a very real——if temporarily painful——contribution to his assessment of reality. Yet it is nonetheless true that as human beings in a very human art, moderators can be caught up in the enthusiasms and the fears of their clients, and as a consequence become unconsciously motivated to "make them happy."

It must be said in passing that knowledge of client hopes and expectations can provoke a very different kind of bias. There can be perverse pleasures in "enlightening" clients, and in dramatically reporting findings which fly in the face of pre-established assumptions. Quite aside from the heady delights of "ego trips," moderators occasionally feel the need to prove the value of the group procedure, and to demonstrate that the technique (and the supplier in question) is essential to client survival. One way to do so, of course, is to "rock the boat," or "find something new," and inevitably, some moderators succumb to the temptation.

For the psychologically trained moderator, these temptations are obvious and are generally held in check. Yet the client-related sources of bias represent a major hazard for the untutored moderator.

(c) The need for consistency

Still another potential source of bias is the need for consistency, both within and across group sessions. Unconscious pressures to bias a group discussion are most powerful during the later stages of a study, particularly when the initial sessions have been highly consistent in their implications. When a group threatens to react in a way which is at variance with research-based expectations, and promises to present us with unexpected and unwelcome analytic and interpretive headaches, our unconscious impulse is to nip this insurrection in the bud ——or, as a last resort, to tune out, or reject such a group as "odd-ball."

Good moderators know, of course, that apparent inconsistencies often have a way of serving up unanticipated insights upon careful analytic scrutiny, and that they can be blessings in disguise. Moreover, inconsistencies and paradoxes can usefully instruct us that an issue is perhaps more complex than we had imagined, or that additional work is legitimately required. Yet in spite of our intellectual willingness to accept occasional inconsistencies, there remains some unconscious pressure to coercively wring conformity out of our group discussions.

It should be said that unconscious efforts to bias a group so that its message is consistent with other groups can backfire, occasionally provoking the "maverick" response that one so wishes to avoid. Respondents tend to be very alert to any covert "signals" which suggest that the moderator is less than objective and has some axe to grind. Once a group recognizes unconscious efforts to bias, the value of that group is often destroyed.

Knowing "what the moderator wants to hear," respondents tend to react in a very different way to this kind of psychological arm-twisting. Some will simply surrender, or withdraw into silence. Yet many will balk and bristle at signs of psychological dishonesty, and will often take vengeful delight in scuttling the moderator ——and his favorite position——in spite of how they might genuinely feel about the issue at hand.

We have seen, then, that there are three major sources of unconscious bias which threaten to challenge moderator objectivity: personal assumptions, client expectations, and the need for consistency. How is moderator bias typically manifested in actual practice? What are its tell-tale signs?

How bias is reflected in practice

It is, of course, true that bias can be introduced at any stage of a group interview study——from guide design to interpretation and presentation. Yet opportunities for unconscious distortion are most accessible in the dynamic, spontaneous give-and-take of the group session itself, where we do not have the time to reflect, evaluate or assess the "objectivity" of each question, comment, nuance of language or gesture.

From the point of view of moderator bias, three different kinds of respondent reactions exist: (a) comments the moderator *wants* to hear, (b) comments the moderator *does not want* to hear, and (c) comments to which he is indifferent. Biasing techniques focus almost wholly on efforts to reinforce "favorable" comments (defined as those which concord with moderator expectation or hope), and on efforts to punish or inhibit the expression of "unfavorable" comments (defined as those which are dissonant with moderator expectation or hope).

How, specifically, are these biasing efforts expressed in practice?

—Most often, by greeting favorable comments with appreciative nods, smiles or reinforcing comments, and by responding to unfavorable comments with indifference, perplexed stares, or body movements which reflect discomfort.

—By being patient, permissive and encouraging when someone finds it difficult to articulate a favorable thought, but by providing no such assistance to one who finds it difficult to express an unfavorable position.

—By more actively directing questions to those who seem most likely to hold favorable views, and by ignoring those who seem most likely to hold unfavorable views.

—By initiating a round of questioning with a favorably-inclined respondent, so that a favorable view will set a precedent and context for subsequent inquiries.

—By failing to probe for contrary sentiments when favorable comments are expressed, but by probing actively when unfavorable comments are articulated.

—By permitting "out of context" favorable comments, while telling those who offer an unfavorable view out of context that "we'll talk about that later."

—In periodic summaries of group positions, understating or omitting "minority" points of view.

—By "turning on the charm" so that respondents will tend to go along with the position you have unconsciously conveyed you want to hear.

—Conversely, by failing to develop any rapport at all with a group asked to assess a competitive product or advertisement, so that not only you, but the product or ad will be rejected.

These examples are meant simply to illustrate rather than to catalogue the many ways in which bias can be introduced. We should note, however, that these devices, when well executed, are often successful in accomplishing their purpose because they are subtle and often escape conscious self-scrutiny.

How moderator bias can be minimized

The group interview technique is a very human art. While one of its unique strengths rests in the character of moderator-respondent interaction, and in the flexibility and scope accorded the moderator, that very freedom poses challenges which must be recognized by client and moderator alike. Absolute objectivity can perhaps never be achieved, yet there are concrete steps which clients and moderators can take to reduce the problem of moderator bias to inconsequential proportions. What, then, can specifically be done to maximize moderator objectivity?

As clients:

—Use moderators with clinical or psychological training, particularly moderators who have had therapeutic experience.

—Understand the unconscious pressures on moderators to "make you happy," and make a conscious effort to keep them in the dark as to your *personal* expectations and hopes.

—Refrain from holding detailed "post-mortems" with moderators after each session, particularly any discussions which attempt to formulate "tentative findings."

—Stay away from "do it yourself" moderation, particularly if in all honesty, you feel you are emotionally invested in the outcome of the research.

—Do not require "top line" findings of the moderator, or even ask him for his "impressions" during the course of a study. Once he commits himself, there are additional pressures to prove himself right.

—Increasingly make "objectivity" one of your criteria for moderator eval-

uation. When in the role of an observer, reward objectivity in your conversations with the moderator, and call him to task when you feel there is evidence of unconscious bias.

As moderators:

—Recognizing the potential hazards of unconscious bias is half the battle. Before a study begins, learn to ask yourself what you expect will happen, what you would like to happen, and why. By doing a little soul-searching and by bringing potential sources of bias to the surface, you will find yourself operating on a much more objective level.

—Learn to be increasingly sensitive to your own feelings during the course of a session. When——and why ——are you feeling angry, uncomfortable, anxious, bored, disappointed, frustrated, relieved or happy? How—— and why——are you unconsciously expressing these feelings to the group?

—When auditing tapes, learn to be sensitive not only to content, but to interaction patterns and to evidence of unconscious bias on your part. Take the time and trouble to analyze your own performance from time to time by way of videotape.

—After completing a given session in a series, try not to discuss your impressions with your client, or to attempt any formulation of tentative conclusions. Do not write interim memos or take notes in lieu of tape recordings.

—Avoid the temptation to prematurely demonstrate your interpretive skills and marketing know-how to observer-clients. The time for synthesis and closure is after the last session has been completed, and not before.

—Recall to mind the times when apparent inconsistencies "made sense" on another level of abstraction, and when they triggered fresh inquiries in unanticipated yet useful directions.

—Though requiring courage, it is sometimes useful at the close of a group session to hold a brief post-mortem with respondents, quite candidly asking them if there had been a full opportunity for all opinions to be expressed, or whether in their view, you have in any way communicated a personal bias.

—Recognize the fact that if your personal expectation or hypothesis is valid, it will withstand the most vigorous scrutiny. By providing full opportunities for contrary positions to be expressed and explored (and in taking the courage to do so), you will be on far more secure grounds in asserting and documenting its validity.

In summary, while the potential hazards of moderator bias are very real, we should not overstate the degree to which these pressures can distort group interview findings, particularly when both client and moderator are aware of the problem and take sensible steps to forestall its expression. Truth is obstinate and persistent, and will generally make itself heard. What is at issue is not the likelihood of massive distortion, but the failure to fully exploit a technique which offers so many unique and valuable rewards to those who use it well.

The Influence of the Researcher and his Procedures on the Validity of Group Sessions

Karen Ida Peterson*

This paper discusses the various ways in which the researcher can influence the validity of focused group interviews.

A researcher can definitely influence the validity of groups. First, by using or recommending groups for a problem or issue which is not well suited for groups; second, by the procedures and methods used to set up the group sessions; and, third, by the moderator's skill. This paper focuses on the first two issues. For those are the issues on which the researcher can influence the validity of the group session approach.

Use of Groups

When are groups appropriate? For what questions, issues, problems is the group session technique an appropriate tool? Groups are almost always appropriate for exploratory research. Most researchers are happy to include groups as a first step in a research program. In this context, the group session can be used for a number of purposes:

  . . . *First to develop an understanding of consumer language and terminology.* The question here is simply to be sure that the researcher understands just how to talk to the consumer, what words he or she uses and will understand in a questionnaire. This is an important and vital use for groups since business executives may not know how to talk with farmers in Mississippi, general aviation pilots, or hunters of small game, etc., etc.

  . . . *Second, to develop cues, insights, hypotheses about behavior or attitudes or motivations relevant to the issues to be studied.* In this instance, it is important both to uncover the hypotheses and to develop ways of expressing the relevant attitudes for measurement.

  . . . *Third, to ensure completeness.* Here the aim is to be sure that the researcher has all the issues in mind, has considered all of the options, and has included all the ideas which could be relevant.

Those purposes are all related to exploratory research. A few years ago, this author would have said that groups are only valid for exploratory research. That indeed there is no finding from a group on which management should take any action.

I'm now willing to accept the fact that there are indeed some decisions which can be made on the basis of group session work.

  . . . *When an initial screening of product ideas is needed.* Here the goal is to use groups as a fast, economical contraceptive procedure. To search out those products from a list of possibilities which apparently have no promise. One can pick out the dogs—the ones which are absolutely impossible and for which management should expend no further development money.

  . . . *When searching for new creative strategies or new product ideas.* In this case the goal is to explore all relevant attitudes and feelings in a product category in order to expose possible new ideas for advertising or products. Even here, however, researchers should not turn to the respondents to invent the new products—they are not equipped to do so. Instead, by exploring their needs, desires, problems, gripes, etc. and in assessing those, the researcher can create the new product or strategy idea.

  . . . *When trying to "flesh out" an existing new product or strategy idea.* Here, the copy writer or research and and development team may have come up with an idea. But the bare bones of that idea need to be fleshed

---

*Principal, Davidson-Peterson Associates, Inc.

Reprinted from Edward M. Mazze, ed., *1975 Combined Proceedings*, (Chicago: American Marketing Association), pp. 146-48.

out, expanded, developed. In this case groups can be used to generate ideas for the further development of products or ads.

In all of these areas groups can provide valid useful guidance for management.

There remain two kinds of research issues which cannot be validly served by groups. Both are derived from the fact that implicit in the group technique is a group of people. That fact of a group means that each respondent interacts with each other respondent. That dynamic is a key plus for groups—and one of the important limitations also. That limitation is important in two specific cases.

... *When the task is to select one among several alternates*—whether it is new products or new advertisements or whatever. Valid research cannot be done by means of group discussions in these areas.

• First, group domination is possible.

• Secondly, there is too much interaction, too much discussion back and forth, too much finding negatives by some which would never have occurred to others. In those instances researchers don't really know what influence another's comments had. That it happened is all that is known.

... *When the object is to explore in-depth an individual's purchase history or experience.* Here the problem is that it is boring for other respondents to listen to one individual recite his history with a product, service or industry.

To summarize, then, groups are appropriate for:

... Generating hypotheses, insights, cues for later confirmation by understanding attitudes, views, feelings of relevant respondents;

... Learning consumer language or terminology;

... Developing interaction among respondents—you don't want or need individual response;

... Eliminating "dogs" from a group of ideas;

... Developing new ideas; and

... Expanding or fleshing-out ideas.

Groups are inappropriate—and indeed, invalid for:

... Selecting a "winner" from among alternates; and

... Recreating long purchase experience histories for individuals.

The researchers' responsibility—whether he be in the research department of a company or agency, or in an independent research company—must be to define the research objectives and decide whether or not groups are the appropriate technique.

Groups are fast, economical and fun to managers. Thus, researchers are often in the position of having to reject groups as the appropriate technique. A marketer says he wants groups on _____ . But he shouldn't necessarily have groups. They may be inappropriate for the problem. If groups are inappropriate, the researcher must recommend the appropriate technique and indicate very clearly why groups are not the right technique. It's easy to get bamboozled by managers into doing groups for the wrong reasons—and thus, getting invalid results. A researcher must stand firmly by his position.

Procedures and Practices

Procedures can be broken down into three basic areas: recruiting, facilities and moderator's guide.

Recruiting

The first question a researcher faces in planning group sessions is "who" should be present in the groups?" In this area, validity can be affected by a number of recruiting decisions.

... First, who is relevant to the topic? That answer depends on whose views are needed to answer the research question, of course. For example, if usage of a brand is declining, only former users might be included in the group. In this event, the researcher focuses completely on the critical group.

In some cases, however, the researcher should also include some current users in order to stimulate the responses among those who are more important—the former users. Questions from those who now use a brand to those who used to can be very revealing in themselves—and the answers can be extremely important in making sure that all of the hypotheses which might be suggested have been uncovered.

The importance of the decisions made on *who* is to be included in a session is difficult to overstate. And, unfortunately, the decision is too often left to chance.

... Secondly, who will be comfortable together in a session? The goal of a session is to set-up a comfortable situation in which respondents feel able to express their views. That comfort is not usually enhanced by diversity of background. On some topics, men and women hinder each other's honest expression of views. More often, those of high and low social station do not "work well" together. Those with less education are hindered by those with more. Those whose age has given them years of experience on a topic tend to make younger people reluctant to discuss their more untrained views. Finally, friends are not necessarily comfortable together in a session. It is often easier to talk about sensitive issues with strangers—than with acquaintance.

... Finally, who will give fresh, unbiased responses? Many have heard the story of the nine housewives in Queens who do all of the group sessions for New York suppliers. Those women have made all the marketing decisions in New York for years.

Seriously, professional respondents can pose a serious problem for the group session research. People simply learn how to answer questions, they learn to understand where the moderator is heading and what he wants to know. Those who have been in group sessions before should not be included in another group wherever possible. Not only will they not be fresh respondents themselves, but they can influence others to respond in particular ways. This is a problem which the moderator can have trouble in sorting out—and it is one which the researcher can help to screen out before it happens.

So, what can be done about these problems in recruiting?

. . . First, carefully review who should be in the sessions, who is relevant to the topic, and who will enhance the discussion.

. . . Then design a tight careful screening questionnaire which will enable the local supervisor to have a group which meets specifications exactly.

. . . Find a supervisor who can be trusted and keep checking on her. Some of the worst mistakes are made where the supervisor and the field director have good rapport and checking becomes perfunctory.

. . . Be precise in telling her exactly what you want. The more information provided to her, the more accurate will be the screening.

. . . Finally, make sure that the moderator has time to review the screening questionnaires before the group begins. He can then identify possible problems and learn the names of respondents who should be probed in particular areas.

Facilities and Equipment

Now that some criteria have been established for selecting respondents who will enhance the study, let's turn to the group facilities and equipment decision which can influence validity.

First, the purpose of the group is to provide a comfortable setting for discussion. Thus, the group location must first be selected so as to help, not hinder, free discussion. This means, simply that groups can be done in homes if, and only if, the home decor and neighborhood surroundings are of the same general type as the respondents'. Clearly, one wouldn't ask low income housewives to meet in the elegant home of one of the community's leading citizens. They will simply feel inhibited initially—or may not even be willing to come.

For the same reasons, an office or hotel conference room may be the most comfortable situation for businessmen when seeking their views as businessmen. If the research is interested in their views as upper-income consumers, then a home setting might even be better.

Another important way to ensure that the group is comfortable is to serve refreshments—and serve them early, as respondents arrive.

Personally, this moderator prefers to have respondents seated around a table. The table becomes a focal point and draws the group together. However, the table must be an appropriate size—long tables tend to destroy the group's cohesion.

A question which is always asked is "what effect does the tape recorder have on respondents' willingness to discuss all types of issues." My reply is "little or none." If the setting is comfortable, and the group is not too diverse in background, and the moderator is good, then the tape becomes irrelevant.

The one-way mirror is often not noticed, but when it is, it should be explained honestly. For this reason, it's often better to have a few observers sit in the room during the session. As long as they don't express views or reinforce opinions taken by the group with facial expressions or comments (a difficult requirement for some clients) then they will probably not have any influence on the group's success. The exception is, of course, sensitive subjects—especially those related to sex. Discussing douching with three male observers in the room will not be productive. Inhibitions will arise simply from their presence and the discussion will be limited. In most cases, it doesn't matter.

The Moderator's Guide

A well-thought out moderator's guide is critical to the completion of good, valid groups. The moderator's guide is just that, a guide. A good moderator doesn't have to use the questions, but the researcher has not done his job if he has not thought through the problems and issues to the point that he has developed a strong guide.

Many have heard a moderator say, "I don't need a guide. Just give me a rough idea of what you want." Such an unstructured approach is a failure on the researcher's part to do his homework. He must carefully review the issues which may arise, allocate the precise emphasis for each topic, and generally provide guidance for the moderator. This is essential. If the researcher fails to do this, then issues can be missed, and topics overlooked which do not arise in the general discussion.

Conclusion

The researcher can affect the validity of group sessions by:

. . . Assuring that they are used only for appropriate issues;

. . . Establishing rigid controls for recruiting the right respondents;

. . . Being sure that facilities and equipment are conducive to a comfortable experience for respondents; and

. . . Providing the moderator with a carefully thought out guide for the session.

PART III

Marketing Applications

In this section, a series of marketing articles are chosen to show how focus group interviews can be utilized for marketing decisions. Major topics include:

1. A transcript of an actual focus group interview.

2. Examples of how focus group studies were used in marketing studies.

3. An illustration of a case study.

4. Use of focus group interviews for consulting and creative purposes.

Focus group interview:
CONSUMERS RAP ABOUT TODAY'S SHOPPING, BUYING

Wainwright: What's going on in the grocery store today?

Alma: I find myself no longer buying meat in the grocery store. I started this about a month ago. I feel that, for those prices, I might as well go to a butcher, pay a few pennies more and get premium meat or prime. I find that whereas just going into the store with no meat used to cost me $30 or $40, now it costs me $60 to $75.

Linda: I bought half a cow a month ago. And I'm still spending the same amount of money in the grocery store every week that I did before I bought the half a cow.

Wainwright: Eileen, how are you making it today? What are you cutting back on and what are you buying more of?

Eileen: I have completely done away with Fritos, potato chips, snacks—we were big on that type of stuff. I'm going back to some of the things my grandmother did. I'm baking. We weren't really taught all that much.

Rose: I sat down with my husband the other night. I do not use that much sugar in baking. Most of my cookies are without sugar. Or they take half a cup of sugar.

Marvella: People during the holidays were complaining because of Christmas baking. They do use a tremendous amount.

Linda: I use a little brown sugar and powdered sugar. I sat down and really thought about it, and normally my consumption of sugar, if I came down to it, even with holiday baking, is 15 lbs. a year.

Wainwright: Are you doing anything different, Sandra?

Sandra: I think so· You know, before I would make a lot of roasts. Now you

What does a "typical" consumer think about the products and prices encountered in today's supermarket . . . in the drug store . . . in the shopping center? How does she/he shop? That information can help the national advertiser's planning. To help get it, ADVERTISING AGE is conducting a series of focus group interviews with shoppers in various parts of the country. Herein is the lightly edited transcript of the first such interview, held in Chicago, using only the first names of the consumer participants. It was conducted by Tony Wainwright of Wainwright, Spaeth & Wright, Chicago agency specializing in new product development.

don't even think about that, except maybe once a week. Now we have more ground meat recipes.

Wainwright: You add anything to it?

Eileen: No.

Wainwright: What's a box mix?

Eileen: Hamburger Helper!

Linda: You can do a lot more yourself. You pay 79¢ for noodles.

Alma: Where I shop, they've been giving us a new cook book each week. So I've been trying some of the things in there. It's nothing you'd buy a mix for. You make it all yourself.

Kathy: Like a meatloaf.

Wainwright: How about side dishes? Anybody serving them?

Rose: Oh, yes.

Wainwright: More or about the same?

Rose: I'm serving less. Of course, they are very expensive so you don't save much.

Wainwright: What is there today?

We Now Buy Pop Only Once a Week

Linda: Well, the only thing I can say is we're just eating cheaper cuts of meat. I haven't had steak since I can't remember when. But I have two teen age sons, and it's hard to tell them: You eat this

piece of meat—you don't get any more. You just can't say this to kids.

Kathy: All of a sudden you don't have the cookies and snacks in the house. Buy pop once a week instead of every time it runs out. All these things are changing.

Linda: I've found what I've done—we get paid twice a month. So my big shopping is twice a month, and I really go in for nothing else but milk and eggs. After they have gone through what I have bought, that's it.

Sandra: I also find I buy things on sale. If it's something I use, I will buy two, because I know when I run out it's going to be up in price.

Marvella: And then, too, don't you shop the specials of the week?

Sandra: If it's something I use, yes.

Wainwright: What about private labels?

Alma: A lot of them are a lot better.

Linda: Oh, I got some Del Monte string beans the other day, and they were about half full of string beans and were about the worst tasting stuff, so I just swore off Del Monte right there.

Rose: The only way you can beat it— is to do comparison shopping. I would suggest you look at the ads on Thursday nights and go to the A&P, go to the Jewel. You have to hit all the stores.

Eileen: By that time, you've wasted a day.

Sandra: That's the only way you can beat the game. Like I work. I don't have that kind of time for it. I'm better off sticking to one store.

Alma: They say that dried beans give you the same amount of protein. Supposedly, I've heard that.

Rose: There's no way my husband is going to sit down and eat a plate full of beans—unless he's at a campfire. He's strictly meat. I have to serve him that.

Wainright: What can you do to meat? If you serve a lot of hamburger, what do you do to vary it?

Ground Turkey Is Cheap

Marvella: Make chili, Sloppy Joes. And then the macaroni.

Linda: You can jazz up anything—a meatloaf, even.

Eileen: I think you get tired of it, though.

Sandra: I've been buying ground turkey because that's cheap, but I'm getting tired of that, too. I'd like a good roast.

Wainright: How about that soy protein?

Kathy: I've used that. You know, my husband couldn't tell the difference.

Marvella: I'll tell you what I've done. I make my spaghetti sauce, but when I cook the soy beans I use the packaged spaghetti flavoring in the water. Then I add that into my spaghetti sauce with maybe ½ lb. of ground meat or my chili sauce and this just extends it.

Alma: I had my sister over to dinner one day and made a hamburger out of it. Plain. It was sort of bland, but it wasn't terrible. It tasted like ground beef.

Wainright: What about sauces? Are any of you ladies using more sauces today?

Eileen: I marinate once in a while.

Rose: I use barbecue sauce mostly in the summer.

Wainright: How about meat tenderizers? Or marinades?

Kathy: Marinades, yes, I use them. I use A.1., Worcestershire, something like that in spaghetti, but I don't use French's or stuff like that—you know, packaged stuff.

Wanna Buy a Car? We'll Wait

Wainright: Let's switch to other areas. One item I'm thinking about is au-tomobiles. Today, they can't sell auto-mobiles.

Linda: No wonder.

Wainright: Do all of you own a car?

All: Yes!

Wainright: Have any of you considered trading it in or buying a new car?

Alma: We had full intentions of buying a new '75, until I looked at it and heard all the stuff about the catalytic converter and everything. My husband said we'll wait until '76. Maybe they'll come out with something better in '76.

Linda: But they are claiming that it is for pollution control and gasoline saving.

Rose: Sure, until the first time you have the wrong kind of gas in your car you have to spend $300 for a new one.

Wainright: Have any of you been to an auto dealer lately?

Linda: We bought a Dodge van, a '74. It's new, and we got it at the beginning of summer.

Wainright: Before you bought it did you go to several places?

Linda: Yes!

Wainright: Why did you pick that model?

Linda: We wanted a van. We didn't want all the extras. Couldn't afford it. They gave us the best deal. We would have gone to Chevy or Plymouth, but Dodge was the best, and we're real happy.

Wainright: What's the feeling when you go into a dealership? Do you feel as though you are being hustled?

Linda: No, no. I didn't. The one place, yes. That was terrible, but it would take me a long time to tell you about it. They kept upping the price every time. In fact, every time we went in. Mostly, they would not accept any trade-in. That was really funny. But where we did buy our car from, he gave us the price the first time my husband went in, and we went together again and looked and we shopped other places—five different agencies, and we came back. He was the lowest, and we're real happy with the service we get.

Wainright: How did you find those dealers?

Linda: My husband found them. We wanted to stay in the neighborhood. With a van, you couldn't order what you wanted. You had to take what they had left. We wanted a '74.

Alma: You bought late in the year?

Linda: Right.

Sandra: We have a Dodge van also. We bought it brand new. It's a '71. My husband shopped around for it. He got a pretty good deal on it. I was talking to Alma's father. He wants to buy a brand new van. He said a new van would cost $6,000. I think we paid $3,700 and we have a sportsman's van. He said there was nothing in it but a radio.

Marvella: That's what I object to.

Kathy: The new Century sport model advertises for $3,800, but there's nothing in it. No heater.

Eileen: All it has is a motor and four tires. All the extras like side mirrors, radio, etc., cost more. The price starts going up.

Wainright: Is there a difference now between the American car and the foreign car?

Rose: You can't get parts for foreign cars.

Wainright: You can't get parts?

Rose: We had an Opel and we loved it! But we couldn't get a $3 part.

Warranty: Nothing for Nothing?

Linda: I took my car in on a warranty . . .

Sandra: A warranty is nothing. They give you nothing for nothing.

Linda: I have a beautiful dealer. I have no complaints with him. As long as that car was under a warranty I could take it in for anything.

Rose: I've heard so many people complain about their warranty. Once the dealer makes a sale, you can forget it.

Wainright: What about Volkswagen?

Marvella: We love ours. We have to get a new car. I don't know if we will get a Volkswagen. Ours is a '71, but we now have a six-month-old baby and we want a heavier car.

Linda: Now they're advertising Volkswagen in bigger models.

Kathy: Volkswagens are beautiful to run, economical, but ours was sideswiped twice. It was not a bad accident, but the sides looked like an accordion. Outside of that, it's a great car.

Alma: My husband has a '68 Plymouth that he wants to turn in. But he goes back and forth to work on a tank of gas for two weeks . . . he says he will run that thing until it runs into the ground.

Kathy: My daughter drives a Vega '74 stick shift. She gets 25 miles to the gallon. I've got a Maverick '74, and I get about 11.

Wainright: What would induce you to go to a dealer this week?

Car Payments, Never—We Pay Cash

Rose: Absolutely nothing. We never

buy a new car. We have only bought used. We pay cash for it.

Linda: Car payments! Never. It's not worth it. The day we buy a new car—we pay cash for it.

Wainright: If you went to a used car lot to buy a used car would you . . .

Rose: I'd bring my own mechanic along!

Linda: Recently, Channel 7 did a story on used car lots. They were trying to crack down on them. They had a reporter drive in an old clunker and have someone come in and want to buy it. The guy upped the price about $600. They drove it for about three blocks and the motor fell out!

Sandra: I don't think I would trust a used car dealer.

Wainright: Would you trust a new car dealer?

Sandra: No, not necessarily.

Wainright: What if someone wanted to sell cars today? What should he do?

Alma: In the first place, he has to be an established dealer and give good service. And if he gives good service, you will go back even if you have to pay another $50 for a car. It all goes down to the service manager. Anybody can sell a car, but the question is how they take care of the car after you buy it.

Marvella: I feel going to the same dealer every two or three years would give you a better chance . . .

Linda: Definitely.

Kathy: They know the car you are trading in because they've been taking care of it. And they've got all the records on that car.

Sandra: If you have a very good relationship with your car dealer, you wouldn't be beyond telling everybody how great he is, and then perhaps they would get a good deal, too.

Wainright: If you were a dealer, how would you advertise your cars?

Alma: I think you should get a big brother image—someone you can trust and put all your faith into. Jim Moran was up there and lived up to everything.

Rose: That I don't know. He got you in there to try his place out.

Wainright: Are there any women who sell cars?

Linda: Yes, at our agency, Keystone, there must have been seven women who sold cars.

Wainright: Would you have more confidence or be more at ease if your salesperson was a woman?

Eileen: I don't think my husband would talk to them.

Alma: My husband would!

Wainright: Who makes the decision as to what kind of car you're going to buy?

Linda: I've been shopping with my husband for the last five years and I finally got him around to my thinking.

Marvella: Nine times out of ten, I've got the time during the day to go out looking for the kind of car I want. Then I'll come home and tell my husband what I found. We go to look at it and both decide.

Wainright: Anybody else?

Linda: I don't drive, so my husband decides. I decide on the color and interior.

Rose: I'm the one who has the time to take the car in to be serviced. My husband doesn't have time.

Wainright: Do you find that when you take the car in for service, they do what you want?

Rose: You better believe it.

Linda: I came in with a list from my husband and it told them exactly what had to be done. When they didn't do it, my husband had to get on their backs.

Marvella: When I drove my car out of the showroom, the rubber bumper in back was hanging off. The dealer told me to bring it in when I had a chance. I brought it in with a long list of what had to be done. One week later they didn't do a damn thing. I went in there and screamed and used language unbecoming to a lady. Everything had to be ordered. I said I wouldn't pay for anything.

Kathy: The only experience we had was when the brakes went out and they claimed it had gone past the warranty. My husband called the district. The next day we took the car in and they fixed it.

Wainright: Who did your husband get hold of?

Kathy: The district manager. In other words, a Ford representative. Don't even talk to the Ford people you bought it from.

Marvella: Whether it be Chrysler, Ford, etc., if you go over their heads, the people who made the car will back it up. Especially if it's something within reason.

Wainright: Now's the time to buy a car, because we should all pitch in and help the economy. Does that make sense?

Rose: Not at the price of new cars. No!

Linda: That doesn't make sense because just last night on tv someone said we're supposed to stop buying.

Sandra: If you know anything about the economy, you have to stop buying everything.

Eileen: I think they mean everything.

Alma: Keep your heat down, throw on a sweater, buy warmer clothing.

$9 for Non-Leather Baby Shoes

Wainright: What other purchases are you concerned about?

Rose: Clothes and shoes. I have two teen age daughters. The prices for their clothing are ridiculous. One's a freshman and one's a junior. They are out of children's sizes, definitely, but I pay the same price for my clothing as I do for theirs.

Alma: I have a six-month-old baby who needs shoes. I went to Sears and a couple of other places. They wanted $9, and he isn't walking yet. I wouldn't mind paying $9 for leather shoes, but they're not leather.

Wainright: Is there a store or a series of stores you have more confidence in?

Eileen: I prefer to shop around my own home. I don't like to run around all those shopping centers to go shopping. I can't stand it.

Wainright: What about Sears, Ward's?

Eileen: I hate Sears in Golf Mill with a passion.

Wainright: Why?

Eileen: My daughter worked there, but I still did not shop there. For one thing, it's too crowded. If you picked up one pen, there would be no one to tell you if there was a better pen. You couldn't get comparison shopping.

Wainright: At Sears there is nobody to help you?

Eileen: Not really.

Kathy: Not really good service.

Alma: They have an awful lot of people, but they don't want to help you.

Kathy: They have their racks overcrowded. You can't push the merchandise apart.

Eileen: I went to Sears one Friday night at 6. I thought I was losing my mind. The crowds were unbelievable.

Alma: Their prices aren't that good.

Kathy: They started out with a very cheap image. They are not cheap any more. Their prices have gone up and up.

Linda: Their prices are equal to any good store.

Kathy: That's right. That's what I'm saying.

Rose: They don't hassle you when you bring something back.

Eileen: Never.

Marvella: You can bring things back a year later. They will not ask you one **single question.**

Alma: That's one plus for Sears.

Sears, Walgreen's Look Good

Sandra: There's another plus for Sears. I just found out this year. They are known for their hardware. If anything breaks, they will take it back, even from a woman, with no argument.

Marvella: Sears also carries the odd sizes.

Wainwright: What about shopping at drug stores?

Linda: I go to Walgreen's. A lot of items are cheaper.

Alma: Toiletries.

Eileen: My son's vitamins and things.

Wainwright: How many of you have savings accounts in banks?

Alma: We have two savings accounts. We used to have one we just put money into and never took out. When we bought our first home, we started a second one for furniture, etc. And we have another account from which we borrow. Hardly anything is going into it now. It's not like it used to be.

Eileen: I feel sorry for anyone living on a pension or social security. I can't imagine how they make out.

Linda: Even if they own their own building, their income is so fixed and so small. Everything is going up, and they still have the same needs.

Sandra: My grandmother is very lucky. She not only has social security, she's got a pension from my grandfather.

Wainwright: It's hard to save money, so where is your cushion coming from?

Linda: That's a good question.

Alma: We have a pension plan, whereby they match dollar for dollar what we put in. You can take it out in stock or saving. We took it out in saving. They take it out of our check.

Rose: That's another thing—an insurance policy.

Wainwright: Have you bought an insurance policy?

Rose: That we have.

Wainwright: How many of you have insurance?

Marvella: At 65 you start collecting on it. Sort of an annuity policy, where you put $1 in and the company puts $10 in—it's like a savings account.

Rose: You want to hear something surprising? My girl friend was making a Halloween costume and it involved play money. She went to the dime store and they don't make it anymore. You know what they have instead for children to play with—a checkbook and credit cards.

Is that a comment on the state of our economy or not?

Linda: I heard that at checkout counters they are now using little magnetic tapes on the packages.

Rose: How can they do that?

Linda: It's computerized.

Marvella: How is the consumer going to know what she's paying?

Alma: It's going to be posted on the shelf.

Linda: I found that computers make mistakes. How many times have you gotten a Diner's Club bill or a Master Charge bill with somebody else's charges on it? Every other month I'm writing them a letter.

Alma: Did you get through to them?

Linda: You know how? I mutilated that card, and when you do, the card pops out and a human being must touch it. Put a couple of staples in it . . .

Rose: I had trouble with Rothchild's. They had my charge up to $200. I wrote them about two months in a row, and I finally got so mad I punched holes in the card and wrote on it: "Now read the letter that came with this card."

Sandra: That's the only way to get an answer from them any more. The trouble is that nobody cares! #

Applications of Focus Group Interviews in Marketing

KEITH K. COX, JAMES B. HIGGINBOTHAM, AND JOHN BURTON

The focus group interview is an effective qualitative technique in marketing research. Three actual marketing applications illustrate the usefulness of this approach for marketing mix problems.

Although focus group interviews have been used by many marketing research firms since the 1950s, their role in the decision-making process is not always clearly understood by marketing management. This article describes three actual applications of the focus group interview in marketing research and management decision making, and discusses the strengths and weaknesses of the technique.

The Focus Group Interview

Basically, there are two types of group interview studies. One is nothing more than a question and answer session: the group moderator asks questions and the respondents give verbal or written answers. A second type is the *focus group interview*, where a group of people (generally eight to twelve) are led through an open, in-depth discussion by a group moderator. The moderator's objective is to focus the discussion on the relevant subject areas in a nondirective manner. Such interviews can be used to develop hypotheses in the planning or qualitative stage of the marketing research process. The interviews provide a basis in depth for the development of additional research, and they may be useful as a source of new and fresh ideas for new products and services, advertising themes, packaging evaluations, and the like.

Marketing Applications

Focus group interviews can be effective research tools in many types of marketing decision situations. The examples given here illustrate the usefulness of the technique in three distinct deci-sion areas: (1) pricing and advertising, (2) a new product, and (3) packaging.[1]

Example 1: Alpha Power and Light

The Alpha company had requested an electricity rate increase in its trading area for the first time in 20 years and wanted to know (1) customer opinions of the rate increase, and (2) reasons for customer resistance to the rate increase, such as general service problems. Alpha company was asking for a rate increase of 6%, which it felt was reasonable and necessary. The company planned to use the research results in its negotiations about price, and for future advertising campaign ideas. Table 1 highlights the three stages of the marketing research process used in this research project.

The first stage of the research project was qualitative in nature. It was designed to identify where the company was at the present time in terms of perceived image of the company and degree of consumer dissatisfaction with rates and services, using the internal interview and audit process described in Table 1.

The information obtained in the first stage was used in guiding the researchers in the second stage of the research, where focus group interview sessions were conducted. The focus group inter-

---

1. Each marketing application comes from an actual marketing research project conducted in 1972 and 1973, but the company names are disguised.

· *ABOUT THE AUTHORS.*
Keith K. Cox is professor of marketing in the College of Business Administration, University of Houston.
James B. Higginbotham is president and John Burton is vice president of Higginbotham Associates, Houston.

Reprinted from *Journal of Marketing*, **40 (January 1976), 77-80, published by the American Marketing Association.**

TABLE 1
STAGES IN THE MARKETING RESEARCH PROCESS FOR ALPHA POWER AND LIGHT

Stage 1 (Qualitative)	Stage 2 (Qualitative)	Stage 3 (Quantitative)
Objectives	*Objectives*	*Objectives*
1. Identify past and current consumer complaints as to service problems and rate dissatisfaction	1. Evaluate consumer attitudes toward utility companies in this area generally	1. Quantify existing consumer attitudes toward service and rate problems
2. Identify perceived image of company as estimated by company employees	2. Develop hypotheses on rate and service problems of customers	2. Quantify existing consumer images of the company
3. Evaluate past advertising and other materials communicated to consumers	3. Develop psychographic profiles of respondents' attitudes about this company and this service	3. Evaluate hypotheses about consumer attitudes
	4. Identify specific topics for questionnaire construction	4. Develop communication ideas for future advertising campaigns
Research Methodology	*Research Methodology*	*Research Methodology*
1. Personal interviews with company executives, complaint department employees, and field linemen	1. Focus group interviews (12 groups of 10 persons in each group), each interview session videotaped	1. Random sample of 700 adult persons using telephone interviews (100 interviews in each of 7 company districts)
2. Audit of past records of consumer complaints	2. Short, self-administered questionnaire for all 120 persons	
3. Audit of past company advertisements		

views were originally intended to obtain relevant information about the following questions:

1. Why were those consumers who opposed the rate hike really opposed?
2. What information should be communicated to those consumers opposed in order to justify a rate increase to them?
3. What reasons were given by those consumers not opposed to a rate increase?
4. How important were general service problems in influencing consumer opinions about a rate increase?

The focus group interviews uncovered a "rate bargaining" phenomenon among the groups, which could be traced back to their fear of an energy shortage and the possibility of fast-rising prices for consumer goods and services. In general, consumers wanted assurances of available utilities and were willing to pay for these services, but they felt that price changes should be negotiated within a bargaining process. In addition, valuable advertising communication themes regarding consumer resistance to the rate increase were suggested by the interviews.

In the third stage of the research process, the hypotheses developed from the first two stages were quantitatively measured. A random telephone sample of 700 people was conducted in the company's trading area. Quantitative results were obtained about consumer attitudes toward service and rate issues, and alternative communicative ideas were evaluated for future advertising campaigns.

Example 2: Johnson Car Air Conditioning Filter

The Johnson company developed a new filter to be used in car air conditioning systems. Management wanted to find out the feasibility of the new product and develop a workable marketing plan. A two-stage research process was followed. Focus group interviews were used in stage 1 to help develop hypotheses to identify potential markets, to determine advantages and disadvantages of the product from the consumer viewpoint, and to identify specific points for questionnaire design.

The focus group interviews indicated that families in which one or more members had allergy or respiratory problems might be the best prospects for the new product. Persons seriously concerned about air pollution were also identified as good potential buyers. The major disadvantages of the product were the performance capability of the filter and the cost of replacement cartridges. Some individuals feared that the filter

102

would cause their car's air conditioning system to malfunction. Nonallergic consumers expressed doubt about their need for the product. An unexpected resistance occurred when consumers were informed that the filter would need to be changed periodically.

After hearing the results of the focus group, the client wanted to proceed immediately with market introduction as a result of the findings that seemed favorable. On the advice of the research firm, the quantitative study in stage 2 of the research process was conducted. An analysis of 1500 respondents in five cities showed that the original marketing strategy for introducing the new product was not economically feasible. This led to the development of an alternative marketing plan.

Example 3: Harris Meat Company

The Harris meat company had declining sales of its luncheon meat wieners and franks in one region during the previous year and needed to identify and isolate reasons for the lack of sales growth. In this case, the focus group interviews exposed a serious packaging problem and minor problems in shelf space allocation and competitive pricing. The packaging problem had extensive ramifications for the product's image, the ease of using the product, the quantity and quality of the shelf space exposure it received, and the consumer's decision to buy certain sizes of the product. The interviews produced very clear hypotheses for explaining consumer behavior and brand penetration in particular market segments. Housewives in the focus groups explained clearly why the packaging was a problem to them. Therefore, the quantitative study was narrowed to specific alternatives for improving the packaging strategy, communicating brand attributes, and increasing distribution penetration.

Evaluation and Implications

Focus group interviews have several advantages for marketing management. First, they help generate hypotheses in the qualitative stage of research. They can provide a stimulus to creative people (copy writers, creative directors, new product managers, etc.), who need to have first-hand contact with how consumers think, feel, use, and talk about the product. Many times, in fact, it is good to involve these people in the evaluation of the group sessions so that they will be more receptive to the findings of the quantitative research results.

Focus group interviews can also give direction and guidelines for constructing questionnaires. Lists of relevant areas of interest of the target audience to be measured can be developed from the groups. With these lists, the risk of addressing the wrong problem is minimized.

The focus group interview can and does bridge the gap between marketing management at the manufacturing level and the end user of the product or service. Although top management should have frequent contact with the users of the product, in actual practice this contact is seldom made. The use of focus group interviews and one-way mirrors or videotape recordings is an effective and efficient means for bridging the gap from busy top executive to the ultimate consumer of the product.

There are also, however, a number of limitations in using focus group interviews. First, the moderator can bias the group results if he or she does not have adequate training and experience in conducting focus group sessions. A poorly conducted group session can be very costly if it misdirects the quantitative stage.

One serious problem that has grown in importance with increasing costs of quantitative research and tight research budgets is the use of focus groups as the only source of information in planning and decision making. For an expenditure of $3,500 to $4,000, the brand manager or advertising agency executive can point to a fat report filled with marketing jargon and page after page of verbatim comments and say—this research backs up our new advertising campaign or our product promotion. But although the advertising campaign or promotion may be great for the segment of the population represented by those in the groups who gave rise to the idea, the key question remains: How big is the segment? What is the expected dollar return?

One way of minimizing the disadvantage of the focus group interview as the only source of information is to take a sample survey. If researchers generalize from the focus group interview results without further quantitative verification, they are on very weak methodological ground. Therefore, one important rule for researchers is: "Don't generalize quantitative results from focus group interviews."

Focus group interviews are widely used by marketing researchers today in such decision areas as new product development, advertising campaigns, and evaluation of existing marketing strategies. The major advantage of this technique is in terms of developing hypotheses that can be quantitatively tested to produce further results. The focus group interview is one of a number of qualitative research techniques that can be profitably employed along with quantitative techniques to help marketing managers make better decisions.

Focus groups can give marketer early clues on marketability of new product

BY MELVIN PRINCE
J. B. Williams Co.
New York

EARLY, TENTATIVE impressions about the marketability of a new product can be of considerable value to the marketer, and it is possible to get such impressions through qualitative methods. The qualitative method to which I refer is the focus group approach, which we have used in connection with a number of men's fragrance products. The focus group involves, typically, eight to 12 participants in a single session.

(In the men's fragrance area, J. B. Williams Co. markets a number of products including Aqua Velva cologne and Mon Triomphe. —Editor)

One of the major purposes of this kind of research for the introduction for a new men's fragrance is to determine how well various elements of the developing product are integrated. The individual strengths of the name, concept, product, packaging, and advertising mean little unless they form a coherent configuration which results in a high level of consumer receptivity.

IN ADDITION TO obtaining impressions about how these marketing elements are coordinated for a new men's fragrance, another objective for qualitative work is to explore weaknesses and suggest refinements in the product, refinements which can maximize its appeal.

In order to implement the qualitative work, the first issue that must be settled concerns sampling—who will be the subjects for focus group sessions? This decision requires some hard thinking about the nature of the target market for the new men's fragrance and the pattern of purchase decision making that can be expected for this market.

The men's fragrance market is multi-tiered; various price and prestige levels stratify the overall market into a number of sub-markets with characteristic consumer profiles.

Sampling decisions for a focus group would use as criteria: age, sex, and brands previously purchased or used. Additional sampling criteria such as marital status and income level might be considered, as well.

There are no hard and fast rules for the format for qualitative exploration in the area of a new men's fragrance. But I can offer some guidelines for this kind of work which the reader may well find useful.

THE NAME of a men's fragrance is regarded as a most important element of the overall appeal, and one strategy is to open the group session with a presentation of the name of the product, while indicating to consumers that it is a new men's fragrance. Reactions to the name alone give a preliminary indication of effect—as well as the kinds of associations and imageries which the name produces. It also provides a set for the consumer's evaluation of the other elements of the men's fragrance product.

Following the exploration of the name, consumers are asked to describe their experiences in purchasing and using men's fragrances. By doing this, they rehearse the criteria used for purchasing, evaluating, and repurchasing these products. Also, it forces consumers to think about the way in which the men's fragrance market is structured, in terms of available brands and benefits.

The consumer is then redirected to the men's fragrance, the name of which has been learned previously. The name is exposed once again: this time it is seen on the packaging. In the interviewing we look for expressions of harmony between the name and the packaging and for projections of product and user imagery that these elements, in combinations, elicit.

Usually this will mean successive exposures to an outer carton and then to a bottle which is removed from the carton. Among the issues at this point are the compatibility of carton and bottle; the esthetics of the bottle, including cap and label design; reaction to the color of the product, if the product is exposed through the bottle; and any physical or "human factor" properties of the bottle which are important to consumers, involving storage or handling and use.

NOW THE CONSUMERS think they are going to sample the fragrance, but *no*. Before this happens they will be exposed to the advertising which relates to the name and package, the imagery, and claims for the product. Once again, name and packaging are appraised—but this time against the backdrop of the product concept.

The product concept itself is analyzed for its appeals and weaknesses, as well as for its distinctiveness.

Only then are the group session's participants permitted to use the product and then to learn of its approximate pricing.

The fragrance itself is appraised in terms of prior expectations, and consumers are probed for their degree of delight or disappointment with the fragrance and for the underlying reasons for their reactions.

With the use of this method it is possible to provide early direction as regards some important issues:

Are certain population segments

Reprinted from *Marketing News,* **XII** (September 8, 1978), 12, published by the **American Marketing Association.**

more receptive than others to this product? For example, do women like it much more than men?

Would women buy it for men?

What is the user image of the brand?

Is this seen as a product for a younger or an older man? For a free thinking or a traditional man?

Is the product aroma strong and overpowering or light and subtle? Is it perfumy or clean?

Does the name, in itself, provide an instant association, or is it devoid of meaning? Does the name project particular kinds of fragrance qualities: lightness of fragrance, etc.?

Does the carton suggest a product image that is different from the image provided by the name alone? Is the name rejected after it has been seen on the carton? Is the carton rejected on the basis of esthetics?

THE ANSWERS to these questions will provide guidance concerning the new men's fragrance's market vitality—the degree of appeal, overall and for the name, the carton design, the bottle, the advertising, and the product. The research will provide also suggested directions for improvement.

AN EARLIER version of this presentation was given by Prince at Metro Expo 6 in New York in the spring of '78.

EXPLORATORY GROUP INTERVIEW IN CONSUMER RESEARCH: A CASE EXAMPLE[1]

Thomas D. Dupont,[2] Oxtoby-Smith Inc.

Abstract

Several applications of focus group interviewing are
described, together with the unique advantages of this
technique. The paper focuses on the use of exploratory
group interviewing as a preliminary to a larger, quantified study. A case example of research conducted for
Volvo of America Corporation is presented as an illustration of the functions of exploratory group interviewing.

Introduction

"Look, my budget's tight and we don't have much time.
Let's just do a couple of groups."

"We need to talk with these people to find out what
they think. We've got to really dig in below surface
opinions. So let's round some up and do some groups."

"I understand the client's problem, but I don't even
know who we should survey or what questions we should
ask. Let's recommend that we start with a couple of
groups and design the quantification after we have a
better idea of what the relevant issues are."

Sound familiar?

I'm not saying that those are the only reasons why
market researchers use focus group interviews, but my
guess is that those three scenarios account for a substantial majority of them.

Is there anything wrong with this?

Certainly not. Those three situations are made to
order for group interviews. In fact, there are a
variety of very good reasons why one would wish to
conduct group interviews:

1. Group interviews can be conducted very quickly,
and relatively inexpensively.

2. They sometimes provide the only mechanism by which
a senior researcher can talk face-to-face with consumers. Individual depth interviews, the alternative,
are simply too expensive in most circumstances.

3. Group interviews provide the opportunity for the
non-research client -- the Product Manager, Vice
President - Marketing, Sales Manager -- to listen to

what consumers are saying about his product and the
way he sells it. What he hears is sometimes painful,
but almost always enlightening.

4. Group interviews are flexible. The moderator is
not tied to a fixed sequence of questions, but can skip
topics which seem to be unproductive and zero-in on
areas which are productive. Sometimes, the ability of
a good moderator to exploit such "targets of opportunity" can result in purely serendiptious findings of
great importance to the client. Such results emerge
less frequently from field interviews.

5. Participants in the group can interact and stimulate
one another. While a group interview is in no sense
similar to a group therapy session, and the moderator
is in no sense a therapist, the plain fact is that the
group situation -- provided it is a secure and comfortable one -- often encourages respondents to dis-
close attitudes and behaviors which they might not
admit in an individual interview situation.

Just as there are a number of good reasons for conducting group interviews, there are a number of
problems which can be addressed in group interviews.
By way of example, within the past year, Oxtoby-Smith
has used group interviews:

1. To explore consumer reaction to new product concepts;

2. To explore consumer response to both advertising
concepts and finished ads;

3. To generate ideas for new products;

4. To explore consumer response to package designs
and labeling; and

5. To explore differences in perception between a live
demonstration of a product and a filmed presentation.

However, the most important function of group interviewing at Oxtoby-Smith is as a device to guide the
design and conduct of a subsequent large-scale quantitative survey. In this context, group interviews
are used:

1. To identify and understand consumer language as it
relates to the product category in question. What
terms do they use? What do they mean?

2. To identify the range of consumer concerns. How
much variability is there among consumers in how they
view the product and in the considerations which lead
them to accept or reject the product?

3. To identify the complexity of consumer concerns.
Are there a few simple attitudes which govern consumer
reaction toward the product, or is the structure complex, involving many contingencies?

---

[1] The author expresses his appreciation to Lars
Samuelson, Vice President -- Marketing, Volvo of
America Corporation, for permission to publish this
paper, and for supporting the research described
herein.

[2] Thomas D. Dupont is Vice President, Oxtoby-Smith Inc.,
New York, N. Y.

Reprinted from *Advances In Consumer Research*, **IV** (1976), 431-33.

106

4. To identify specific methodological or logistical problems which are likely to affect either the cost of the subsequent research, or our ability to generate meaningful, actionable findings at all.

I'd like to describe a project we recently completed which illustrates these four functions of exploratory group sessions.

A Case Study

Background Of The Case

For the past six years, Oxtoby-Smith has been conducting consumer research for Volvo of America Corporation. During that period, we have witnessed a substantial change in the marketplace as it affects Volvo:

1. Consumers seem increasingly interested in cars like Volvo -- functional, durable, compact and safe.

2. Until very recently, Volvo and a few other imports had this segment to themselves; prior to Ford's introduction of the Granada there was little direct domestic competition in this segment.

3. Most importantly, because of successive devaluations of the dollar and other economic factors, the price of the least expensive Volvo has risen from about $3,300 in 1972 to about $5,500 in 1975.

It became increasingly apparent to Volvo marketing management, and to Volvo's advertising agency, that whereas Volvo used to compete primarily with a small group of imports (mainly Audi), in the future Volvo, because of its price level, would be increasingly competing with domestic luxury cars (Buick Electra, Chrysler Cordoba, Ford Elite, and even Cadillac and Lincoln Continental).

In consequence of these changes, we decided to undertake a study to explore the differences between Volvo buyers and Volvo considerers (people who thought about buying a Volvo, but in the end bought some other car). We wanted to learn the reasons for buying a Volvo, and the resistances to buying a Volvo.

The Study Design

Our study design, as you might guess, involved inquiry among two respondent populations -- people who had recently bought Volvos, and people who had recently considered buying Volvos, but instead bought competitive makes.

Finding buyers is easy -- Volvo has lists. Finding considerers is not so easy, especially since a previous attempt at getting Volvo dealers to record the names and addresses of all prospects was a dismal failure.

Accordingly, we decided to buy lists of buyers of new car models who we felt would be most likely to have considered Volvo. This selection of models was based upon the premise that the cars Volvo buyers reject are the same cars which Volvo considerers buy. Since we knew from previous research what other cars Volvo buyers consider, we had our list of models. The design called for two phases of research:

1. An exploratory stage, involving four group interviews -- two with Volvo buyers and two with Volvo considerers (prior research had taught us that buyers

and considerers don't mix well; buyers dominate the sessions by proselytizing about Volvo).

2. A quantification phase involving telephone interviews with 400 first-time Volvo buyers and 200 Volvo considerers.

In the remainder of this paper, we'd like to describe what we learned in the exploratory group sessions, and how what we learned affected the design and conduct of the quantification study.

What We Learned From The Sessions Themselves

We had conducted a great deal of research for Volvo in the past and had generated a number of hypotheses about what makes a considerer become a Volvo buyer. In spite of this extensive background in the product area, however, we still learned important things in the groups which permitted us to conduct a quantification study which was both more insightful and less expensive than we would otherwise have conducted.

Let me give you a few examples.

Volvo considerers differ sharply in the way in which they consider Volvo. One of the most important things we learned -- which confirmed what we suspected -- was that there are a number of different ways in which considerers considered Volvo. Some considered Volvo very seriously, and narrowed the choice of cars to Volvo and one other make. Others considered Volvo seriously, but it was not among the cars which survived until the final decision. (In selecting respondents for the groups, we asked whether they seriously considered a Volvo, and only serious considerers were recruited. Prior experience had taught us that a question like, "Did you consider buying a _____" is a very weak question. Many consumers will say they considered buying a product even if that consideration was very fleeting and casual.) Even within the "serious considerers," the ways of considering Volvo varied enormously:

1. Some test drove the car and haggled over price with the dealer.

2. Others evaluated the car carefully, but did not get to the point of negotiations with the dealer.

3. Some considered the car seriously without ever visiting a showroom, relying instead on word-of-mouth and ratings of the car in magazines like "Consumers Report," "Motor Trend," and the like.

Accordingly, we felt it crucial in our quantification study to include questions which would enable us to segment considerers according to the degree to which they seriously considered Volvo and the methods they used to arrive at their purchase choice. To that end, we designed a question to determine which specific actions were taken in considering Volvo, such as talking with Volvo owners, reading evaluative articles in magazines, paying more attention to Volvo advertising, visiting a Volvo showroom, negotiating over price, and others.

Volvo buyers and considerers are highly segmented. Since Volvo's share of the U.S. auto market is less than 1%, it would be reasonable to expect that Volvo buyers, and to a lesser extent, Volvo considerers, are relatively homogeneous in terms of demography, attitude and preference. However, while it is true that these groups are more homogeneous than U.S. car buyers at large, it is nevertheless the case that segmentation is very real within Volvo's market.

1. Volvo buyers range from those who bought Volvo as a less expensive alternative to Mercedes to middle-income Americans who must strain to afford the car. They range from first-time import buyers to those who would never consider a domestic car.

2. Volvo considerers vary even more widely than do Volvo buyers, from "typical domestic buyers" interested in styling, power, status, and a familiar name to "typical import buyers" interested in economy, functionalism, durability, and "foreign craftmanship." These group interviews strongly suggested that the primary variable differentiating the Volvo buyer from the Volvo considerer was the set of concerns that individual brought with him to the car-buying process. Further, it was readily apparent from the groups that these concerns varied widely, implying that it would be necessary in the quantification to measure the importance to the consumer of a number of characteristics of a car, such as safety, exterior styling, anticipated cost of service, and so forth. In consequence, we prepared a list of 26 automobile attributes -- some drawn from prior research and some new ones based upon the group session findings to present to consumers in the quantification. It was our hope (subsequently realized) that importance ratings of these items would prove to be extremely powerful in discriminating between Volvo buyers and Volvo considerers.

However, the desirability of this approach left us with a methodological dilemma. It was important that we not only learn the importance of these 26 factors to Volvo buyers and considerers, but also that we learn, among considerers, how Volvo stacked up, on the factors they considered important, against the car actually bought.

The logical alternative, after having the respondent rate all 26 factors for importance was to have him rank the five factors which played the largest role in the automobile selection decision, and then rate Volvo versus the competitive car on those top five factors. Clearly, it would be expecting too much to have the respondent perform this task in a telephone interview. It was critical, we felt, that the respondent have the 26 factors in front of him while he was going through the rating process. Thus, we were left with two alternative methodologies -- personal interviews or mail. As we will see, the screening experience in recruiting respondents for the sessions strongly influenced our choice between these two alternatives.

What We Learned From The Recruiting Process

As was mentioned earlier, prospective participants for the group sessions were recruited from lists of recent buyers of cars felt to be competitive with Volvo. In order to be invited to a session, the respondent had to indicate that he seriously considered buying a Volvo.

As it happens, the results of the screening for serious considerers proved very instructive; we had to contact about 1,000 recent new car buyers to recruit approximately 20 focus group respondents. While we knew we could expect a higher cooperation rate in the quantification, since respondents would not have to leave their homes, the fact remained that the incidence of

Volvo considerers, even among buyers of selected models, was very small. Accordingly, a quantification study conducted via telephone interviewing, to say nothing of personal interviewing, would substantially exceed the budget which Volvo had set aside for this project.

In that circumstance, we decided to conduct the study as a mail survey -- a decision which permitted us to collect the rating information which we could not collect over the telephone, while at the same time saving Volvo a considerable sum of money (we estimate about $10,000). The mail survey went smoothly, the quantification verified some of the hypotheses we had generated in the group sessions (and refuted others), and the results of the study have since played an important role in the development of Volvo advertising and marketing strategies for 1976.

Summary

In summary, this example illustrates quite well the value of conducting a few exploratory group interviews prior to a larger, quantified study. Such an exploration will not always pay for itself in a more efficient final research design, as this one more than did, but it will nearly always lead to a subsequent survey richer in content, more adroit in interpretation, and more actionable to marketing management. That is why Oxtoby-Smith -- as well as many of our competitors -- makes a standard practice of conducting some exploratory group interviews prior to any extensive data collection effort, even when the product area is one with which we are highly familiar.

Group depth interviews also have consulting and creative uses

BY ALFRED E. GOLDMAN
President
National Analysts Inc.
Philadelphia, Pa.

ALL GROUP DEPTH INTERVIEWS AREN'T NECESSARILY MARKETING RESEARCH. Many are conducted for consulting and creative purposes. Let's look at these three overlapping and interacting uses—consulting, creative, and research—and see what the group interview can and cannot contribute.

Such a review of the technique's functions should help understand much of the support for and criticism of the group interview. Those who enthusiastically laud the technique seem to assess its virtues within the context of its legitimate use while critics often cite "deficiencies" that group interviewing was never intended to provide.

The group interview isn't necessarily a **research** technique and should not be assessed exclusively as such. Perhaps even more important is that use of the group interview solely within a research context unnecessarily constrains its usefulness.

Although the boundaries between the technique's consulting, creative, and research functions are blurred by definition and intention, I'll describe how varying objectives can be served by this remarkably versatile technique.

CONSULTING — Management, whether marketing, advertising, manufacturing, or finance, often is confronted with an unfamiliar area—a product manager assigned a totally new product, a corporate planning director asked to assess a potential acquisition of which relatively little is known, or an ad agency required to learn about the products or services of a potential client prior to making a presentation seeking the account.

The principal objective is learning about a field quite alien to those given the management responsibility and usually having to do so under time pressure. Though much valuable secondary source data is available in the public domain, the prudent manager will want direct, immediate exposure to the ultimate purchaser involved. He needs a personal, in-depth understanding, particularly the determinants of purchase and the perceived assets and liabilities of competition.

Such consulting group interviews work best when the qualitative researcher is a member of a total consulting team, which may consist of marketers, financial people, and technical specialists, whose attention is focused on relevant issues and whose questions are translated into probing inquiries of session participants.

Some examples may illustrate the role of group interviews in a consulting assignment:

1. A conglomerate considers acquisition of a high technology company. The product line of the potential acquisition is well known to some of the firm's management, but it is less confident about how this line is viewed by the market.

Groups are convened with dealers, institutional purchasing agents and administrators, and also the medical experts who, in this case, play a major role in determining purchase. The research professionals who conduct the groups are prepared for the task by other team members:

A. Technicians orient moderators with as much detail as they will need to create sufficient technical credibility to establish rapport with group members, to recognize important issues raised, and to permit meaningful, incisive probing.

B. Marketers suggest the most relevant components of the market to interview and to identify how and where relevant participants may be found.

C. Financial specialists focus the moderator's attention on areas of inquiry that will assist them in assessing the future financial viability of the acquisition (for example, price elasticity, alternative methods of purchase, etc.).

2. A company considers an acquisition that produces an energy product that is subject to public controversy. Management is concerned that such an acquisition may adversely affect its own corporate image, fail to engender support of its shareholders, and perhaps ultimately impact negatively on the price of its stocks.

Group interviews are conducted with each of the relevant universes—shareholders, financial analysts, and the public as a whole—and the findings are integrated into the final report of the consulting team. Thus, these attitudinal issues are weighed along with those conventionally analyzed when an acquisition is contemplated.

3. Still other examples of situations in which group depth interviews have been included as an integral part of the consulting assignment are: exploration of the potential of

Reprinted from *Marketing News*, **IX (January 16, 1976), 11, 15**, published by the **American Marketing Association.**

a new building material prior to entering into a royalty agreement and searching for a means of utilizing a technology that had required considerable investment to develop, but seemed inapplicable to consumer needs based on early product and concept work.

In summary, the characteristics that distinguish the consulting mode of group interviewing from creative and research modes are the kinds of problems it addresses, its location within the context of a consulting team, and the infrequency with which it is followed by subsequent phases of research.

CREATIVE—A copywriter who carefully fashions a commercial to address a given market segment, may ask whether his words communicate the message he intends.

Are the words understood? Is the copy platform a meaningful one? Does the story line support the message? Other members of the creative team may ask, Are the music and lyrics congruent in tone and mood with the main theme? Is the creative execution appropriate to the underlying theme of the campaign? Is the executional context of the story line relevant to the message and theme?

The ad team may not only need feedback on completed creative efforts but also may welcome initial provocative insights to get the creative juices flowing. The group interview conducted in the creative mode requires that the moderator play a more active role in the creative process.

In the mid 1950s when National Analysts introduced group interviewing as a service to its clients, a rather rigorous objectivity was observed by the moderator. In accordance with the academic environment from which most moderator-analysts emerged, it is not surprising that their own opinions were carefully screened from exposure either in the group or in the final report. Group interview results often reflected only a comprehensive summary of what occurred.

Today moderators do not hesitate to offer creative insights as hypotheses to client marketing and advertising staffs. The

objectivity with which the group is moderated is **still** observed; the moderator cannot lead the group in the direction of his prior convictions.

However, aggressive probing of areas uncovered in the group that seem creatively fruitful, and exploit fully the moderator's past experience with the category, is not only acceptable but also frequently a criterion of moderator selection and success.

An example may clarify the creative role of the moderator. An ad team acquired an account from another agency and wished to assess the slogan long used in the brand's ads.

The central focus of the group interviews was to explore the slogan's motivating equity with current brand users and rejectors. It was initially hypothesized that abandonment of the slogan would alienate loyal buyers, a group that was already diminishing.

Probing suggested that the slogan itself generally was not appealing to users or nonusers. Even to its users the slogan, and the concrete symbol it embodied, was experienced as mildly distasteful to decidedly objectionable.

However, at a more covert level, the slogan did address an important need gratified by the product category as a whole. Discovery of this distinction between concrete slogan and implicit communication of salient meaning led to the suggestion that a new theme be developed in which the need, that was implied only inadvertently in the slogan, be made central and the slogan itself abandoned.

The moderator not only provided the initial insight that distinguished between manifest and latent communication but also recognized that the current users seemed particularly responsive to the latent message due to needs the product gratified for them.

Thus, abandonment of the slogan would not alienate loyal buyers. Indeed, *explicit* focus upon the more basic, latent, previous theme would address their needs even more directly.

The qualitative analyst identified and resolved another strategic issue. Implementation of

the new theme would require presenting women in an historically traditional role, catering to the needs of men.

Wouldn't this merely serve to alienate those with more liberated, current views of women? This conflict was tentatively resolved in terms of the immediate sales objectives of the brand sacrificing potential long-term appeal to those who would find this approach objectionable, in return for more immediate appeal to those to whom the theme was meaningful.

The suggested theme raised yet another issue. Conventional marketing wisdom held that women should not be central in commercials selling a product category traditionally oriented to men.

Here, the qualitative analyst reasoned that taking a calculated, yet prudent, risk was justified because it would directly speak to those men most likely to be threatened by the emerging liberated role of women. In addition, the uniqueness of this theme implementation would be likely to attract and sustain attention to a brand that desperately needed broader top-of-mind awareness.

Critical time constraints precluded the opportunity to structure and complete a quantitative study. Thus, these issues were confronted without descriptive market segmentation statistics.

The need for a new campaign was immediate. In this decision environment the qualitative analyst accepts creative responsibility.

The role of the group is to provide provocative stimuli to mobilize the analyst's own experiential and creative resources. The group interview provides **leads** to ideas, not developed ideas themselves. And surely, it does not confirm the reliability or validity of those ideas.

The group interview, used in the creative mode, serves needs other than those related to advertising. New product development managers may call upon group interview specialists to provide informational grist for their own creative mill.

Marketing and R&D staffs are eager to learn about consumers' unfulfilled needs. Since consumers are rarely particularly insightful or innovative about new products, and since marketing and R&D executives may not feel comfortable translating consumer needs into product concepts, an experienced intermediary is often welcomed. This role is frequently assigned to the qualitative analyst.

Hordes of new product and service ideas may emerge from a company's creative staff and require critical evaluation to screen out those that either grossly violate the consumers' needs or assume needs that simply do not exist. The objective in this mode is not to establish how many people would be receptive to a new product concept, but rather, to determine whether the concept makes sense from the consumer's viewpoint.

It subjects to scrutiny the inherent logic of the concept to different user segments, not the breadth of its appeal. In doing so, it not only screens out those concepts that are unlikely to gratify consumer needs, but equally important, it provides insights to the R&D designers and technicians as to how "protocepts" may be modified so that they do fulfill consumer need. Procedures used in this manner serve creative, rather than research, functions.

I'm not here concerned with whether this may legitimately be called marketing research. The most meaningful criterion by which this technique is assessed is its ultimate usefulness.

Hypothesis generating always has been an accepted part of the total research process. Whether or not it falls within the purview of "research" is not quite relevant to the marketer or advertiser who needs creative assistance.

This very question, and the issues that prompt it, lead to the suggestion that group interviews that serve the objectives described above should be distinguished from others as conducted in a creative, rather than research, mode.

RESEARCH—Techniques serving this mode adhere to the conventions and rigor of scientific methodology. Thus, the market researcher who seeks to establish the incidence of a particular consumer behavior, or the way in which a market is segmented in accordance with attitudes or needs, often requires exploratory steps to enchance the fruitfulness of quantitative research to follow.

These exploratory procedures are designed to answer questions such as: What are the most relevant and meaningful hypotheses to test in a quantitative phase? In structuring questions, what language is most likely to be understood by the respondent? What data collection procedure (mail, phone, personal interview) is required to yield meaningful results? What eligibility criteria should be used to screen respondents?

In segmenting needs, values or life-styles, the questionnaire designer must develop items that are comprehensive and meaningful to respondents. The usefulness of segmentation research is dependent upon the degree to which items represent the full array of relevant needs or life-styles and are presented in terms that are relevant and comprehensive to respondents.

Further, segmentation results are dramatically enhanced by items that are directly related to the product under study. Exploratory techniques provide the insights that generate such items.

The hypotheses developed in this manner are generally subjected to verification or rejection by the survey instruments that also emerge from this initial phase. In this sense, such procedures serve a research function.

It is in acknowledgement of the functions described above that the group interview was introduced. It has flourished because it has been useful in all three modes—consulting, creative, and research—often more so than other approaches.

The alternatives are generally the unstructured individual interview or some variant of a structured, quantitative technique. The group interview, when compared with these other techniques, provides the following advantages:

1. It exposes the dynamics of decision making. The permissive, supportive context provided by the group interview allows the emergence of decision dynamics at a more profound level of inquiry than does the individual depth interview.

2. It provokes new ideas. The stimulation provided by other involved group members generates ideas that individual participants may not think of alone. Unrecognized needs, unusual uses of new or old products, misperceptions of product positionings, or misunderstanding of messages may emerge from group effort.

3. It provides a level of candor and spontaneity unobtainable in other techniques.

4. It provides direct observation by the research professional and the client, allowing the attentive researcher to pursue serendipitous avenues of inquiry that emerge only in the course of the interview and allowing the well-trained moderator to observe and interpret non-verbal behavior, such as facial expression and physical gestures. These physical cues then become platforms from which further, more penetrating inquiry can be launched.

Not only the researcher, but clients as well, can directly observe the group without intrusion. This capability is especially valued when groups are conducted in consulting or creative modes.

The principal liabilities are:

1. It is not representative. The findings of group interviews are not generalizable to the universe from which participants were recruited, because of the very limited number of participants ordinarily included, the nonrandom manner in which participants are invited, and the potential bias introduced by selective acceptance of the invitation.

2. It provides less time per respondent than individual interviews. Most group interviews run about two hours. Except in special circumstances, most participants become restless and may be unproductive beyond that time. Information must be sought from eight people in a 120-minute period,

permitting an average of 15 minutes per participant, if all participants contribute equally, which rarely happens. The usual 45- to 60-minute individual interview can devote much more time to any given respondent than ordinarily can be given to a group participant. For example, the details about purchase behavior may have to be sacrificed in deference to assiduous pursuit of purchase motivation.

3. **Experienced moderator-analysts are in short supply.** Finally, use of the group depth interview is handicapped by the perennial shortage of soundly trained and broadly experienced moderators and analysts.

PART IV

Advantages and Limitations

The final section examines some of the advantages and limitations of focus group interviews. Major topics include:

1. A study of the validity of focus group interviews.

2. Using focus group interviews as a form of quantitative analysis.

3. Developing telephone focus sections for hard-to-reach groups.

4. Using focus groups more than once.

5. How focus groups can be abused as a form of research.

Validity of Focus-Group Findings

Fred D. Reynolds and Deborah K. Johnson

Focus-group reports often start with a disclaimer: "Qualitative research is exploratory in nature. Findings should not be considered conclusive or projectable." This disclaimer deserves close examination because it sums up a self-contradictory attitude toward the validity of focus-group research: "Believe me, but don't believe me" or perhaps "Believe me, but not too much." Indeed, the warning has become the marketing equivalent of the surgeon general's warning about the hazards of cigarettes. Like committed smokers, users of focus groups ignore the warning on the package and find great delight in practicing what is warned against. Is this prudent behavior? Or should qualitative reports be regarded as purely speculative?

Such questions become fundamental when the consequences of focus-group addiction are considered. It is generally accepted that quantitative studies are needed to make definitive inferences, and that "only in emergencies" are groups to be used in lieu of quantitative studies. But emergencies are the daily facts of marketing life, and qualitative studies frequently do indeed substitute for quantitative studies as the basis for making decisions—especially "no go" decisions. Marketing practice, if not marketing theory, holds that group interviews, even with their acknowledged limitations, are better than no research at all.

But are they?

An affirmative answer suggests that the results of a group study have predictive and/or convergent validity. A negative answer suggests hazards ahead for the brand manager and the researcher.

This article presents a tentative answer by offering a point-by-point comparison of some qualitative and quantitative research.

Two Studies

Two studies conducted at Needham, Harper & Steers Advertising, Inc., provide the basis for comparing findings. The first, the qualitative study, was a large-scale focus-group study conducted for the benefit of Needham, Harper & Steers's food clients. The report, called "The Shopping Crisis," was based on an analysis of 20 group interviews conducted in 10 U.S. cities during December 1974 and January 1975. The discussion focused on food shopping and food preparation, on reactions to inflation and concerns about nutrition, and on what was different then from the way it was the year before. Respondents were homemakers responsible for food shopping and food preparation, selected so as to vary in age, family size, and social class.

The second study was a nationwide life-style survey conducted in spring 1975. It employed a 19-page questionnaire mailed to 2,000 female members of Market Facts' Consumer Mail Panel. Usable questionnaires were returned by approximately 90 per cent of the initial sample. Demographic checks indicated that the obtained sample matched the U.S. homemaker population on age, education, income, and area of residence.

The questionnaire included sections on interests and opinions, activities, product use, media use, and perceived changes in behavior. The section on changes is of particular interest here because it provided opportunities for many comparisons between the trends it indicated and the trends set forth in the qualitative "Shopping Crisis" report. The quantitative-change question read:

As times and circumstances change, people do less of some things and more of others. Below is a list of activities. For each activity, please indicate, compared to this time last year, whether you yourself are engaging in the activity a lot more, a little more, about the same amount, a little less or a lot less. Remember the comparison is with what you yourself were doing *this time last year*.

There followed a list of activities, many of which had been covered in the "Shopping Crisis" interviews.

In addition to the perceived changes, several of the interest and opinion statements in the life-style survey touched on matters that had been discussed in the "Shopping Crisis" groups. These statements are presented along with the percentages of respondents reporting agreement to them.

Our way of addressing the supportability of the focus-group findings is straightforward: comparisons are based on direction rather than magnitude. This approach fits the notion that group interview findings, including those reported in the "Shopping Crisis," are not—and should not be—reported in statistical form. The comparisons between the qualitative results and the quantitative results are presented in Table 1.

Reprinted from the *Journal of Advertising Research,* **(June 1978), 21-24. Copyright © 1978 by the Advertising Research Foundation.**

Table 1
Consumer Changes and Opinions

Qualitative (Groups)   *Quantitative (Life Style)*

Price Conscious

Check prices   1. I find myself checking prices even on small items—90% agree.
Pay more attention to food prices
Pay more attention to food prices   2. I pay a lot more attention to food prices now than I ever did
                                          before—90% agree.

Nutrition

Concerned about nutrition   3. I am very concerned about nutrition—87% agree.

Concerned about cholesterol—especially older women   4. I try to avoid foods that are high in cholesterol—total, 62%
                                          agree; 55 and older, 79% agree.

And worrying about cholesterol a little more   5. Worrying about cholesterol—total, 35% change, 22% more; 55
                                          and older, 52% change, 35% more.

Try to avoid additives, but   6. I try to avoid foods that have additives in them—56% agree.

Concerned about salt—especialy older women   7. I am concerned about how much salt I eat—total, 56% agree;
                                          55 and older, 66% agree.

How They Shop

Specials   8. Shop a lot for specials—84% agree.

Comparison shopping   9. Shopping around for the lowest prices on food—68% change;
                                          65% more.

Coupons   10. Saving and using "price off" coupons—56% change; 52%
                                          more.

Labels   11. Looking at labels in the grocery store—64% change; 62% more.

Quantity   12. Purchasing larger-size packages of food products—52%
                                          change; 41% more.

Eliminate runs to store   13. Going to the grocery store—30% change; 19% less.

No fun to shop   14. Shopping is no fun anymore—54% agree.

What They Buy/Do Less

Snacks   15. Buying snack foods—67% change; 58% less.

Snack cakes   16. Buying snack cakes—% change; 59% less.

Cookies   17. Buying cookies—59% change; 51% less.

Sugar   18. Buying sugar—70% change; 67% less.

Candy   19. Buying candy—70% change; 48% less.

Soft drinks   20. Buying soft drinks—58% change; 48% less.

Jam or jelly   21. Buying jam or jelly—50% change; 42% less.

Entertaining at home   22. Entertaining in my home—51% change; 28% less.

Dining   23. Going out to dinner—60% change; 35% less.

Movies   24. Going to the movies—52% change; 43% less.

Cutting down on hard goods such as a house   25. Thinking about buying a new house—78% change; 63% less.

Cutting down on hard goods such as a car   26. Thinking about buying a new car—78% change; 56% less.

Cutting down on hard goods such as an appliance   27. Thinking about buying a new appliance—61% change; 40%

What They Buy/Do More

Fruit   28. Buying fruit—48% change; 40% more.

Do-it-yourself gardening   29. Gardening—61% change; 44% more.

Canning   30. Canning things at home—59% change; 32% more.

Discussion

In only one comparable instance—baking—were qualitative and quantitative findings not in accord. In this one instance later sales data showed the qualitative finding to be the more accurate reading of the market.

With a confirmation rate of 97 per cent, brand managers, copy writers, and other users of group interviews should rest a bit easier about the validity of focus-group findings. Even with their acknowledged methodological limitations, a set of focus groups produced much the same information as a large-scale quantitative survey.

This conclusion is tempered by two "Yes, buts." Yes, but "Shopping Crisis" was not a typical group study. It was based on 20 groups conducted over a period of two months in various parts of the country instead of the more typical two to four groups conducted at one site. Would it have been possible to have arrived at the same conclusions within the typical two-to-four-group format?

Our experience with the "Shopping Crisis" findings suggests that it would have been possible to obtain similar results from a much smaller number of groups. Certainly, the most salient points were apparent early. But our understanding of some important details did change as the groups accumulated, and we do not have a firm conviction on when it would have been safe to stop. Certainly this issue merits empirical investigation.

The other "Yes, but" concerns the rather broad descriptors focus-group reports employ—"some women," "they say," "most women," "women agree." The range of meaning implied by such descriptors leaves room for much doubt. For instance, if a group study reports that "women agree they are concerned about salt," does this mean a general consensus or a simple majority? Clearly, where quantitative rather than directional conclusions are required, quantitative data are necessary.

We do not mean to imply that quantitative data are always preferable or even always right. Quantitative findings depend on respondents' ability to make sensible replies on issues that are often difficult to frame as simple, straightforward interview questions, and the circumstances of the normal questionnaire survey do not permit the flexible give and take between interviewer and respondent that assures the question was correctly understood. In this connection, it should be remembered that in the present comparison, in the one flat contradiction between qualitative and quantitative, the qualitative data later proved to be correct. We believe this occurred because the respondents in the quantitative survey did not understand the question the way it was intended.

Conclusions

The comparison presented in this article should prove reassuring to users of group interviews. We think it shows that if interest is in detecting the direction of changes in the behavior of consumers—in getting the drift of the market—the group study has a viable position as a research tool for decision making as well as for hypothesis generation.

We do not deny that quantitative studies are often necessary. But we do contend that qualitative information is important as a double check, because quantitative studies have their own set of vulnerabilities. In fact, we believe that it would not be unreasonable to insist that reports of questionnaire surveys begin with the disclaimer "Warning: This study was purely quantitative. Findings should not be considered conclusive without confirmation from focus groups."

Quantitative—yes, quantitative—applications for the focus group, or what do you mean you never heard of 'multivariate focus groups'?

BY ALVIN J. ROSENSTEIN
Associate Professor of Marketing
Graduate Division, School of Business Administration
Adelphi University, and
President,
Alvin J. Rosenstein Associates
New Rochelle, N.Y.

QUALITATIVE ANALYSES ARE IMPORTANT IN INTERPRETING FOCUS GROUPS, but the stigma attached to quantitative uses of such group research still somewhat puzzles me. After all, much Freudian theory originally was based on intelligent nose counting among a sample of less than 30 disturbed and atypical people.

For example, some of the participants in the *Marketing News* "focus group on focus groups" were bending over backwards so as not to be accused of mundane nose counting within the confines of the focus group. Consequently, I found that edited transcript, published in the Jan. 16, 1976, Special Marketing Research Issue of the *Marketing News* under the headline "Research buyers of major corporations tell why, how they use focus groups, work to avoid or solve problems groups might cause," useful and provocative but disturbing in this one regard.

They were reflecting a sentiment prevalent among qualitative researchers that the gestalt-like "mystique" of the focus group is inconsistent with unsophisticated activities such as nose counting. This sentiment results partly from the fact that many focus group moderators (like myself) are current and former clinical psychologists who (unlike myself) analyze sessions almost wholly in the clinical mode.

One reason for this approach is that many associate the focus group with techniques used in group therapy, T-groups, and the like, which generate "depth" material. Here, counting noses is considered inconsistent with the analytical processes designed to yield qualitative "insights."

THE LOGIC OF NOSE COUNTING IN THE FOCUS GROUP: Obviously, the focus group is used to investigate a marketing and not a clinical situation. The discussants do not come to the group as atypical individuals with repressed wishes to be uncovered.

Rather, they are typically normal people paid to sit and talk with a moderator, who asks questions about things probably not too important to them, and over which they have few, if any, inhibitions or hang-ups. The questions asked are designed to elicit information useful for making marketing decisions and usually they are direct as are the answers.

In this situation, the focus group's unique strength lies in its ability to engage participants in an interactive exploration, in which the contributions of one discussant stimulate those of the others. In this manner, a broad range of material is generated, including considerations that might not occur to any of the members individually. However, even these considerations should be assessed in a way that reflects incidence as well as the intensity and logic of expression.

However, prime methodological weaknesses of the focus group lie in the subjectivity employed in conducting the group and in its lack of replicability. The research conclusions that emerge from the focus group are based upon subjective procedures and analyses which not only are likely to vary among different moderators and analysts but also might even for one moderator-analyst at different times. This is because the trend of any focus group discussion not only depends upon moderator-analyst stimulation but also upon spontaneous comments that are, in turn, probed.

Pragmatically, replicability is handled by conducting several groups on a given problem and seeking the common threads that run throughout. However, obviously, even in several groups, it is difficult to intensively explore more than a limited number of questions and certainly there cannot be many pollings with a group without destroying a good interactive discussion.

Reprinted from *Marketing News*, **IX (May 21, 1976), 8,** published by the American Marketing Association.

Therefore, although some quantification is important within the focus group, the procedures for quantifying are not always convenient or feasible. Here are several solutions that have worked for different kinds of marketing problems.

THE "MULTIVARIATE FOCUS GROUP": Often before starting a large-scale marketing study incorporating segmentation, perceptual mapping, or some other multivariate technique, focus groups are conducted to develop hypotheses and to get a "feel" for the areas of investigation.

In this situation, I've had some success with what might be termed a "multivariate focus group," which **develops hypotheses** not only with regard to traditional issues but also **with regard to aspects of market structure, such as consumer segments, brand positioning, and the like.**

In brief, the multivariate focus group procedure provides the kinds of input and analyses currently associated with multivariate segmentation or perceptual mapping studies, while maintaining, in all other respects, the format and qualitative nature of the traditional focus group. Specifically, the following procedures are employed:

1. A standard focus group discussion guide is developed, relevant to the marketing problem to be explored, for example, consumer benefits, problems, brand positioning, etc.
2. After several initial sessions, a self-administered questionnaire is developed, much like that which might be included in a full-scale segmentation and-or perceptual mapping study. Usually, this consists of some 50 to 100 items, requiring less than 30 minutes to complete.
3. The remaining focus groups (that is, a minimum of four) are conducted as focus groups, with the exception that subsequent to each session, the discussants are given the self-administered questionnaire to complete.
4. During the analytic phase, qualitative focus group analyses are performed, while independently appropriate multivariate analyses (for

example, R and A factor analyses) also are executed. The final report is largely similar to current qualitative analyses, except for two sections, one which presents the hypotheses developed from the multivariate analyses and another which integrates the joint qualitative and quantitative findings.

Although the multivariate aspects of these procedures are obviously non-projectable and represent output from a small sample of sensitized discussants, as does much of the focus group itself, still there is much value to the numerical analyses performed.

These analyses can be used to anticipate the kinds of output planned for subsequent full-scale studies. Here, a valuable contribution of the method is the development of empirically derived hypotheses regarding market and brand structure, prior to committing large sums to more definitive work.

Such preliminary studies can enhance the probability of successfully conducting subsequent full-scale multivariate studies by suggesting item omissions and redundancies as well as new areas of inquiry. In this regard, they are more useful than the focus group alone, while the additional time and analytical costs incurred are minor.

Finally, the systematic procedures employed provide a structural framework for interpreting the dynamics of the group. It makes it less likely that the analyst will be misled by the output of one atypical group or by the contributions of a relatively few vocal but atypical discussants. The probability of developing replicable findings, which is important even for the exploratory focus group, is thereby significantly enhanced.

SCREENING OF CONCEPTS, PRODUCTS, AND ADS: A second use for systematic nose counting within the focus group is in the initial screening of concepts, products, and advertising. Since similar procedures are used for the three types of screening, only concept testing will be discussed here.

The procedure involves obtaining ratings on one or more concepts from the discussants at

the outset of the group prior to any discussion. This procedure accomplishes two objectives:

1. It minimizes the dangers of discussants influencing one another.
2. The procedure commits a discussant to a viewpoint (which may later be changed).

Even if the viewpoint is an unpopular one, having committed him or herself, the discussant is more inclined to defend the rating than if the commitment was not made. In this way, material which might not otherwise be divulged is generated within the group setting.

Rarely, in my experience, have products that have performed strongly (or weakly) within the context of the group reversed their performance in subsequent testing. Moreover, this initial nose counting provides valuable direction in terms of later probing within the focus group for sources of unusual product strengths and-or weaknesses and in providing insight into significant sources of product acceptance or rejection.

Also, if there is much consistency in voting and if the rationale for this voting, in the moderator's view, supports the positions taken, then there is justification for eliminating certain concepts from consideration or in making sequential modifications in concepts, as the sessions progress.

Here, while we do not achieve the 95 percent level of confidence in the correctness of the decisions made, the process takes advantage of empirically developed odds in attempting to maximize the probability of correct client decisions. This is especially useful in early exploratory work, where firm directions are not yet set and where large-scale research is not yet appropriate.

Systematic polling tied to thoughtful use of quantitative procedures can be a valuable adjunct in interpreting focus group sessions and in providing a basis, superior to traditional qualitative analyses alone, for marketing decisions.

Incomplete use keeps focus group from producing optimum results

BY ROBERT J. KADEN
President
Goldring & Co., Chicago

THE KEY TO SUCCESSFUL FOCUS GROUPS comes when the participants begin *hearing* each other and responding accordingly.

Unfortunately, this happens all too seldom in the typical two-hour focus group — or when it happens, it happens just as the session is about to end because:

1. The group has reached its peak as far as rapport is concerned.
2. Fear of expressing ideas, (or not saying something stupid or silly) seems to be reduced.
3. The participants in the group are presumably getting some enjoyment out of the process and have loosened up.
4. The real reason for the existence of the group will have been reached. The group is into the crux of the subject under discussion.
5. Sometimes the group moves away from a bunch of individual "me's" and starts working as a group.
6. A two-hour session is like taking a snapshot of consumer attitudes at a specific moment. Yet, the participants may not have had any time to really think about any new information thrust upon them during the session.

The simple way to avoid such problems is to have the groups come back for additional sessions.

THE RELATIONSHIP OF focus groups to therapy groups is an interesting one. Some therapy groups go for years before the participants feel a sense of personal expression. Focus group interviews go for two hours — and we feel we've reached a depth of consumer concern.

It's just not enough to do a bunch of different groups and then go into the quantitative phase. The consumer expression we've uncovered is no more valid, in terms of what consumers really think, than is the problem we've gone ahead and quantified — and solved — as a result of that expression.

We have learned a great deal about communicating. From Synectics we can see the value of positive communication. From the Creative Education Foundation there are problem-solving seminars which teach practical application. From Adlerian thought, gestalt, TM, TA, est, there are new models for understanding human behavior.

Yet we, as qualitative market researchers, remain practically static in advancing our art.

Qualitative research is an art, and it always will be. But, altered qualitative techniques can allow us a fuller and more direct understanding of consumer attitudes. Given this, our quantitative output can't help being more on target.

MY ADVICE to "Bring 'em back — again and again" is based on four basic premises or theories:

I. CONSUMERS ARE CREATIVE — and neither we nor they believe it.

Yes, I really mean that, and you'll rarely, if ever, see creativity happen in a conventional two-hour group discussion.

Creativity can be taught, but it takes breaking conventional lines of communication. It's hard to do. It takes training. It takes commitment. And it can work with consumers. It will require several things:

1. Invite the same groups back two times, three times, four times — whatever is indicated.
2. Maybe have their husbands or kids come along on one of the sessions.
3. Between sessions, assign them tasks related to the problem.
4. Allow these tasks to be the stimulus helping their minds to incubate ideas. Have them keep "thought diaries."
5. Encourage them to develop relationships within the group — personal relationships.
6. Encourage them to write songs about their ideas; draw illustrations communicating the ideas; maybe (OH NO!) even write an ad.
7. Teach them that an idea is fragile and easy to attack. Teach them to ask "What do I like about that idea?" rather than "Yes, but it'll never work."
8. Use your own imagination. Have fun — and out of fun will come thoughts and ideas that require special care and feeding.
9. Realize that neither you nor they think you're getting anywhere — and all of a sudden you'll be somewhere.

II. CONSUMERS ARE EXPERTS — and it's also okay to make them experts when conducting a focus group.

Well, they do have the final judgment. Through their experience your product will live or die. In a qualitative research sense, if you do not observe what happens when a consumer reaches the level of expert with your product, you'll never know what comes next. Try this:

1. Let consumers come in and talk about your product concept. Get all that background stuff.
2. Give them some prototype products or something that approaches your idea. If you don't have any product, give them a concept board to take home.
3. Let them "incubate" your product or idea for a week and have them back.
4. Between groups, rewrite your concept statements on the basis of what you've learned. Present your new positions in week two.
5. Experts can be critical and suspicious of their own ideas. When your group comes back a second or third time, have the members bring a friend who doesn't know anything about what's going on.
6. Watch what happens when the "expert" tries to explain the "developed" idea to a friend. Sparks fly, and you learn.

III. CONSUMERS DON'T KNOW HOW THEY FEEL about things until those things are viewed on a time continuum.

Reprinted from *Marketing News*, XI (September 9, 1977), 4, published by the American Marketing Association.

Feelings and expressions about feelings change as more information and experience are received and "incubated."

If someone came up to you and asked you, "How do you like the new Cadillacs?" chances are you'd think about the question for a moment then reply "Great lookin' machines, but they're probably real gas eaters."

The problem is that your answer may or may not reflect your real long-term attitude. Yet others can form distinct impressions about us as a result of such answers.

Thus, after test driving a new Cadillac, listening to a salesman for an hour, and reading a brochure, your answer might be "Great lookin' machines that don't use as much gas as I thought they did. In fact, they use less than my present old one."

Similarly, a group participant will probably give you an answer to every question you ask. Yet the answers cannot reflect a long-term feeling or attitude. Each answer reflects only one moment in time.

To get a greater sense of consumer feeling and attitudes, try:

1. **Giving consumers an opportunity to know how they feel about the problem at hand. Let them work on the idea for a while.**

2. **Repeating to yourself, "Consumers don't give a damn about my product unless I do something to force awareness and thought" ... or they will give you answers based on "not giving a damn" every time.**

3. **Saying, "the initial impression is fine and it's worth something," but after a while that will be altered. Know what happens when they begin to "give a damn."**

If you are using groups to uncover theories on how consumers think about food or shampoo or bank services or tractors or whatever, try analyzing consumer responses this way:

● Analyze their motives after Group Session 1.

● Analyze the same group of respondents after you've had them back a second time.

● Analyze the same group of respondents after you've had them back the third time.

● Give the tapes from the third group session to another qualitative analyst and have that person write a report independent of yours. Compare the analysis of that third group with where you were after Group 1.

● Remember — and keep remembering — that attitudes and feelings are altered as the actual buying experience is created or recreated.

As long as we remain stuck with the notion that a consumer's *perception* of a product or concept or buying situation is valid, we will be stuck in a big mistake. Perceptions are for the birds. Actual experience is the only truth.

Attitudes and feelings change as one gets closer to the buying experience. In a two-hour group session you get about as close to the buying experience as a man on the moon. In a four- or six- or eight-hour recurring series of sessions, you can simulate the attitudes and feelings of the buying experience to a much greater extent.

IV. IF WE EVER HOPE TO

get any sense of depth from consumers, we had better know what establishing rapport within a group situation really means — Webster's defines rapport as "a relationship marked by harmony."

In the focus group sense, harmony does not mean getting everyone to agree with each other. It refers to that kind of harmonious feeling and openness which develop when people truly understand that it is okay to disagree.

Rapport among people can take years to develop, but we researchers think we're approaching it in a two-hour session. Often we're just guessing, and then patting ourselves on the back when a respondent tells us something we haven't already thought about.

Before we take everything we hear as truth, or at least truth worthy of quantification, I suggest we shake up a few taboos:

1. **At the end of the first session, tell members of the group what they told you. Tell them the real reasons for their visit. Tell them the things you think you've learned. Let them in on the big secret.**

2. **Tell the group a little about yourself — your hobbies, your joys in life, maybe even a fear or two you have.**

3. **Send them home with their tasks.**

4. **When they come back in a week, spend the first half-hour of the discussion talking about something innocuous, like vacations or raising kids.**

5. **Realize that rapport within the**

group has been enhanced, and if you look at your original outline guide, your same questions will likely produce different responses.

6. **When rapport is heightened, it's okay for a group participant to take on the moderator's role. You be a respondent for a while (maybe even the client would like to come into the room and play a role).**

7. **Answer the questions put to you as honestly as you can. Take turns being group moderator and be sensitive to the new moderators.**

8. **The character of the group will change drastically the more frequently the members come back. The greater the rapport, the greater your understanding of consumer motivation.**

9. **Know when to quit! That's when the group members become so involved in personal matters that the issue under discussion starts to get lost in the shuffle.**

Rapport is a goal that comes with work and effort, is dynamic in character, and is never totally reached.

But bringing the groups back again and again for better rapport and more significant results is an expensive proposition. Right? Not necessarily. By juggling the subject matter and using fewer groups, though more fruitful ones, it is possible to get better results without spending more money. But sometimes this is not possible; and then, yes it may cost more.

Focus Groups:
The Most Abused Form of Research

Alex Biel, Canada

Alex wrote this piece while Managing Director of our Montreal office. He has since left O&M to work for a research firm in California.

It is time to put the group interview into perspective.

On one hand, the group interview—also known as the "focus group" or "group depth interview"—is a useful and important technique for advertising agencies and their clients.

On the other hand, it has become market research's *most atrociously abused procedure!*

Let's look first at the major advantages of the group interview:

1. Properly utilized, focus groups are an excellent method of generating hypotheses about product categories, brands, and general subject areas. In particular, how consumers react in group interviews can stimulate a great number of ideas for subsequent investigation using more rigorous methods.

2. They are also useful in learning the ways consumers describe products and the ways these products fit into their lives.

3. They are a good starting point: for a product upon which little or no research exists they return a great deal of insight at low cost.

4. Group interviews allow a "surprise" factor to emerge that is often not possible in more structured methods. Because of this they can sometimes (though certainly not always) compensate for a less than brilliant designer of research or a less than superior interviewer.

The chances of operating on misleading, pseudo information masquerading as fact are very large.

All well and good. And in the U.S. group interviews are more often than not properly utilized as a useful first step in a research project.

Not so in Canada, alas. Although much lip service is paid to going on to more substantial research, the great majority of group studies are not only the first step, but the final research step as well!

When this happens, the chances of operating on misleading, pseudo information masquerading as fact are very large.

Under these conditions, it is worthwhile to consider whether the marketer can truly afford the high cost of being misled.

But let's be specific: what's really all that wrong with groups?

Here—for starters—are nine major di:

advantages that Ogilvy & Mather has identified:

1) Groups are simply not quantitative This is true whether there are two groups or twenty involved. We can learn that an attitude, perception, or even a motive exists, but it is impossible to know the extent to which it is held. In fact, we may not even know the size of the sample involved. Is it the number of respondents, the number of groups, or, perhaps, even the number of interviewers? Do we perhaps see the shadow of "mother-in-law" research emerging, albeit in fancy clothes?

2) Groups are not useful in examining problems of communication, comprehension, or awareness. The interaction of respondents, an advantage in detecting and describing attitudes, is, of course, a liability in determining what people understand. Because of this, the potential for false information pretending to be truth is enormous!

Focus groups have a dangerously misleading appearance of reality.

---

3) Focus groups have a dangerously misleading appearance of reality. Since it is

Reprinted from *Viewpoint*, (Spring 1978), 6-7, published by Ogilvy & Mather, Inc.

usually convenient to see and/or hear group interviews, some people come away with an impression that this is "reality." It isn't. Unfortunately, more representative research, using summary devices such as collation of response and numerical description, seems artificial by contrast.

4) Usually, the number of groups is not enough. It is not unusual to see marketing plans formulated on the results of two—or even one—group interview. In fact, sound practice says that these should be increased to at least four or six for completeness even in the hypothesis development phase of research.

5) Group interaction is appropriate for product research and attitude investigation but *misleading for advertising studies.* Interaction in advertising studies is inappropriate since respondents quickly stop acting as consumers and become "experts" and "critics." Unfortunately, they are properly experts as consumers but amateurs when it comes to advertising.

When discussing a floor polish, for example, consumers concentrate on what the product does or does not do to their floors. When they focus on advertising their discussion is based upon what they like or dislike about the ads. Unfortunately, advertising is not an end in itself as an art form. It is a means to an end: a positive statement about a product.

Reactions to advertising in groups in the vast majority of the scores of the cases we have examined tend to interact with attitudes towards the product.

Unfortunately, by using group interviews in investigating advertising effects, we end up destroying what we actually wish to measure.

6) Group interviews appear to be less costly than they actually are. While two group interviews with eight women each might result in direct costs of say $1,200-$1,800 (including analysis), the cost per respondent works out to between $75.00 and $112.50. And these costs do not account for the staff time that is often expended in viewing the groups, briefing the interviewer, etc.

Small sample individual interview studies can often provide a lot of information more efficiently and at less cost.

7) It is well known that a strong personality can dominate a group and an in-ept interviewer can influence a discussion (usually without intending to, of course).

Today there is hardly a research firm, or individual practitioner, that does not offer group discussions to clients. The best use considerable discretion in so doing; the worst use none at all.

While the number of qualified group interviewers has increased, the number of amateurs dealing in groups has grown far faster. Unfortunately!

While the number of qualified group interviewers has increased, the number of amateurs dealing in groups has grown far faster. Unfortunately!

As well, even among professionals, great differences in interviewing styles occur that can importantly affect results.

8) As demand for focus group interviews has grown, an army of "instant" group gurus has emerged, ready to take the money and pontificate.

Eager, but ill-trained, the group interviewer of today is often spared the hard job of thorough analysis of her work; group interviews are now thought to be largely self-analyzing by those who commission them. A so-called debriefing is all that is required!

9) Sampling is often largely neglected. All too often, groups are put together on the basis of convenience rather than any other reason. Often, that means that the individuals are likely to be more homogenous than is desirable.

For example, an easy source of groups has been clubs and service organizations. The problem here is that the values and attitudes of members of the same organization are likely to be more alike than those of people drawn at random.

Why—with all these drawbacks—are groups so popular?

Well, groups can be done quickly.

And it is impressive to hear real live consumers talk about our products—there's a sort of magic "touchy-feely" quality to groups that no table or graph can quite match.

There's a sort of magic "touchy-feely" quality to groups that no table or graph can quite match.

All heightened, of course, by the slightly voyeuristic aspect of eavesdropping by watching through one-way glass or closed-circuit TV.

And somehow it's always easy to find brand managers willing to fly to a faraway city to watch a group (but harder to find volunteers to pour over text and tables).

Perhaps a more serious reason for the overabundance of group research, however, is that research bought in Canada is commissioned by brand managers and marketing managers. This in turn reflects the fact that only the largest companies here maintain professional research staffs in-house.

And to the inexperienced research buyer, the group interview has an undeniable attractiveness. Here, every man can be his own analyst, and who is to say that one interpretation is better than another.

To summarize, it would obviously be wrong to claim group interviews have nothing to offer.

They can help develop hypotheses—but so can a host of other procedures.

But as they are used today in Canada, the marketing community would clearly gain more than it would lose by turning away from groups to more meaningful methods. □

How Useful Is Focus Group Interviewing? Not Very . . . Post-Interviews Reveal

by Dr. William A. Yoell, Director
Behavior Research Institute

Focus Group Interviewing (FGI), the process whereby eight to ten consumers meet and discuss a product, a product category, a new product concept, an activity or a company, has been part of market research for almost two decades. The value of the technique has its opponents and proponents.

Proponents state that the purpose of FGI is to establish hypotheses and to give Research & Development or creative people direction. However, if the material from FGI is based on artifacts, invalid material, there is not only considerable time and effort wasted, but the hypotheses and directions will be misleading.

An extensive search of the literature has revealed nothing with respect to the basis of or justification for FGI in psychological fact. Nowhere in marketing literature could this writer find any written material that has considered the dynamics of FGI, which most certainly affects the result of the group session: for example, the type of "personality" of each group member. Consumers are selected without standards or criteria for either the subject matter of the FGI or for psychological typology. Neither are the factors of low interest considered; or the lack of self-assertiveness of individuals; or such affective states as anxiety, awkwardness, shyness, tenseness; interest in people; the positive or negative reinforcements that operate prior to or during the group session.

Group interviewing was originally a curative process used in psycho-therapy, Freudian analysis specifically, designed to hasten the psychoanalytic process of transference; counter transference; repressed infantile sexual material, etc.[1][2] Goldman (1962) discusses the psychoanalytic character of focus group interaction using such terms as slip of the tongue; psychic conflict; unconscious, repressed material.[3] It is extremely doubtful that such dynamic processes operate or that meaningful material emerges from a *single* FGI session.

How reliable is the data that emerges from an FGI? Not very, based on a behavioral post-FGI interview study. Before discussing the results of the study, a history of group processes is necessary.

Prior to Freud, Dr. Joseph Pratt made use of group interaction in his tuberculosis clinic. Ruitenbeeck (1970) cites the work of a French physician who utilized the group approach and who stated in 1913, "group depends wholly and exclusively upon the beneficial influence of one person on another."[4] Much disagreement exists today as to the efficacy of group therapy and group processes. Marsh (1931), for instance, determined that his groups were effective because each member of the group was supportive of one another.[5] Burrow (1925) became dissatisfied with psychoanalysis because it excluded social factors.[6]

One wonders how the results of FGI, limited to the use of products or activities that occur as infrequently as twice a year up to daily activities which have become habituated, can have any meaning or significance.

Moreno (1927) has written at length on "acting out" that occurs within groups, casting even more doubt on the meaningfulness of material that emerges.[7]

The emotional states that occur in a group have not been considered by marketing people; or the relationship between the individual and group culture. Bion (1952) has stated that in this relationship the individual moves along valences: the valence of pairing; of dependency; of fight or flight.[8] He also realized that lack of structure and direction led to anger, confusion, isolation, alienation, boredom.

One vital question asked by psychotherapists must be asked by marketing people: "Can an experience, highly concentrated in time, created in a situation with a built-in sense of urgency, produce a significant personality change?"[9] Marketers would have to substitute useful, meaningful data for the words "personality change."

The setting and dynamics of FGI create artificial interaction, making the one-shot session a passing experience, a free-for-all. Psychotherapy and problem-solving groups meet over a period of months, even years, and the group composition is stable throughout this time period. Hoch (1972) states that the group environment imposes certain restrictions on the individual.[10] The free association questioning process that goes on in groups is avoided by many therapists and sociologists, until the individual has been thoroughly

Reprinted from *Marketing Review*, 29 (April 1974), 15-19, published by the New York Chapter/American Marketing Association.

124

analyzed in terms of traits, characteristics, personality, etc. Hoch also points out that in a conference, questions are selective and because it *is* a group, inhibitions often occur. Others like to hear themselves talk. The method creates the findings including the possibility that the analyst (moderator) becomes a determinant in the results.

Much has been written about body movement (Perls, 1951, for example). To what extent is the FGI moderator capable of observing, interpreting such actions and reactions? Goldman (1962) states an advantage of groups is that respondents react to each other and their behavior is directly observed. In experimental studies conducted over many months, inter-observer rating reliability has been a problem, and experiments are not conducted until inter-observer ratings or observations correlate at an .85 level. It is questioned whether one individual, untrained, is capable of observing or interpreting a member's behavior in the group. Shifts in posture, facial expressions, arm, leg movements are as important as, if not more important than, vocalization. Skinner (1957) includes body movements, gestures as verbal behavior since they do mediate responses.[11] Gantt (1970) discusses various parts of the body as a means of transmitting information.[12] Lieberman (1972) points out that Darwin utilized the method of correlating details of facial expression, body movements, with emotion.[13] Lieberman further states "the key to a behavioral analysis of emotions is what is the person *doing* when he experiences an emotion! Our interest is in facial expression, motor movements, not vocalizations and speech."

In FGI no consideration is given to the effects and affects of the setting in which group members behave. In individual face-to-face behavioral interviews that consumed an average of five hours, consumers, when asked, "are there times, situations when you take a particular type of medication more often than usual?" answered with such statements as "yes, when there are headlines in the paper" (stating her son was a juvenile delinquent); "when my husband doesn't get home on time, he has a drinking problem," etc. Such statements were not made in a group, although in the post-FGI inter-

views it was established similar conditions existed within the family.

FGI is indeed moving away from a science of marketing or a science of consumer behavior. All behavior occurs in an environmental context with stimuli and events preceding and following it. The regularity of interaction between environment and behavior, assessed by careful observation and measurement, allows us to build a science of consumer behavior. The cake baking example, cited later, is a perfect example of how unconditioned responses become attached to neutral or conditioned stimuli when paired with unconditioned stimuli.[14]

FGI advocates overlook several vital facts: the fact that group reactions may have no counterpart in the behavior of the individuals[15]; that all cues that convey a certain attitude or hypothesis to an individual about the supposed purpose of an interaction, potentially modify behavior——a dynamic that weakens the significance of any response made in groups.[16]

An FGI study revealed acceptance for a new method of packaging luncheon meats. In a test market, the accepted package did not sell. Subsequently, behavioral interviews in the home revealed that women were responding in the group, away from "living" behavior. Heavy users of luncheon meats had no problem with restoring. Light users had been conditioned to the concept that "you can't eat liverwurst, bologna that has been stored for four days; you get sick." More importantly, *every* woman had had the experience of "fishing the lid out of the applesauce, the gravy when leftovers were stored in containers, because family members didn't put the cover back on."

What women *said* in groups, and how they *behaved* in the home, were two different things.

There is also the fact that the correlation between a person's description of his attitudes or emotional state and his actual execution of the behavior may vary as a function of the specific conditions under which each of these two behaviors take place (Kanfer and Phillips, 1970).[16]

Participants in FGI play games, similar to those described in Berne's transactional analysis (1966), such as "I'll be a good respondent and help

you"; or, "I'll show him who's boss"; the Greenhouse game described by Berne; or the "Gee, you're wonderful, Mr. Moderator" game; or the "you people are wonderful, but you'll never budge me" game.[17]

In the search of marketing literature only one reference to sociological, psychological literature on group dynamics has been found, despite the fact that in *one* book there are several hundred references involving research, experiments, analysis of group dynamics.[18] What are the defenses operating in a group? What roles are people playing? In our post-FGI studies, women revealed they selected a *particular* style of dress; a *particular* style of wig for the group session. How does the moderator "come off" to members? Does he (the moderator) act, as several post interviewees said, "like he was our father." People project a mask in groups. What identity is a member taking on? What interpersonal anxieties exist? We administered the Wolpe-Lang Fear Schedule to 25 of the 50 people in our post-FGI study. On a 0 to 5 rating, 15 of these consumers revealed high fear and anxiety in the inter-personal matrix; fear of rejection; of being ignored; of looking foolish; of making a mistake; of hurting someone's feelings. Any data from the FGI sessions these people were in, could only result in misdirection in solving the marketing problem.

Where were FGI proponents during the '50's when such a considerable volume of research was being done on groups? Such research, in fact, was going on in the '40's——the Lewin-Lippitt-White studies, for example.[19]/[20]

The internal validity of FGI seems to have been overlooked. Internal validity refers to the confidence that the conclusions we draw from the research are the correct ones, whereas external validity refers to the confidence we have that the conclusions we draw will apply to any group or situation other than the ones on which the research was accomplished.[21]

In the use of FGI only "feelings," reactions are expected and the use of control groups is virtually unheard of. Moreover, feelings, or any other affective state is accidental, and is the result of a particular situation. The literature on this subject is so vast, it is impossible to begin to cite references.[22]

Campbell and Stanley[21] discuss eight threats to the internal validity of any research, any experiment as well as to the results of groups. One of them is the "plaguing factor of statistical regression."

How much attention is paid to the dynamics involved in hetero-versus homogeneity in groups? Many differences are involved between invited-accepted group members; invited-refused subjects; uninvited-controlled subjects.

Such factors are not at all considered in the stampede to "get ideas," without regard to "how valid the ideas" from FGI are.

Orne has pointed out (1962) that a threat to the external validity of research is the mere fact of being in a group, is of considerable importance for most people and that their reactions are often rather special and not representative of their ordinary performance.[23] (See also Yoell, "Abuses & Misuses of Psychological Techniques by Business & Industry.")

A second factor that can limit external validity is the selection of the sample. If the sample consists of extroverts; or of socially adaptive, or socially submissive consumers, then the results are limited only to the particular group. This author is not aware of any sort of pre-test or pre-analysis in the selection of members for an FGI session.

Yet, the universality of behavior is never considered. Pretty much the same things happen in a frame as in a brick house; students, freshmen in one school behave pretty much like those in another school with respect to certain variables.

In generalizing the results of FGI we are working without prior knowledge and a history of the behavior of the individual with respect to the area under study. There are no matched variables between groups, such as, for example, the space in years between children. A household with three children, aged 3, 5, 7 has different needs than a household with a 3, 8, 18 spacing.

FGI proponents must ask the question, "is individual interviewing indistinguishable from group interviewing?" If so, either one is vitiated.

A science of marketing or a sci-ence of anything cannot advance or evolve on the basis of variables that defy observation: "attitudes," beliefs, opinions, affective states (feelings).

So much has been written concerning the dynamics of groups that marketing remains oblivious to. Schatz (1966) has mentioned some of the simple and obvious factors involved in FGI.[24] More subtle dynamics occur, such as "the leader's helper."[25]/[26] Research has been done on the size of groups (Hare, 1962, for example) and such dynamics have emerged that as size increases or decreases, the propensity to talk or remain silent follows accordingly.[27]

The question of whether or not group members demonstrate (or are) high authoritarian group members in contrast to their equalitarian counterparts, must be considered. Sanford and Medalia (1950, 1955) have demonstrated the former prefer status-laden leadership, strong authority and direction from the top.[28]/[29] High authoritarian individuals are usually more hostile to non-assertive leaders. The equalitarian-type member strives for approval. There is a tendency for the high authoritarian types to reject quickly those who deviate from their position.

Many more variables exist than the few cited. Group size is a factor.[30] Six-member groups, in contrast to eight or 12 permit more observer (leader) agreement in perceiving, tracking and judging group members. In groups larger than six, members perceive and react to other members in terms of sub-groups or classes, rather than as individuals.

Kelly & Thibaut (1954) report groups are less productive on essentially intellectual tasks.[31] The group setting, on a more qualitative basis tends to result in more moderate individual positions on judgmental subject matter. Bos (1937) has explained this process in groups as the process of leveling and sharpening.[32] Allport(1955) explains "when working with others we respond in a measure as though we were reacting to them."[33]

It is questioned by this author whether FGI proponents have ever studied the Bales Interaction Process Analysis (BIPA). The BIPA involves 12 categories of group members ranging from "shows solidarity" to "asks for orientation" to "shows antagon-ism."[34] The Bales Study also reveals the stages through which groups proceed and was based on 22 group problem-solving sessions. As phase transitions occur from emphasis on orientation (BIPA categories 6) to evaluation (categories 5 and 8), the frequency of both positive and negative categories in interaction, increases. The Bales Study also revealed the nature of the average profile of group members. The average profile, for instance, shows 50% attempted answers; 25% positive reactions; 12% negative reactions; 6% questions and 7% attempted answers (reactions). Talland (1955) in commenting on groups that meet in order to discover problems, reactions, stated that neither have to reach a solution nor must they finally close a case unresolved at the end of the session.[35] This is a different process of interaction that occurs in problem-solving groups that meet over a period of time.

Janis and Hovland discuss high and low persuasibility and the individual differences in attention, comprehension and acceptance of messages.[36] Cohen has done considerable work on the influence of the communicator's vividness of personality, status, expertise, admiration or affection for the communicant.[37]

There are too many sociometric techniques used (the interpersonal behavioral inventories of Lorr and McNair or Leary, 1957), to cite here.[38]/[39] But far more usefulness might be derived from FGI if these dynamics were understood——instead of the potluck results obtained from such sessions by marketing people.

The structure of contemporary group interviewing rests on a body of literature consisting overwhelmingly of anecdotal and impressionistic reports. There is a gross absence of evidence that FGI is anything more than purely descriptive. No hypothesis testing, experimental research has appeared concerning the value or validity of FGI. Cartwright (1951), a leading contributor to group dynamics, formulated eight principles by which group characteristics are held to influence attitudinal and behavioral change in group members.[40] Bach (1954) carries matters much further in suggesting that small group variables such as cohesiveness, clique formation, etc. operate in a largely specifiable manner in problem-solving groups.[41] Group dynamics tend to homogenize the membership to create an apparent (psychological) uniformity and so block the emergence of healthy differentiation.[42]/[43]

To what extent are group members inhibited; excitatory; submissive; insightful? No one knows in advance because no "pre-testing" has been done on group members.

Goldstein, et al[18] pose a hypothesis: on a variety of interactive communicative and comparability criteria, prediction of subsequent in-group behavior will be more accurate when based on direct behavioral measurement than on interview or psychometric measurement. Bales also found that the interaction rate actually demonstrated by a given member was an inverse function of the characteristics rate of his co-participators.

Breer found that when a subject's and another member's ascendance-submission scores were considered, it accounted for 37% of the variance in the person's ascendance toward the other person.[44] Twenty-one per cent of the variance was accounted for in a member's behavior toward others in the group solely on the basis of what was known about the others.

Others too numerous to mention have researched the effects of self-need orientation and its effect on groups; the member who can be labeled the "energizer"; the "information seeker"; the "initiator"; the "harmonizer"; the "expeditor"; the "encourager"; the "elaborator" and other active member roles, all of which make the comments, discussion subject to much doubt and reduce their meaning to mere verbiage, rather than meaningful material.

Here are some findings relevant to group dynamics.[45] As the size of problem-solving groups is increased, the following is noted:

1. The differences between the relative interaction rates of members tend to disappear.

2. The difference between the relative interaction rates of the group leader and the average member becomes greater.

3. The absolute rate of interaction for any given member tends to decrease because the interaction rate for each member is inversely related to the rates of other group members.[46]

4. The proportion of very infrequent contributors to the group interaction increases (Kelly & Thibaut[31]).

5. An increasing proportion of the members report feelings of threat and inhibition regarding participation.[47]

Bales and Borgatta (1955) also report the group size interaction relation via the BIPA, as the size of problem-solving groups increases from two to seven, the rate of giving information and suggestion increases, whereas the rate of asking for opinions and showing agreement decreases. As an explanation hypothesis for such interactional change, these investigators suggest that as group size increases, there is a tendency toward a more mechanical method of introducing information, less sensitive exploration of the viewpoints of others and more direct attempts to control others, all of which are associated with the increasing restriction of time available per member.[46]

There is also a relationship in the proportion of increasing or decreasing verbalizations vis a vis either the leader or members. Miller (1950) reports an increasing proportion of verbalizations, as groups increase in size, addressed to the group leader and a decreasing proportion to other members.[48] In turn, as size increases, the leader tends to address more and more remarks to the group as a whole and less and less to specific individuals within the group. Size affects tolerance of group members toward the leader and toward other members. Carter, Haythorn and Shriver and Lanzetta (1951) comment: in the group of four, each individual has sufficient latitude or space in which to behave and thus the basic abilities of each individual can be expressed; but in the larger group only the more forceful individuals are able to express their abilities and ideas since the amount of freedom in the situation is not sufficient to accomodate all the group members.[49]

Larger groups are more disruptive than smaller ones; size affects feelings of frustration. Hare[27] reports degree of satisfaction, consensus is lower in 12-member groups than in 5-member groups. Member status and overall group hierarchy becomes more resistant to change with increasing ties.

Despite the quality of the group leader, and regardless of the group leader, the group dynamics are subtle; far too subjective to control or even be perceived by the group leader.

Even versus odd-sized groups affect the working of the group——even-sized groups (4, 6) are characterized by more disagreement and antagonism and less asking for suggestions or showing agreement than are odd-sized groups (3, 5, 7). Five-member groups have been found to be most harmonious.

Thus, the artificiality, misdirection, invalid data, unrealistic data, data based on artifacts, results. The reason for so many product failures?

It makes a difference if the group is leader-centered or group-centered; so, too, does the fact of whether the leader is reflective or leading. The silence of two or one group member influences productivity and increases other member defensiveness.[50]

Taken as a group, studies of communication networks and leadership orientation consistently demonstrate that in diverse settings, laboratory, industrial, educational and other settings, group-centered leadership orientation results in more favorable member affective reactions and attitudes than does a leader-centered group orientation. Successful accomplishment of the group task also appears more often to follow from group-centered leadership. Certainly, more research is needed in the area of group dynamics *per se*, much less in FGI.

Factors that affect group cohesiveness, such as motivation of group members; the attraction of the group for members; the coordination of efforts of group members, have all been examined by researchers in this specific area of group dynamics. FGI considers cohesiveness not at all. Schachter (1960), to name one, demonstrated that groups toward which members are highly attracted may develop norms resulting in low group productivity, low achievement motivation, low degree of effort.[51] Group cohesiveness does have 12 vital consequences that concern anxiety, more equal participation, exerting of pressure on marginal members, etc. Cohesiveness, in turn, has 15 consequences, among them the influence of within group status hierarchies; the real rate and nature of verbal interaction; hostility, etc. The consumer's attitude and expectancies are also factors that affect results as well as the interaction of group members. The effect of pre-instructions or of instructions, beginning with what the interviewer tells the prospective group member, vitally affects what comes out of the group.[52]/[53] Pre-meeting expectations affect both behavior and perception by each group member.[54]

Attention concentrated on a member rather than on the problem at hand, again, has been the subject of study by innumerable people——in addition to those already cited. Bass noted (1960) that if we see others sharing our attitudes, we increase our attraction to them. There is no opportunity to determine such attitudes in FGI, since there are no pre-sociometric or other measurements applied.[55] Wolf and Schwartz[43] found that sub-groups result in isolation in some members (1962).

The post survey

The author conducted his behavioral type study among 50 women who had participated in an FGI within two to three days of the actual FGI session. These consumers re-created their behavior from the time they were first contacted for the FGI, until they had returned home, after the FGI session. In fact, post-behavior included any discussion of the FGI with friends, family, etc. This re-creation was, in effect, a blow-by-blow, word-by-word re-creation as presented in a monograph.[56]

The 50 consumers were located in three different geographical areas, the interviews spanning eight months, from April 1972 to November 1972.

Some survey results

Schatz (1966) has taken cognizance of the fact consumers may well be saying what is expected of them, not what they feel.[24]

It is also a fact of group dynamics (or even a dyadic interaction) that the moderator unawaredly reinforces a line of thought——by a raised eyebrow, a more intense look, etc. Thus, creative or R&D people are using data that is not based on something real.

In a few cases we taped the post-interview and then played it back to the consumer. After the playback consumers responded with such comments

as (numbers in parentheses indicate the number of people who made the same or nearly the same comment):

"Did I say that?" (to our interviewer). "I sure was mad at him." (the moderator).

"Yes, that one (referring to a group member) was stuck on herself."

"I really sounded unsure of myself, didn't I?"

"I must have said that because I felt sorry for her."

"I was really trying to make him (the moderator) look good." (5)

"I identified with her and went along with what she said." (11)

"I felt she was full of crap but I didn't say it."

"I guess I felt she was nervous so I backed her up."

"I think he wanted that answer and if it pleased him, that was okay with me." (4)

"I went to be entertained and I was——some of those women are real weirdos."

"He smiled but I think he (the moderator) was nervous. I felt embarrassed for him." (2)

"I wouldn't say anything, I felt I was ignored." (6)

"I wanted to show her up, she sounded like a real bitch."

"I was just turned off by the whole thing. Everybody was acting. I know I don't brush my teeth every day ——things go on and you forget——especially when you're rushed." (2)

"No, I didn't say anything, I'm not good at expressing myself." (7)

"He asked me if I was a meticulous housewife. Oh, God, no——sometimes I am and sometimes I'm not. It depends on my mood."

"I wouldn't bother to tell her off ——Miss-know-it-all."

"I can't stand that motherly type ——too, too sweet; nothing bugs her."

"She bugged me. I don't know, her attitude, not so much what she said. I decided to bug her back."

"I wanted to say you're crazy like my sister, putting _____ on a good roast beef, but you can't start a fight."

"I felt left out. I wanted to leave but I couldn't bring myself to do it." (2)

A rainy day is the trigger for cake baking, even if other desserts are available. So, too, is a grouchy family because a cake has the capacity to re-

store cheerfulness——facts which the housewife has learned. These are learned, conditioned responses to situations and have become so habituated that consumers are not aware of them. They have virtually become reflex responses. Goldman's use of "projective techniques," limited to one or two such questions, bastardizes this area of psychology.[3] Moreover, projective techniques have lost their acceptance by clinicians, diagnosticians, etc.[57]

In our post-FGI study, when women were asked why they described the type person they thought was represented by a picture, or who bought a particular type (or brand) of product, as they did, responded with such comments as:

"She reminded me of my sloppy sister——she'd do anything to get out of housework."

"That's my neighbor——the worst-looking house on the block."

"I went to gripe and to talk. My husband never talks to me about my problems or concerns about the house. He couldn't care less."

These comments reveal that cognitive affect was not directed to the product, not to the member's own in-home behavior, problems (or thoughts). Too little, if any, attention is given to cognitive affects or to members' cognitions. It is doubtful that a moderator not specifically trained in group dynamics would be capable of perceiving them——when even *trained* observers disagree.

In real life consumers do not react to eight strangers, but to each other member of the family; to on-going situations plus family. Nor is there any evidence for Goldman's (1962)[3] statement, that in the group, the purchasing or marketing situation is created. The marketing situation is created in real life when, as our behavioral studies reveal (interviews conducted within two hours of actual grocery shopping), consumers keep lists; family members write down, "don't forget shampoo, Mom"; the housewife leafs through the newspaper; asks a relative or neighbor, "what store do you need stamps from?"

In assuming, as Goldman does, that a range of attitudes is revealed, marketing and R&D people will be receiving misinformation——because attitudes are evoked by a particular situation. A range of attitudes always exists——what triggers off an attitude is the key.

FGI may be an economical way of obtaining data and information, but the chances of misinformation, artifactual data, misdirection make it a risky and potentially-expensive operation.

References

[1] Perls, F., *Gestalt Therapy*, Delta, N.Y., 1951.

[2] Lazell, W.W., "The Group Treatment of Dementia Praecox," *The Psychoanalytic Review*, Vol. 8, 1921.

[3] Goldman, A.E., "The Group Depth Interview," *Journal of Marketing*, July 1962.

[4] Ruitenbeeck, Hendrick M., *The New Group Therapies*, Discus, N.Y., 1970.

[5] Marsh, L.C., "Group Treatment by the Psychological Equivalent of Revival," *Mental Hygiene*, Vol. 15, 1931.

[6] Burrow, Trigant, "The Group Method of Analysis," *Psychoanalytic Review*, Vol. 14, 1927.

[7] Moreno, L., *The Theater of Spontaneity*, Boston, Beacon House, 1947.

[8] Bion, W.R., "Group Dynamics, A Review," *International Journal of Psychoanalysis*, Vol. 33, 1952.

[9] Stoller, F.H., "Accelerated Interaction: A Time Limited Approach Based on the Brief Intensive Group," *International Journal, GAP Psychotherapy*, Vol. 18, No. 2, April 1969.

[10] Hoch, Paul, *Differential Diagnosis in Clinical Psychiatry*, Science House, N.Y. 1972.

[11] Skinner, B.F., *Verbal Behavior*, Appleton, Century, Crofts, N.Y., 1957.

[12] Gantt, *Pavlov Approach to Psychopathology*, Pergamon, N.Y., 1970.

[13] Lieberman, R.A., *Guide to Behavioral Analysis & Therapy*, Pergamon Press, N.Y. 1972.

[14] Lieberman, R.A., *Ibid.*

[15] Sidman, M., *Tactics of Scientific Research*, Basic Books, N.Y., 1960.

[16] Kanfer, F.H. & Phillips, J.S., *Learning Foundation of Behavioral Therapy*, Wiley, N.Y., 1970.

[17] Berne, Eric, *Principles of Group Treatment*, Grove Press, N.Y., 1966.

[18] Goldstein, A.P.; Heller, K.; Sechrest, L.B., *Psychotherapy & Behavior Change*, John Wiley & Sons, N.Y., 1966.

[19] Lewin, K.; Lippitt, R.; White, R., "Patterns of Aggressive Behavior in Experimentally Created Social Climates," *Journal of Social Psychology*, Vol. 10, pp. 271-299, 1939.

[20] Asch, S.E., "Forming Impressions of Personality," *Journal of Abnormal Social Psychology*, Vol. 41, pp. 258-290, 1946.

[21] Campbell, D.T. & Stanley, J.C., "Experimental Designs for Research in Teaching," in N.L. Gage, Editor, *Handbook of Research on Teaching*, Rand McNally, Chicago, pp. 171-246, 1963.

[22] Yoell, W.A., Monograph: "Does Marketing Need the Construct of Attitudes?"

[23] Orne, M.T., "On the Social Psychology of the Psychological Experiment," *American Psychologist*, Vol. 17, pp. 776-783, 1962.

[24] Schatz, L., "The Group Session or Obsession," *Marketing Review*, Oct. 1966.

[25] Katz, D. & Hahn, R.L., "Leadership Practices in Relation to Productivity and Morale," in D. Cartwright & A. Zander, *Group Dynamics*, Evanston, Ill., Row, Peterson & Co., 1953.

[26] Crockett, W., "Emergent Leadership in Small Decision Making Groups," *Journal of Abnormal Social Psychology*, Vol. 51, 1955.

[27] Hare, A.P., *Handbook of Small Group Research*, Free Press of Glencoe, N.Y., 1962.

[28] Sanford, R.H., *Authoritarianism and Leadership*, Philadelphia, Institute for Research in Human Relations, 1950.

[29] Medalia, N.Z., "Authoritarianism, Leader Acceptance and Group Cohesion," *Journal of Abnormal Social Psychology*, Vol. 51, pp. 207-213, 1955.

[30] Bass, B.M. & Norton, F.M.,"Group Size and Leaderless Discussion," *Journal Applied Psychology*, Vol. 35, pp. 397-401, 1951.

[31] Kelly, H.H. & Thibaut, J.W., "Experimental Studies of Group Problem Solving and Process," in G. Lindsey, Editor, *Handbook of Social Psychology*, Cambridge, Mass., Addison-Wesley, 1954.

[32] Bos, M.C., "Experimental Study of Productive Collaboration," *Acta Psychologica*, Vol. 3, pp. 315-426, 1937.

[33] Allport, R.H., "The Influence of the Group upon Association and Thought," in A.P. Hare, E.F. Borgatta & R.F. Bales, Editors, *Small Groups*, N.Y., Alfred A. Knopf, pp. 31-43, 1955.

[34] Bales, R.F., *Interaction Process Analysis: A Method for the Study of Small Groups*, Cambridge, Mass., Addison-Wesley, 1950.

[35] Talland, C.A., "Task and Interaction Process," in A.P. Hare. Ibid.

[36] Janis, C.I. & Hovland, I.L., Editors, *Personality and Persuasibility*, New Haven, Yale University Press, 1959.

[37] Cohen, A.R., *Attitude Change and Social Influence*, Basic Books, N.Y., 1964.

[38] Lorr, M. & McNair, D.M., "An Interpersonal Behavior Circle," *Journal of Abnormal Social Psychology*, Vol. 67, pp. 68-75, 1967.

[39] Leary, T., *Interpersonal Diagnosis of Personality*, Ronald Press, N.Y.

[40] Cartwright, D., "Achieving Change in People: Some Applications of Group Dynamics Theory," *Human Relations*, Vol. 4, pp. 381-392, 1951.

[41] Bach, G.R., *Intensive Group Psychotherapy*, Ronald Press, N.Y.

[42] Lowrey, L.G., "Group Therapy for Mothers," *American Journal of Orthopsychiatry*, Vol. 14, 1944.

[43] Wolf, A. & Schwartz, E.K., *Psychoanalysis in Groups*, N.Y., Grune & Stratton.

[44] Breer, P.E., "Predicting Interpersonal Behavior from Personality and Role," unpublished Doctoral Dissertation, Harvard University, 1960.

[45] Stephan, F.F. & Mishler, E.G., "The Distribution of Participation in Small Groups: An Experimental Approximation," *American Social Review*, Vol. 17, pp. 598-608, 1952.

[46] Borgatta, E.F. & Bales, R.F. in A.P. Hare, ibid.

[47] Gibbs, C.A., *Handbook of Social Psychology*, ibid.

[48] Miller, N.E., "Effects of Group Size on Group Process and Member Satisfaction," University of Michigan Conference, 1950.

[49] Carter, D.; Haythorn, W.; Shriver, E. & Lanzetta, J., "The Behavior of Leaders and Other Group Members," *Journal of Abnormal Social Psychology*, Vol. 46, pp. 589-595, 1951.

[50] Berkowitz, L. & Levy, B., "Pride in Group Performance and Group Task Motivation," *Journal of Abnormal Social Psychology*, Vol. 53, pp. 300-306, 1956.

[51] Schachter, S.; Ellerston, N.; McBride, D. & Gregory D., "An Experimental Study of Cohesiveness and Productivity," in D. Cartwright & A. Zander, Editors, *Group Dynamics*, Evanston, Ill., Row, Peterson & Co., 1960.

[52] Back, K.W., "Influence Through Social Communication," *Journal of Abnormal Social Psychology*, Vol. 46, 1951.

[53] Festinger, L.; Schachter, S. & Back, K.W., *Social Pressures in Informal Groups*, Harper, N.Y., 1950.

[54] Beilin, H., "Effects of Set Upon Impression Formation," Paper presented at APA, Chicago, Sept. 1960.

[55] Bass, B.M., *Leadership, Psychology and Organization Behavior*, Harper, N.Y., 1960.

[56] Yoell, W.A., Address to the AMA International Conference, "Attitudes at Sea—the Determination of Consumer Concepts, Attitudes and Motivations," 1966.

[57] Yoell, W.A., in press, 1973.